Teaching Materials —————————

by Kenneth L. Weimer

to accompany

COMPUTING ESSENTIALS
Annual Edition 1994–1995

Timothy J. O'Leary
Linda I. O'Leary

 Mitchell McGRAW-HILL, INC.

New York St. Louis San Francisco Auckland Bogotá Caracas Lisbon
London Madrid Mexico City Milan Montreal New Delhi
San Juan Singapore Sydney Tokyo Toronto

The creation of this manual was made possible through the efforts of the following people:

Timothy J. O'Leary
Linda O'Leary
Roger Howell
Rhonda Sands
Rich DeVitto

and many others on the McGraw-Hill Staff.

Mitchell McGRAW-HILL

Teaching Materials to accompany
Computing Essentials Annual Edition 1994–1995

3 4 5 6 7 8 9 0 MAL MAL 9 0 9 8 7 6 5 4

P/N 048985-8

ORDER INFORMATION
ISBN 0-07-911751-1 (Teaching Materials with 3.5-inch Test Questions Disk)

Table of Contents

TO THE INSTRUCTOR

In <u>Microcomputing Annual Edition, 1994-1995</u>, Timothy O'Leary and Linda O'Leary have written an informative, comprehensive, and readable text in a format that will enable the publisher to keep it up-to-date with the changing technology.

In this instructor's manual, to accompany the O'Leary & O'Leary text, resources are provided to assist the instructor in successfully teaching an introductory course on microcomputing.

This manual was designed to be flexible to accommodate varying teaching styles and experience levels of the instructors adopting this text. For those instructors with considerable teaching experience, there is a "Chapter at a Glance" outline for each chapter. For those that are new to teaching or to the course area, there are extensive lecture notes of each chapter. These lecture notes contain references to the accompanying transparency masters and the answers to the questions found at the end of each chapter.

Chapter Resources

Each chapter in this manual is constructed in a format that is consistent throughout the manual. The components of each chapter are as follows:

Chapter at a Glance - This is a brief outline of the chapter that highlights the key themes of the chapter. It may be used in preparing the general course outline or in introducing the chapter material in a manner that best accommodates the instructor.

Chapter Objectives - The major themes to be emphasized in the text reading and in the class discussions are stated in the text and in the instructor's manual for each chapter.

Vocabulary - Key terms that are introduced in the chapter are listed alphabetically, and highlighted in the lecture notes for easy reference by the instructor.

Detailed Lecture Notes - The lecture notes follow the lecture outline and the text format exactly with page number references. Key terms are highlighted and the italic print notates instructor tips and prompts for transparency master sheets that accompany the text.

Transparency Master Sheets - Each chapter has a set of transparencies that are referenced in the detailed lecture notes to assist the instructor in communicating course content material. The lecture prompt to the instructor identifies each transparency referencing its chapter and sequence number in the chapter. There is an additional set of "Color Transparencies for the Introductory Computer Course" provided by Mitchell Publishing, Inc., you can secure this set by talking with your book representative (**SEE pp. V**).

Answers to Review Questions - At the end of each chapter in the text, a set of true/false, multiple choice, fill-in and open-ended questions can be found. The instructor's manual duplicates these questions with answers for each question.

Supplemental Video Guide - A <u>Student Video Guide - Computers at Work second edition</u> by Joe M. Kinzer may be very helpful at supplementing and enhancing the lecture course. This guide is published by Mitchell Publishing, Inc. ISBN: 0-394-39404-6.

The sample course schedules found in this manual make reference to the lab text that can supplement the <u>Microcomputing Annual Edition, 1994-1995</u>. To give the student a comprehensive and balanced experience, it is strongly suggested that the text material and lab activities both be taught concurrently.

The suggested lab exercises can be culminated with a relevant personal application project for each of the applications of word processing, electronic spreadsheet, and database management. Ideas for these projects include making a resume, a yearly income/expense budget, and a personal name and address database.

Course Title and Section
Course Time/Location
Course Schedule

The following is a tentative schedule for discussion topics, lab assignments, quiz/daily exercises, exams, and projects. The reading assignments should be completed prior to class discussion. Changes, if any, in this tentative schedule will be announced in class by the instructor.

10 Week Course Schedule

Week	Project	Text Assignment	Lab Assignment	Quiz/ Exercises	Exam
1		Chapter 1 and Chapter 2	DOS Overview & Lab 1	1	
2		Chapter 3 & Exam	Word Perfect Labs 1-2	2	1
3		Chapter 4 & Chapter 5	Word Perfect Lab 3	3 & 4	
4	Word Proc.	Chapter 5 & Chapter 6	Lotus Labs 1 & 2	5	
5		Exam / Chapter 7	Lotus Lab 3	6	2
6		Chapter 8	Lotus Lab 4	7	
7	Elec. Spr.	Chapter 9 & Exam	dBase Lab 1	8	3
8		Chapter 10 & Chapter 11	dBase Lab 2	9/10	
9		Chapter 12 & Chapter 13	dBase Lab 3	11/12	
10	Database	Chapter 14 & Exam	LAN Lab 1	13/14	4

Course Title and Section
Course Time/Location
Course Schedule

The following is a tentative schedule for discussion topics, lab assignments, quiz/daily exercises, exams, and projects. The reading assignments should be completed prior to class discussion. Changes, if any, in this tentative schedule will be announced in class by the instructor.

16 Week Course Schedule

Week	Project	Text Assignment	Quiz/ Lab Assignment	Exercises	Exam
1		Course Intro & Chapter 1	DOS Overview		
2		Ch. 1 & Introduce Ch. 2	DOS Lab 1	1	
3		Chapter 2	Word Perfect Lab 1	2	
4		Chapter 3	Word Perfect Lab 2	3	
5		Exam & Introduce Ch. 4	Word Perfect Lab 3	4	1
6	Word Proc.	Chapter 4	Lotus Lab 1	5	
7		Chapter 5	Lotus Lab 2	6	
8		Chapter 6	Lotus Lab 3	7	
9		Exam & Introduce Ch. 7	Lotus Lab 4		2
10	Elec. Spr.	Chapter 7	dBase Lab 1	8	
11		Chapter 8	dBase Lab 2	9	
12		Chapter 9	dBase Lab 3	10	
13		Exam & Introduce Ch.10	dBase Lab 4		3
14	Database	Chap. 10 & Chap. 11	LAN Lab 1	11	
15		Chapter 12 & Chapter 13	12/13		
16		Chapter 14 & Exam		14	4

Videocourse
for the
Introductory Computer Course

Transparency Master List

CHAPTER 1
YOU AND COMPUTER COMPETENCY
Chapter at a Glance

I. Introduction to the Application of Microcomputers

    A. Common tools in all areas of life.
    B. Developing new forms of learning.
    C. Making expert knowledge readily available.

II. End User and Computer Competency

    A. Definition of end user
    B. Definition of "prewritten programs"
    C Solving business problems
        1. information-related
        2. decision-related
    D. Definition of computer competency

III. Four Kinds of Computers

    A. Microcomputers
    B. Minicomputers
    C. Mainframe computers
    D. Supercomputers

IV. The Five Parts of a Microcomputer System

    A. People
    B. Procedures
    C. Software
    D. Hardware
    E. Data

V. Software

    A. Applications Software
        1. Packaged software
        2. Custom-made applications software
    B. Systems Software

VI. Hardware
  A. Input devices
  B. The system unit
    1. processor (CPU)
    2. primary storage

  C. Secondary Storage
    1. floppy diskettes
      a. program diskette
      b. data diskette
    2. hard disk
    3. tape drive

  D. Output devices
    1. monitor
    2. printers
    3. secondary storage as output

  E. Communications devices
    1. modem
    2. outside information

VII. Organization of data

  A. Character
  B. Field
  C. Record
  D. File
  E. Database

VIII. Connectivity

IX. Computer competency and your future.

  A. Expanding computer competency
    1. understanding the rules and the power of microcomputers including "basic tools"
    2. powerful software
    3. powerful hardware
    4. connectivity

  B. Applying computer competency effectively to your career
  C. Emerging microcomputer applications
  D. Workplace issues of ergonomics, computer crime, privacy, security, and your future

2

OBJECTIVES

The student should be able to:

1. Explain "computer competency" and identify its personal importance.

2. Distinguish four kinds of computers: microcomputer, minicomputer, mainframe, and supercomputer.

3. Explain the five parts of an information system: people, procedures, software, hardware and data.

4. Distinguish applications software from systems software.

5. Describe hardware devices for input, processing, storage, output, and communications.

6. Describe document, worksheet, and database files.

7. Explain computer connectivity.

8. Identify a personal goal you hope to achieve by completing this course.

VOCABULARY

applications software	document files	microcomputers	program
central processing unit	end user	midrange computers	reads
computer network	floppy disks	minicomputers	secondary storage
computer competent	hard disk	modem	software
computers	hardware	monitor	supercomputers
connectivity	information systems	mouse	system unit
cursor	information	operating system	systems software
custom programs	input devices	packaged software	video display screen
custom-made software	keyboard	personal computers	worksheet files
data	local area networks	primary storage	write
database files	mainframe computers	printer	
disk drive	memory	procedures	

INTRODUCTION TO THE APPLICATION OF MICROCOMPUTERS (page 2)

Identify and discuss examples of how end-users apply computers in their everyday lives (three general examples are listed below):

* Microcomputers are used in all areas as common tools.
* Home computers are used as learning tools or as a vehicle of the learning process.
* Microcomputers provide a means of imparting expert knowledge to the masses.

END-USER and COMPUTER COMPETENCY (pages 2-3)

Developing a personal level of computer competency is important for people to improve productivity and increase their value in the workplace. To develop this competency end users may:

* Work with microcomputers as tools for their personal and professional lives.
* Work with output produced by large computer systems or microcomputers. This output can be produced directly by the end user or by others, including programmers.
* Learn to manage their personal computer systems for the purpose of solving problems.
    * Use "prewritten programs" to play a video game, produce documents, do calculations and/or a variety of other tasks.

A practical reason for using computers is to improve productivity; which is very important to employers.

* End users can implement available programs to solve their own problems which may involve solutions to **information-related** or **decision-making** problems that will improve productivity.

Computer competency is having a practical working knowledge of computers that allows one to obtain the necessary information to solve problems.

The focus of this book is to help you become competent in computer related skills. After developing this competency, you will hopefully feel more comfortable in using a computer for personal and professional applications.

THE FOUR TYPES OF COMPUTER SYSTEMS (page 3-4) *TM 1.01*

Computer systems are classified into: **microcomputer** (with subclassifications of personal computer, portable laptop or transportable, and workstation); **minicomputer**, also known as midrange computer; **mainframe**; and **supercomputer**.

These classifications become less distinct over time because of constant improvements in computer technology. Generally, classifications are determined by applying present technology standards in clock speed, memory size, storage capacity, costs, and processor size (data word length processor). These differences are discussed in Chapter 4.

4

THE FIVE PARTS OF AN INFORMATION SYSTEM (pages 5-6) *TM 1.02*

People that are more productive as a result of using a computer.

Hardware as the physical equipment of the computer system that includes a keyboard, monitor, printer, the system unit, and other peripheral devices that may be part of the system. *TM 1.03*

Software consists of instructions (programs) in a step-by-step sequence telling the computer how to do its work.

Data consists of raw (unprocessed) facts that are input to the system. Organized (processed) data is usually called **information**.

Procedures (manuals) contain rules and guidelines for using software, hardware, and data.

SOFTWARE: APPLICATIONS VERSUS SYSTEMS SOFTWARE (pages 6-8) *TM 1.04*

Applications software enables end users to perform practical tasks and may include the popular "basic tools" of: word processing, electronic spreadsheet, database management, graphics and communications. These application programs can be packaged ("prewritten") or custom made to the specific needs of an individual by a programmer.

Systems software are essential programs helping the computer manage its own resources. It interacts between the computer and the application program transparently. An important part of the systems software is the **operating system** which controls the execution of programs, stores data and programs, manages the processing tasks (manipulating data), and has built in programs for file management. The most popular operating systems include: DOS; Windows, and Windows NT; OS/2; and Macintosh.

You may wish to assign and discuss SECTION 1: DOS COMMANDS LAB 1 (see Instructor's Lab Manual).

HARDWARE (pages 8-11)

The five categories of hardware are:

*   <u>Input devices</u> allow raw data into the system in a form that the computer can process. The most common input devices on a microcomputer are the **keyboard** and a mouse.

*   The <u>system unit</u> is the electronic circuitry made up of the **processor** and **primary storage**. Usually, the system unit also contains secondary storage devices. The **processor**, also called the **central processing unit (CPU)**, processes the input data. **Primary storage** (also known as **main memory**, **internal storage**, or **memory**) temporarily holds the data for processing, programming instructions, and processed data before it is output. It is a volatile memory.

* **Secondary storage** is designed to hold data and programs permanently on a **floppy diskette, fixed disk**, or **magnetic tape**. Secondary storage is non-volatile.

* **Output devices** allow the computer user to see the results of processing. The two most common output devices are the **monitor** and the **printer**. Disk drives are also considered to be output devices because information can be sent to the disk as output after the data has been processed.

* **Communications** devices allow the sending of data and programs from one computer system to another. The communications process can happen by telephone, other kinds of cable, microwave, earth-orbiting satellites, or a combination of all of these communication channels. A **modem** is a device that is used **modulate** and **demodulate** electronic signals so they can be transmitted over the telephone lines. A modem can be an internal device or an external device.

If you plan to have the students begin working on the computers, this may be a good time to discuss data disks, program disks, formatting, and booting the computer.

DATA (page 12)

Discuss the four classifications or levels of **data** listed from lowest to highest in the following sequence:

* A **character** is a letter, number, or special symbol usually found on the keyboard. It is the equivalent to one byte.

* A **field** is an item of data made up by one or more logically related characters.

* A **record** is a collection of related fields.

* A **file** is a collection of related records.

These four categories can collectively make up a sophisticated structure known as a database. A **database** is a collection of data that can give different people access to the same data. This data is accessed for the purpose of creating information to serve the needs of the individuals using the database.

CONNECTIVITY (pages 13-14)

The concept of connecting a microcomputer to the outside world. Using a modem, telephone lines and other means of telecommunications, people can "connect" to numerous sources of data and information. An important aspect of connectivity is the network (attaching two or more computers and their peripheral devices). These networks can be local, regional, national and international in scope.

YOU AND COMPUTER COMPETENCY (pages 12-15)

Computer competency is in a constant state of change in terms of what an individual must know. The basic foundation to computer competence is having the knowledge and understanding of the rules and power of the microcomputer and use of software applications referred to as "Basic tools". Having this foundation enables the individual to benefit from more powerful software, hardware, and connectivity to outside information systems.

In addition, competency is awareness of:

Emerging Microcomputer Applications including:

* Personal Information Managers
* Project Management Software
* Desktop Publishing involving Hypertext and/or Multimedia
* CAD/CAM
* Artificial Intelligence (AI) involving Robotics, Knowledge-based Systems, and Expert Systems
* Virtual Reality

Workplace Issues involving:

* Ergonomics
* Computer Crime
* Security

REVIEW QUESTIONS
True/False

T 1. Microcomputers are also known as personal computers.
F 2. Hardware consists of monitor, keyboard and <u>software</u>.
F 3. <u>DOS</u> is the standard operating system for <u>Apple Corporation's Macintosh</u>.
T 4. Memory is also known as primary storage.
T 5. A modem is used to send electronic signals over telephone lines.

Multiple Choice

A 1. Computers are electronic devices that accept instructions, process input, and produce:
   Answer; information
D 2. High-capacity computers used primarily for research purposes are:
   Answer; supercomputers
B 3. The central processing unit (CPU) is located in the:
   Answer; system unit
C 4. When electrical power is disrupted or cut off, data and programs are lost in:
   Answer; memory
C 5. Files containing highly structured and organized data are:
   Answer; databases

Open Ended

1. What is computer competency?

   Having the knowledge to use a computer for personal and professional applications to solve problems.

2. Describe the five parts of a microcomputer system.

   The five parts of a microcomputer system include:

   People — **that are more productive as a result of using a computer.**

   Procedures — **manuals containing rules and guidelines when using software, hardware, and data.**

   Hardware — **the equipment including the keyboard, monitor, printer, CPU and other peripheral devices that can be attached to the system.**

   Software — **the step-by-step instructions that tell the computer how to process data and to perform the desired tasks.**

   Data — **the unprocessed facts that are processed into information. Processing data into information occurs in the steps of input, processing, storage, and output.**

3. Distinguish between applications software and systems software?

   Application software are computer programs that can perform useful work. Systems software are programs helping the computer to manage its own resources. Part of the system software includes the operating system, which makes it easier to use the hardware.

4. Name the five categories of microcomputer hardware.

   Microcomputer hardware can be classified into input devices, the system unit, secondary storage, output devices, and communications devices.

5. What is the difference between memory and secondary storage?

   Memory is the part of the system unit that holds data and instructions temporarily. Secondary storage consists of devices that separate from the CPU and are designed to hold data and programs permanently.

8

CHAPTER 2
APPLICATIONS SOFTWARE:BASIC TOOLS
Chapter at a Glance

I. Using Software Off the Shelf

    A.   Identify the purpose and forms of application software

    B.   Define "off the shelf" software

II. Common features found in Application Packages

III. Word Processing

    A.   Define the purpose of word processing

    B.   Identify key features found with most word processing programs

IV. Electronic Spreadsheets

    A.   Define the purpose of an electronic spreadsheet
        1.   Review the history and development of a spreadsheet
        2.   "What if" possibilities

    B.   Identify key features found with most spreadsheet programs

V. Database

    A.   Define the purpose of a database program
    B.   List hierarchy of organization of data from the DBMS to a character
    C.   Identify key features found with most file managers or DBMS

VI. Graphics

    A.   Analytical graphics
    B.   Presentation graphics

VII. Communications
    A.   Databanks
    B.   Message exchanges
    C.   Financial services

VIII. Integrated Software

IX. New Software Developments

9

OBJECTIVES

The student should be able to:

1. Explain the features common to all kinds of applications software.

2. Describe applications software for word processing, electronic spreadsheet, database management, graphics, and communications.

3. Describe integrated software that combines all the tasks listed in number 2.

VOCABULARY

analytical graphics	dynamic file links	labels	scrolling
block	electronic spreadsheet	macro	special-purpose keys
block move	exporting	mail merge	spelling-checker
boldface	form letter	menu bar	spreadsheet cursor
cell	format	menus	thesaurus
cell address	formulas	off-the-shelf software	unjustified
cell pointer	function keys	outlining programs	value
column headings	help menu	presentation graphics	word processing
database manager	help screen	pull-down menu	word wrap
DBMS	highlighting	recalculation	worksheet area
desktop publishing	importing	replace	WYSIWYG
documents	integrated package	row headings	
drawing programs	justified	search	

GENERAL-PURPOSE APPLICATIONS PACKAGES (page 20)

* Programs performing useful work (usually business related) which are usually user friendly and are referred to as off-the-shelf software.

* Enable end users to perform tasks previously requiring a programming specialist.

* The most common applications include word processing, spreadsheet, database management, graphics, and communications.

COMMON FEATURES FOUND IN APPLICATION PACKAGES (pages 20-23)

Identify the features found in many of the popular application software packages include:

* **a cursor -** a blinking symbol indicating the present location on the screen.

* **scrolling -** the ability to move quickly forward or backward through text.

* **menus -** list options to select actions for the computer to perform. Menus are of two kinds: **menu bar** (a line or two across the top or bottom of the screen) and **pull-down** (a list of commands that "drops down" from a menu bar at the top of the screen). *TM 2.01*

* help screen -	an explanation of operations of a software package. It is usually called to the screen by pressing a function key. *TM 2.02*
* format -	the ability to change the appearance of output so that it can be presented to the user in the most informative manner possible.
* special purpose keys -	keys like Esc (Escape) and Ctrl (Control), which are used in the data entry, edit, and execution process.
* function keys -	the keys labeled F1, F2 and so on, used for commands or tasks that are frequently performed.
* WYSIWYG	what you see is what you get.
* macros	key command which starts a user-defined program of useful tasks.
* Import/Export	non-text files (ie. spreadsheet file) can be **imported** (retrieved) into a word processing document. Saving a file in a form so other applications may retrieve it is called **exporting**.

WORD PROCESSING (pages 23-25)

Define **word processing** as the ability use of a computer to create, manipulate, store, and print documents. A **document** is any kind of text material such as letters, memos, term papers, reports, and contracts.

Some key features of word processing programs may include:

block operations	menu options
block commands	search and replace
cursor movement	special purpose keys
desktop publishing	spell-checking
document formatting	text justification
function keys	text scrolling
highlighting	thesaurus
mail-merge	word wrap

SPREADSHEETS (pages 25-28) *TM 2.03*

Describe an **electronic spreadsheet** as a tool much like an accounting worksheet. It can be used to perform the same tasks that one would use a pencil, paper, calculator, and an eraser. It allows one to do automatic recalculation that permits one to experiment (playing **"what if"**) with the numeric data, determine possible outcomes, and help in decision-making tasks.

Some key features of an electronic spreadsheet include:

cell pointer   functions
column and row headings   macros
data formatting   replication
formulas   windows

DATABASE MANAGERS (pages 28-30) *TM 2.04*

Discuss the purpose of a **database** to keep track of interrelated data in an organized way for the purpose of producing decision making information. Highlight the following items:

* A **database manager** or a **database management system (DBMS)** is a program that allows the user to easily create, edit, access, and retrieve the information stored in a file (or possibly several files with a DBMS).

* A database can be a single file or several files that work together with common data links to access the desired information.

* A **file** is a collection of records holding the same type of data for each record in the file.

* A **record** is defined by identifying each field name, length, and the type of data.

* A **field name** is unique and holds one item of data for each record. The data type is specified as **numeric, alphanumeric, alphabetic,** or as a special type.

* Some common features of a file or database manager include:

calculate   program control languages
data entry forms   report
editing   retrieve and display
format   sort
index   updating
mail label

GRAPHICS (pages 30-32) *TM 2.05*

Discuss the purpose of **business graphics** to help convey information and to show relationships in numeric data. Identify the two types of graphic programs:

* **Analytical graphics** convert numeric data into a picture form such as a bar chart, line graph, high-low graph, or pie chart. This conversion can make it easier to analyze data and to help the user make more informed decisions. Viewing the numeric data in a graphic form may allow the user a comparative analysis that is not readily

12

apparent when working with raw numbers.

* **Presentation graphics** allow the user a method of communicating a message to other people. Presentation graphics may use color, titles, free form art, dimensionality, and analytical graphic output. Presentation graphics allows the user to produce output similar to what would be done by a graphic artist. *TM 2.06*

COMMUNICATIONS (pages 32-33)

Describe **communications** as the sending and receiving of information/data between two or more computers. This task is accomplished with a **communications software** program.

Discuss the principle of **"connectivity"** established by communications programs opening a plethora of computer services to the microcomputer user, including:

* **Data Banks**, which are enormous computerized databases that resemble huge electronic encyclopedias.

* **Message Exchanges**, which are communications programs that enable you to receive and leave messages on **electronic bulletin boards** or to use **electronic mail services**.

* **Financial Services**, that can make inquiries into airline reservations and stock quotations; bill payments; home banking and shop at home services possible.

INTEGRATED SOFTWARE PACKAGES (pages 33-35) *TM 2.07*

Contrast an **integrated package** as software providing the user with multiple application programs packaged together versus a **stand-alone** package that has only one application.

* The most common integrated packages (**"basic tools"**) include spreadsheet, word processing, graphics, database manager, and communications.

* An integrated package may include only two applications, possibly all five of the above, or some other type of application software.

* The advantage of an integrated package is that the programs work together and share resources and use the same commands to do similar functions.

* It also allows the user to merge data from one program into another such as, taking a list of names from a database and merging them into a form letter created with the word processing program.

LEARNING COMPLEX SOFTWARE TASKS (STAYING CURRENT) (page 35)

Emphasize that applications software is in a constant state of change and the need to use available means of staying current with the newest versions of software. Some of the means available include:

* **tutorials** (step-by-step instructions and practice sessions).

* **add-on consoles** plugged into a microcomputer keyboard having special cartridges containing instructions to assist students with complex software commands.

* **windowing software** allowing the user to work on several applications at once.

* **context sensitive help screens** which indexes to the help text related to the user's task.

REVIEW QUESTIONS
True/False
T 1. The cursor indicates where you may enter data next.
F 2. Word wrap is a feature common to <u>database managers</u>.
F 3. Quattro Pro is a widely used <u>word processor</u>.
F 4. Spreadsheet programs are <u>typically</u> used to <u>store and retrieve records quickly</u>.
T 5. With communications programs, you can look up airline reservations and stock quotations.

Multiple Choice
C 1. The feature common to most application packages that allows you to store a sequence of keystrokes as a single command: **Answer; macro**

B 2. When using a word processor, the portion of text that you wish to move is called a: **Answer; block**

C 3. In spreadsheets, the common feature that specifies instructions for calculation is: **Answer; recalculation**

E 4. A tool used frequently by marketing people to communicate a message or to persuade clients: **Answer; presentation graphics**

D 5. A collection of applications software packages that work together and share information: **Answer; integrated**

Fill in the Blank
1. The <u>exporting</u> feature is common to many applications programs and allows word processing files to be retrieved into spreadsheet files.

2. The <u>electronic spreadsheet</u> is based on the traditional accounting worksheet.

3. <u>Database management</u> programs are used to keep track of details such as inventory records or client lists.

4. **Communications** software lets you send and receive data from another computer.

5. Microsoft Works and Lotus Works are **low-end** integrated packages.

Open Ended

1. What is a Help screen? What is Help used for?

    A help screen provides an explanation of operations of a software package. It is usually called to the screen by pressing a function key. Help menus are particularly useful when assistance is needed for quick reference rather than lumbering through an instruction manual.

2. How do formulas and recalculation work in a spreadsheet?

    The real power of a spreadsheet is the recalculation feature that recalculates all formulas in the spreadsheet after each single change of a data cell occurs. With most spreadsheets recalculation will happen automatically with each new entry or change in data within the worksheet. This feature can usually be turned off to a manual mode.

    The formulas are written much like they are in any math equation. However, variables can be referencing different cells within the worksheet by using the cell address. Numeric values are held and can be changed in these other cells. When these changes occur the formulas will automatically reflect the new results.

3. Explain the purpose of analytical graphics. Explain the purpose of presentation graphics.

    Analytical graphics help put numerical data into a graphic format that is easier to analyze than voluminous numeric data.

    Presentation graphics are designed to help communicate a message to other people. Generally, they are more sophisticated than analytical graphics and employ special equipment, color, titles, dimensionality, and other features similar to those used by a graphics artist.

4. Name three common types of graphs and charts used in analytical graphics.

    Analytical graphics include bar charts, line graphs, and pie charts.

5. Describe some computer connections.

    Connectivity establishes the connections between personal computers and the world of services that were previously only available to large computer systems. They include connecting to data banks, message exchanges, and financial services.

CHAPTER 3
SYSTEMS SOFTWARE
Chapter at a Glance

I.   Why Learn About Systems Software?

    A. Industry standards are changing for microcomputers
        1. Limitations of DOS
        2. Possibility of running more than one system software on one computer
        3. More sophisticated users
    B. Purchase decisions should be based on knowledge

II.   Four kinds of programs

    A. The bootstrap loader
    B. Diagnostic routines
    C. Basis input output system
    D. The operating system

III. DOS
    A. Industry standard for IBM PC, XT, AT, PS/2 and Compatibles.
    B. Versions
    C. Advantage
        1. Popularity
        2. Number of applications
        3. Economical expense when building a system
        4. Easy to use
    D. Disadvantage
        1. Limited primary storage capacity
        2. Inability to do multitasking
        3. Character based interface

IV.   DOS with Windows
    A. Advantages
        1. Multitasking
        2. Dynamic data exchange
        3. Graphical User Interface (GUI)
        4. More primary storage

    B. Disadvantages
        1. Inherent limitations of DOS
        2. Minimum system configuration (memory and processor)
        3. Unrecoverable errors
        4. Limited network capabilities

C. Windows NT
   1. Powerful New Operating System
   2. All the advantages listed above
   3. Networking capability
   4. Memory manager (well above 640K)
   5. Multiprocessing capability
   6. Multiuser capability

D. Windows NT Disadvantages
   1. Requires a minimum system configuration
      a. At least a '386 processor
      b. Needs four times more memory than DOS
   2. Unrecoverable application error
      a. Occurs when running earlier versions of DOS for Windows
      b. Must restart application

V. OS/2
    A. Developed for the new hardware technology
    B. Versions
    C. Advantages
       1. Protected mode
       2. Multitasking
       3. Ability to utilize more primary memory
       4. Compatibility with DOS
       5. Common graphical user interface
       6. Communications link between applications
       7. Flexibility to run older DOS and Windows applications
    D. Disadvantages
       1. Fewer users (1/7 that of DOS for Windows)
       2. Fewer applications developed specifically for OS/2
       3. Minimum system configuration
          a. Should have at least a '386 processor
          b. Twice as much memory and hard disk space as DOS with Windows
       4. None of the disadvantages apply when compared to Windows NT
VI. MACINTOSH
    A. Apple Macintosh hardware environment
    B. Versions
    C. Advantages
       1. High quality graphical user interface
       2. Ease of use
       3. Quality graphics
       3. Consistent interfaces
       4. Multitasking
       5. Shared data communications
    D. Disadvantages
       1. Is it a business machine?
       2. Compatibility difficulties with DOS

VII. UNIX
   A. Portable programming language
   B. Versions
   C. Advantages
      1. Multitasking
      2. Multiprocessing
      3. Multiuser
      4. Networking
   D. Disadvantages
      1. Limited applications software
      2. No UNIX standard
      3. Difficult to learn and use

VIII. Future Operating Systems
   A. Continued use of DOS, Windows, UNIX, and Macintosh
   B. Microsoft's Windows NT
   C. IBM & Apple's Taligent
      1. Object-oriented programming
      2. Faster, less expensive development
   D. Government and Large Organizations
      1. OS/2
      2. UNIX
      3. Windows NT

OBJECTIVES
The student should be able to:

1. Understand the importance of learning about systems software.

2. Distinguish among the five kinds of operating systems.

3. Explain the advantages and disadvantages of DOS.

4. Discuss the difference between DOS and Windows and Windows NT.

5. Describe the pluses and minuses of Windows.

6. Discuss the benefits and drawbacks of OS/2.

7. Describe what's good and bad about Macintosh systems software.

8. Explain the advantages and disadvantages of UNIX for microcomputers.

VOCABULARY

backup	command line interface	icons	operating system
Basic Input Output System (BIOS)	copy	initializing	OS/2
	diagnostic routines	memory manager	portable
booting	Disk Operating System	multiprocessing	Taligent
bootstrap loader	formatting	multiprogramming	UNIX
character based interface	graphical user interface (GUI)	multitasking	utility programs
		networking	virtual memory

WHY LEARN ABOUT SYSTEMS SOFTWARE (PAGES 42-44)

* Systems software is essential to the operation of the microcomputer system.

* End users must determine which systems software best fits their needs. To help in this determination end users should consider **competing systems software**.

* Recent developments in computer hardware and software technology have created a situation where there are now several competing forms of systems software.

  The circumstances that created this situation include:

* DOS limitations.
* the ability of microcomputers to run more than one type of systems software.
* more sophisticated microcomputer users wanting the full potential of the newer hardware systems.

FOUR KINDS of PROGRAMS (pages 44-45)

Identify the four kinds of programs found in systems software.

* The <u>bootstrap loader</u> is stored permanently in the computer's electronic circuitry. This loader performs two essential tasks:
  1. it starts up the computer when you turn it on.
  2. it obtains the operating system from the default disk and loads the operating system into primary memory.

* The <u>diagnostic routines</u> are programs also stored into the computer's electronic circuitry. These routines automatically start up when the computer is turned on. They test the primary memory, the central processing unit, screen, keyboard and other components of the computer system. These routines are for the

* The <u>basis input output system</u> consists of service programs stored in primary memory which enable the computer to interpret keyboard strokes and/or to transmit characters to the monitor or to a disk.

* The <u>operating system</u> is a collection of programs taking care of numerous internal details while interacting directly with the end user. These details include interpreting commands used to run and interact with programs.

  The operating system contains a set of **external** programs called **utility programs**, performing tasks such as **formatting** disks. Another set of DOS programs are **internal programs** held in a file called COMMAND.COM. Some commonly used DOS internal commands include: COPY, ERASE, RENAME, and DIR.

  Multiprogramming (interrupts and switches back and forth between several programs as they execute) and **multiprocessing** (divides the CPU into separate, independent parts) allow more than one person to use a computer system.

19

MS-Disk Operating System software was developed by Microsoft Corporation. PC-DOS is a version that Microsoft licenses to IBM for its personal computers (PC, XT, AT and PS/2). Other manufactures also have license to use MS-DOS. DOS is the standard operating system for all "IBM compatible" hardware systems.

Versions - DOS has developed and changed since it was first introduced in 1981. The original version DOS 1.0 has had several minor revisions and four major revisions. The most recent version of DOS is 5.0.

Discuss and demonstrate the use of the DOS internal commands and external commands.

Advantages of using DOS include:

* **Popularity** - DOS is the most popular microcomputer operating system ever sold. It has been installed on an estimated 85% of all microcomputers in the world.

* **Number of applications** - More than 20,000 application programs have been written for the DOS environment.

* **Runs on inexpensive hardware** - The IBM Personal Computer set the standard for the microcomputer business environment. The makers of the IBM "clone" have created a very competitive microcomputer market. This competition has driven prices of hardware and software down to a very affordable level for many people.

* **Ease of use** - Operating systems can be difficult to install and operate. DOS is installed easily and has a vast amount of resources available to assist users.

The **disadvantages** of DOS include:

* **Limited primary storage** - An applications program running in the DOS environment difficulty accessing more than 640,000 bytes of primary memory. Many programs being written today, require access to more than 640,000 bytes.

* **"Single tasking" only** - Dos can only work with one user and a single applications program at a time. **Multitasking** is an operating systems ability to run several applications programs at the same time. The demand in the workplace for multitasking capabilities is growing rapidly.

* **Character-based interface** - Working with DOS, users issue commands or select menu items. This method requires more knowledge or experience with the application than a graphical user interface method.

Industry observers believe DOS will have a following of users for many years, as newer updated versions are designed to minimize its disadvantages. Adding new Windows software, users are able to eliminate some of the previous disadvantages of DOS.

DOS with Windows is an operating environment. **Windows NT** is a powerful new operating system. Windowing software extends the capability of DOS by creating an environment that allows **multitasking, graphical user interface, more primary storage,** and **networking**. Windows NT permits **multiprocessing** and **multiuser** capabilities.

The **advantages** of enhancing DOS with Windows, include:

* **Multitasking** - the computer can work on more than one application simultaneously.

* **Graphical user interface (GUI)** uses a mouse to point at **icons** or pull-down windows for performing tasks previously requiring the user to type a command.

* **More primary memory** can be managed by the windows program. DOS can only access 640 kb of primary storage by itself. DOS with Windows can access billions of bytes in primary storage.

The **disadvantages** of Windows, include:

* **Unrecoverable errors** when running earlier versions of DOS for Windows indicates there are still technological limitations in the software. These errors require a restart of the program. These errors are rare with the newer versions of Windows.

* **Minimum system configurations** - Windows requires a more expensive system using at least a '386 chip, a hard disk, and four times as much memory as DOS.

OS/2 (pages 49-51) *TM 3.03*

OS/2 (Operating System/2) - jointly developed by IBM and Microsoft for IBM's Personal System/2 (PS/2) line of computers. These two companies have since separated from this joint venture. Standard Edition 2.0 - Utilizes the 386 and 486 Intel microprocessor chip.

Advantages of OS/2 over DOS with Windows include:

* **Common User Interface** - meaning applications have a common graphics interface that is consistent when working with micro, mini, and mainframe computers.

* **Flexibility** - without the constraints of DOS, it processes more efficiently.

* **Multitasking** - OS/2 has true multitasking capabilities that allows more than one application program to share the CPU.

The **Disadvantages** of OS/2 include:

* **Expense** - Requires twice the memory and hard disk space of DOS with Windows.

21

*   **Fewer applications** - OS/2 has sold about 1 million copies. This narrow market share makes the price of programs for OS/2 expensive. Many programmers have opted to write programs for windows, which is in greater demand than OS/2.

*   **Fewer users** - (1/7) that of DOS with Windows and far less users than DOS.

Compared to **Windows NT**, flexibility is not an advantage for OS/2, however, none of the disadvantages apply. OS/2 only operates on IBM and compatibles, while Windows NT can operate in a wider variety of microcomputers. In addition, OS/2 does not have built in networking, multiprocessing, and multiuser capabilities.

MACINTOSH OPERATING SYSTEMS (pages 51-53)

The "graphical user interface" was available in the Apple Macintosh even before OS/2. Apple introduced new models on frequent intervals and there are several unique versions of its operating system. Unfortunately, these versions are not "backward compatible" (not like DOS), meaning that many applications designed for the newer Macintosh will not run on the older versions of the Macintosh. **System 7** allows applications to exchange both data and instructions.

Advantages of the Apple Macintosh include:

*   **Quality graphics** - This has been the principal reason for its success because users can easily merge pictures and text to produce near professional quality output.

*   **Ease of use** - The graphical interface is popular with novices to the microcomputer. The reason for the popularity is because the need and effort required for learning to use this operating system is half as much as that of learning DOS.

*   **Consistent graphics interface** - The user has similar screen displays, menus, and operations across all applications.

*   **Multitasking** - The Macintosh System 7.0 has multitasking capability.

*   **Communications between programs** - The System 7.0 allows programs to easily share data and commands with other applications programs.

Disadvantages of the Apple Macintosh include:

*   **Lacks serious consideration as a business machine** - The general perception of the business community has not been favorable to the Macintosh as a business computer.

*   **Difficulties in compatibility** - In the past, DOS and Macintosh have had incompatible microprocessors. Hardware and software are now available for the Mac allowing it to run DOS applications. Recently, Apple developed links with Digital Equipment Corporation (DEC). They have made DOS-compatible circuit boards available and have developed ways of connecting the Macintosh into communications networks that use DOS.

Originally, **UNIX** was developed by AT&T as a minicomputer operating system; it now runs on microcomputers. Its popularity exists because for many years it has been used at universities. As the computer science graduates became employed, many of them promoted it as the operating system to use to their respective employers.

This operating system is less well known to the business community.

The more powerful development of the '386 and '486 chip technology has created a situation where UNIX has the possibility of competing in the microcomputer arena.

Versions

The principal microcomputer versions of UNIX include: AT&T's UNIX System V; the University of California's Berkeley 4.2 UNIX; IBM has AIX; and the Open Software Foundation is trying to create a UNIX standard. This foundation is a consortium of seven major computer suppliers led by IBM and DEC.

Advantages of UNIX include:

* **Portable programming language** - This means that it is able to be used with many different computer systems. The other operating systems are not nearly as portable as UNIX.

* **Multitasking** - means the CPU is shared to do more than one program at a time.

* **Multiuser** - UNIX can also share the CPU and the system resources with multiple users. OS/2 does not have this capability, however, because hardware costs have dropped substantially, this is not as big a factor in the selection of an operating system.

  Networking - Unix is able to share files over electronic networks with many different kinds of computer equipment. Other operating systems can now perform this service, but UNIX has successfully been accomplishing this for several years.

Disadvantages of using UNIX include:

* **Limited business applications software** - There are many engineering applications programs, but there are very few business applications programs. Businesses are very dependent on running off-the-shelf software. The few applications that do exist usually require customizing, usually an expensive proposition. Many DOS users lack the experience to customize UNIX programs.

* **No UNIX standard** - There is no UNIX standard at any level. As discussed above, there are several different versions of UNIX available. The significance of this is when an application is written for one version of UNIX, it will not likely work in a different version of UNIX.

23

* **Difficult for the novice** - The commands in UNIX tend to be cryptic and difficult for new users to learn.

FUTURE OPERATING SYSTEMS (page 55)

What will replace DOS? What is the best choice for an operating system?

These questions are difficult to answer even for those considered to be "in-the-know" regarding computers. Although other operating systems may be easier to use, DOS has a great many users. And, at present, other operating systems do not seem to offer many of these users enough benefit to make them want to change operating systems.

As we prepare for the future, some observers believe **windowing software** and Macintosh will be the solution for many users who are waiting for the dust to settle to determine the best choice of an operating system for the future, especially home users and small businesses.

Large organizations, universities, and major governmental units will likely use Microsoft's **Windows New Technology (NT)**; OS/2;or, UNIX. In addition, a joint venture of Apple and IBM known as **Taligent** which uses a technology called **object-oriented programming**. This involves creating an operating system with a series of interchangeable software objects or modules (quite different from the layers of computer code that other operating systems employ) making the development of applications software less expensive and more expedient.

REVIEW QUESTIONS
True/False

F   1.   One computer can <u>only run one</u> kind of system software.

T   2.   Virtual memory increases the amount of memory available to run applications programs.

T   3.   Mainframe and minicomputer systems tend to focus on multiple users of a single computer system.

F   4.   Macintosh computers are designed to use the <u>'486 microprocessor</u>.

F   5.   One of Unix's primary strengths is the <u>large number</u> of applications written for it.

Multiple Choice

C   1.   The collection of programs that helps the computer manage its resources: **Answer; operating system**

A   2.   The most widely used microcomputer operating system: **Answer; DOS**

D   3.   The ability to have a number of applications running at the same time: **Answer; multitasking**

B   4.   An operating system developed jointly by IBM and Microsoft Corporation: **Answer; OS/2**

A   5.   The multiuser microcomputer operating system: **Answer; UNIX**

Fill in the Blank

1. <u>Booting</u> the system means that the computer has been turned on and the operating system has been loaded into memory.

2. Of all the microcomputer operating systems, <u>DOS</u> is able to run on the least expensive hardware.

3. Window NT is an operating <u>system</u>.

4. The System file and the Finder are the two primary files in the <u>Macintosh</u> operating system.

5. The lack of a standard version for <u>UNIX</u> is likely its most significant disadvantage.

Open Ended

1. What, in a phrase, is the difference between applications software and systems software?

   Application software are computer programs that can perform useful work. Systems software are programs that help the computer to manage its own resources.

2. What are utility programs?

   The operating system contains one set of programs called utility programs which perform routine tasks such as formatting blank disks. This set of programs are known as external programs because they reside on the disk after DOS is loaded.

3. What is meant by multitasking?

   Multitasking is the capability of more than one application program to share the CPU at the same time.

4. What is a graphical user interface?

   A graphical user interface is a graphical windowing system. For every program running a window appears on the screen. These windows can be repositioned, made larger, smaller, expanded to fill the whole screen, and even shrunk to the size of a single character.

5. What is meant by the term multiuser?

   A multiuser system means that the CPU is shared with several programs and with several different users all at one time.

CHAPTER 4
THE CENTRAL PROCESSING UNIT
Chapter at a Glance

I. The Four Types of Computer Systems

    A. Microcomputer
       1. word size
       2. storage capacity
       3. clock speed
       4. cost
       5. type
          a. workstation
          b. portable
             1. laptop
             2. transportable
             3. notebook
             4. pocket

    B. Minicomputer
       1. word size
       2. storage capacity
       3. clock speed
       4. cost

    C. Mainframe computer
       1. word size
       2. storage capacity
       3. clock speed
       4. cost

    D. Supercomputer
       1. word size
       2. storage capacity
       3. clock speed
       4. cost

II. The CPU

    A. Control unit
    B. Arithmetic logic unit

III. Primary Storage

    A. Define its purpose
    B. Describe how it works

IV.   The Binary System

    A.   Identify its practical use with computers
    B.   Describe the classifications in bytes (characters)
    C.   Translate the two popular coding schemes
       1.   ASCII
       2.   EBCDIC
    D.   Parity Bit - Error Checking

V.   The System Unit

    A.   system board
    B.   microprocessor chips
    C.   memory
       1.   random access memory (RAM)
       2.   read only memory (ROM)
    D.   system clock
    E.   expansion slots
       1.   open and closed architecture
       2.   memory expansion boards
       3.   network adapter cards
       4.   combination cards
       5.   PC cards
    F.   bus line architecture
       1.   ISA - Industry Standard Architecture
       2.   MCA - Micro Channel Architecture
       3.   EISA - Extended Industry Standard Architecture
    G.   ports
       1.   serial
       2.   parallel
       3.   peripheral devices

OBJECTIVES

The student should be able to:

1.   Describe the four classifications of computer systems.

2.   Explain the two main parts of the central processing unit and identify their function.

3.   Understand the workings and the functions of memory.

4.   Describe how a computer uses binary codes to represent data in electrical form.

5.   Describe the components of the system unit in a microcomputer.

VOCABULARY

adapter cards	EBCDIC	microseconds	pocket personal
addresses	EISA	MCA	computers
ALU	EPROM	megabyte	processor
ASCII	expanded memory	megahertz	PROM
binary system	expansion boards	memory	RAM
bit	extended memory	motherboard	registers
bus line	firmware	notebook personal	RISC chips
bytes	gigabyte	computers	ROM
cache memory	interface cards	open architecture	register
client/server systems	internal storage	palmtops	semiconductor
closed architecture	integrated circuit	parity bit	silicon chip
coprocessor chip	ISA	peripheral devices	subnotebooks
control unit	kilobyte	PCMCIA cards	system board
controller cards	laptops	personal computers	system clock
conventional memory	local bus	plug-in boards	terabyte
distributed data	main memory	ports	upper memory
processing	massively parallel	primary storage	word
environments	processing		workstations

THE FOUR TYPES of COMPUTER SYSTEMS (pages 60-65) *TM 4.01*

Microcomputers are of two types: personal computers and workstations.

Personal computers perform personal computing needs at home and in the office and are classified as desktop or portable. **Portable computers** are growing in popularity because of the more powerful and smaller size of this class of computer system. There are four categories of portable computers:

* **Transportable computers** weigh from 18 to 25 pounds and feature greater computing power and higher quality screen output.

* **Laptops** are lightweight portables ranging from just under 10 to 16 pounds. They can be powered by a battery and can fit into a brief case or be carried using a shoulder strap.

* **Notebook**-size computers (weigh between 8 and 10 pounds) fit inside a briefcase and are most popular for note taking.

* **Pocket PCs** are hand-held, weigh as little as one pound, and are too small to fit in one's lap. These **palmtops** are intended to complement personal computers, not replace them. They can connect with desktop computers or networks and exchange data with them.

Workstations - The concept of workstations is changing dramatically due to technological advances. Until recently, workstations were expensive, powerful machines that engineers, scientists and other used for multitasking and powerful networking links. The powerful processor of the work station was the major difference between a workstation and a microcomputer. Today, the microprocessors used in many popular personal computer systems are providing workstation capabilities to end users.

Minicomputers were developed as special-purpose mainframe computers which are faster and can store more than a microcomputer.

Mainframe computers process millions of instructions per second. They are often used as a decentralized computer system meeting the computing needs of banks, airlines, insurance companies, and most of the large corporations.

Supercomputers can process over one billion program instructions per second; measured in **nanoseconds** (billionths of a second) and possibly even in **picoseconds** (trillionths of a second). A select few have the computing needs to justify the expense of a supercomputer system. It is used principally for worldwide weather forecasting, oil exploration, and weapons research. The most powerful supercomputers use **massively parallel processing** consisting of thousands of interconnected microprocessors.

The CPU (page 66) *TM 4.02*

The **Central Processing Unit** is the part of the computer system that executes the program instructions. It consists of the **control unit** and the **arithmetic-logic unit**.

* The **control-unit** tells the computer system how to carry out a program's instructions. It directs electronic signals between main-memory and the arithmetic-logic unit. The control unit also controls signals to and from the input and output devices.

* The **arithmetic-logic unit** (ALU) performs arithmetic operations (+,-,/,and *) and logical operations (=, <, and >) which compare two pieces of data.

MEMORY (pages 67-69)

Discuss the purpose of **main memory** (also known as primary storage, internal storage, RAM, and memory) to hold data for processing, the program, and information waiting to be output or stored in secondary storage.

Clarify the purpose of registers and how they are employed in the processing cycle.

Registers are additional storage locations which are part of the control unit and ALU. They make processing more efficient by acting as a high speed staging area that holds data and instructions temporarily during processing.

The processing cycle involves the interaction of primary storage and the CPU to process information. The computer stores characters of data or instructions in main memory at locations known as **addresses**. During each cycle of the computer's clock, a data word is fetched, decoded, executed and stored. The main memory uses an **address** that keeps track of the location of stored data and instructions. The address is a permanent label while the contents stored at a particular address can change continuously.

THE BINARY SYSTEM (pages 69-71) *TM 4.03 and TM 4.04*

Discuss how a computer is made up of electronic circuitry that controls electronic signals that represent data and instructions. These electronic signals have two conditions--ON and OFF.

Describe how the **binary number system** (with only two digits--0 and 1) is used when working on the computers level. In the computer, the 0 represents an "off" signal and the 1 represents an "on" signal. Each 0 and 1 is called a **bit** (binary digit) in the binary system. In order to represent numbers, letters, and special characters, bits are combined into groups of eight bits called **bytes**. A **byte** is the equivalent of one character.

Discuss how memory capacity and secondary storage is expressed in numbers of bytes:

A **kilobyte** (**K, KB,** or **K-byte**) represents   1,024 bytes (two to the power of ten).
A **megabyte** (**MB,** or **M-byte**) represents   1,024,000 bytes. (Million bytes)
A **gigabyte** (**GB,** or **G-byte**) represents   1,024,000,000 bytes. (Billion bytes)
A **terabyte** (**TB,** or **T-byte**) represents 1,024,000,000,000 bytes. (Trillion bytes)

Identify two popular coding schemes used in the conversion of a character into a byte.

Extended binary coded decimal interchange code (**EBCDIC** pronounced "eb-see-dick") is used predominately by mini- and mainframe computers.

American standard code for information interchange (**ASCII** pronounced "as-key") is most widely used as the binary coding scheme for microcomputers.

Discuss the use of a parity bit as a means of having the computer detect erroneous data. An extra bit is added to a byte during keyboarding as a means to test accuracy. There are even or odd parity systems and the value of the parity bit will always keep the character's value (added sideways) even or odd depending on the parity system. *TM 4.05*

The SYSTEM UNIT (pages 71-79) *TM 4.06 and TM 4.07*

The components of the system unit include: the system board, microprocessor chips, memory chips (RAM and ROM), system clock, expansion slots and boards, bus lines, and ports.

The system board (also called the **motherboard**) usually contains the CPU and main memory chips that are mounted on **carrier packages** that can be plugged into sockets on the system board. The system board also usually has expansion slots.

The processor chip is a single silicon chip containing the computer's CPU.   This **microprocessor-- "microscopic processor"** will vary in **word size** (the number of bits in a common unit of information that the computer reads in each cycle of its clock). The most common computer word sizes are 8, 16, 32, and 64. As the word size increases so does speed and power. The **RISC** (**reduced instruction set computer**) chip is beginning to supplant the present form of **CISC** (**complex instruction set computer**) chip.*TM 4.08*

The <u>random access memory</u> (RAM) is temporary storage. A microcomputer will contain a limited amount of RAM ranging from a few hundred thousand to several million.

Contrast conventional memory (the first 640K); with upper memory (from 640K to 1MB); extended memory (directly accessible above 1MB); and expanded memory (from 1MB to 32MB holds information which is swapped in and out of conventional memory).

* The **read-only memory (ROM)** consists of chips that have built-in instructions (programs) made part of the system board by the manufacturer of the computer. These chips cannot be changed by the user and provide the necessary instructions that the computer reads to perform basic operations. Variations of ROM include:

* **PROM (programmable read-only memory)** allows a software manufacturer to write instructions on a chip, with special equipment, that cannot be changed.

* **EPROM (erasable programmable read-only memory)** can be erased with special ultraviolet light so that new instructions can be written on it.

* **EEPROM (electrically erasable programmable read-only memory)** is another type of EPROM but is erased electronically.

The <u>system clock</u> controls the speed of operation of the computer system. The speed is expressed in **megahertz (MHz** which equals a million cycles of the computers clock in one second). The faster the clock speed, the faster the computer can process information.

The <u>expansion slots</u> and <u>expansion boards</u> can provide the user with a great amount of versatility. Computers having expansion slots are known as **open-architecture** computers permitting the user to insert expansion boards. Some common expansion boards include:

* **Memory expansion boards** contain RAM chips that increase the computer's memory.

* **Network adapter cards** allow the user to connect to one or more computers.

* **Combination cards** are multifunction boards combining several expansion activities on one board. These cards are especially useful for systems with a small number of expansion slots available.

* **PC cards** are credit card-sized to meet the size constraints of portable computers. They are called **PCMCIA (Personal Computer Memory Card International Association)** cards. They perform the same variety of functions described above in the larger expansion cards and boards.

Computers having no expansion slots or capabilities are said to have a **closed-architecture.**

The <u>bus line</u> connects the CPU with peripheral devices and other parts of the computer system. It is a data roadway on which bits travel resembling a multi-lane highway. The greater the number of lanes the faster data can travel. The three principal bus line architectures are:

* **Industry Standard Architecture (ISA)** was first used by IBM as an 8-bit wide data path. This was later widened to 16 bits when the IBM AT was introduced.

* **Micro Channel Architecture (MCA)** developed when IBM decided to support the new '386 chip with a 32-bit bus line. This architecture lacks the compatibility to allow owners of IBM AT computers to utilize old expansion boards in this new architecture.

* **Extended Industry Standard Architecture (EISA)** was proposed by nine manufacturers of IBM clones to work as a 32-bit standard that extends from the old ISA standard. The significant difference between EISA and MCA is that the former will allow all existing expansion boards to work with the new 32-bit architecture.

* A <u>Port</u> is a socket on the outside of the system unit allowing the user to plug other devices into the computer system. A **parallel port** allows lines to be connected that will transmit several bits simultaneously. This type of port is often used by printers and other devices physically located close to the computer. A **serial port** transmits bits one after the other on a single communications line. This type of port is used frequently to link equipment physically located at a distance from the computer system. *TM 4.09*

Clarify the devices used outside of the system unit--but not necessarily outside the system cabinet--are called peripheral devices. A peripheral device would include printers, plotters, phone modems, monitors, disk drives, keyboard and other devices attached to the computer.

A LOOK AT THE FUTURE (pages 72-73) *TM 4.10*

Discuss four new technologies that could make computing faster:

RISC (Reduced Instruction Set Computer) microprocessors will probably begin to replace the present **CISC (Complex Instruction Set Computer)** form of chip design. It is believed by some observers the RISC chip will triple the performance of the desktop processor.

New **superconducting semiconductors** allow electricity to flow through the chips without resistance. This improvement over the present day silicon chip offers the possibility of faster on-off processing to permit lightning-quick computers. This technology was thought to be impractical because the material had to be at extremely low, subzero temperatures. Recent research is now being done on "warm" superconductors.

Optical computing uses laser technology which operates with light rather than currents of electricity to represent the on-off codes of data. Light is much faster than electricity so this technology is getting much attention from the computer industry.

Neural networks differ from the **von Neumann architecture** of which most present day computers are based. Instead of having a single processor, a neural network consists of layers of processors interconnected somewhat like the neurons of a biological nervous system. This arrangement allows data to be transmitted to and from a processor many times faster than the old von Neumann architecture.

These new technologies will allow us to build smaller and faster computers that may permit us to have desktop computers, in the year 2000, that are as powerful as the first supercomputer.

REVIEW QUESTIONS

True/False

F   1. Workstations are classified as <u>minicomputers</u>.

F   2. <u>Mainframe</u> computers are also known as midrange computers.

T   3. Registers are high-speed areas for temporarily holding data and instructions.

T   4. Another name for a system board is a motherboard.

T   5. Network adapter cards are used to connect the system unit to a communication network.

Multiple Choice

D   1. The type of portable microcomputer that fits comfortably into most briefcases: **Answer; notebook**

E   2. The computer system used for large special-purpose applications like predicting weather worldwide: **Answer; supercomputer**

B   3. The measure of capacity that represents 1 million bytes: **Answer; megabyte**

D   4. In a microcomputer, the CPU is contained on a single chip called: **Answer; microprocessor**

A   5. The new bus that IBM developed to support the '386 chip: **Answer; MCA**

Fill in the Blank

1. A <u>pocket</u> personal computer is very small and can easily be held in one hand.

2. Another name for internal storage and primary storage is <u>memory</u>.

3. An extra bit automatically added to a byte to test for transmission errors is called a <u>parity</u> bit.

4. <u>RAM</u> memory chips are volatile and lose their contents if the power to the computer is turned off or disrupted.

5. <u>Serial</u> ports are widely used for a variety of purposes including connecting a mouse, keyboard, modem, and other devices to the system unit.

Open Ended

1. Distinguish between the four kinds of computer systems.

    The following classifications identify the four types of computer systems:

    Microcomputer systems are the smallest form of computers. They range in price from a few hundred up to fifteen thousand dollars. The size of the system allows it to fit nicely on most office desks, some are even portable. The processing capability of these machines can rival minicomputers and easily surpass the power of some older mainframe model computers.

    Minicomputer systems range from several thousand to half million dollars in cost. Generally, they are more powerful, faster at processing, and can store more data than contemporary microcomputers.

    Mainframe computer systems costs several thousand dollars but can easily range into the millions of dollars. They can process millions of instructions per second and can permit a multiple user environment.

    Super computer systems can cost several million dollars. The power of a supercomputer allows it to process over one billion instruction per second.

2. Describe how the control unit, arithmetic-logic unit, and memory work to process information.

    The main memory and the CPU work together in a five step process that turns data into information.

    1. Data enters the computer from an input device.
    2. The data and the program are held temporarily in memory.
    3. The control unit supervises the transfer of data between main memory and the arithmetic-logic unit.
    4. The arithmetic-logic unit performs the calculations on the data (processing the data according to the program's instructions).
    5. Processed data is sent to an output device.

3a. What is the difference between the decimal system and the binary system?

    The decimal system is based on ten digits (0-9). Each place value is a unit of ten for the place value to the immediate right. The first five whole unit place values starting on the right and working left are: 1s, 10s, 100s, 1000s, 10000s, etc.. The binary system works on the same principal, however it is based on a unit of two digits 0 and 1. Each place value is a power of two greater than the place value on the right. The first five whole unit place values starting on the right and working left are: 1s, 2s, 4s, 8s, 16s, etc..

3b.   Why is the binary system used in computers to represent data and instructions?

A computer is made up of electronic circuitry controlling electronic signals representing data and instructions. These electronic signals have two conditions--ON and OFF. When a program or a user communicates with the computer it must be translated into ON and Off signals. A convenient number system representing the ON and OFF signals is the binary number system. The binary system has only two digits--0 and 1. In the computer, the 0 represents an "off" signal and the 1 represents an "on" signal.

4.   What kinds of expansion boards are available for what purposes?

Some common expansion boards include:

Memory expansion boards containing RAM chips that increase the computer's memory.

Network adapter cards allowing the user to connect to one or more computers.

Combination cards with multifunctions combining several expansion activities on one board. These cards are especially useful for systems with a small number of expansion slots available.

PC cards (credit card-sized) meet the size constraints of portable computers. They are called PCMCIA (Personal Computer Memory Card International Association) cards. They perform the same variety of functions described above in the larger expansion cards and boards.

5.   Name the three alternative bus architectures.

The three bus line architectures are Industry Standard Architecture (ISA, Micro Channel Architecture (MCA), and Extended Industry Standard Architecture (EISA).

CHAPTER 5
INPUT and OUTPUT
Chapter at a Glance

I.   Input: Keyboard versus Direct Entry

   A. Keyboard Entry
     1. typewriter keys
     2. function keys
     3. numeric keys
     4. directional arrow keys
     5. special purpose keys

   B. Terminals
     1. dumb
     2. smart
     3. intelligent

   C. Direct Entry
     1. pointing devices
       a. mouse
       b. touch screen
       c. digitizer
       d. light pen

     2. scanning devices
       a. image scanner
       b. dedicated fax machines
       c. bar code
       d. magnetic-ink character recognition (MICR)
       e. optical-character recognition (OCR)
       f. optical-mark recognition (OMR)
       g. point-of-sale terminal (POS)
       h. touch-tone device

     3. voice input devices

     4. other direct-entry devices

II. Output
  A. Types of Monitors
    1. color
    2. monochrome
    3. resolution
    4. technology
      a. flat-panel display
        1. liquid-crystal display (LCD)
        2. electroluminescent (EL)
        3. gas plasma
        4. color
          a. passive-matrix panel
          b. active-matrix panel
      b. Cathode Ray Tube (CRT)
        1. color graphics adapter (CGA)
        2. enhanced graphics adapter (EGA)
        3. video graphics array (VGA)
        4. super video graphics array (SVGA)
        5. extended graphics array (XGA)
  B. Printers for Microcomputers
    1. dot-matrix
    2. laser
    3. ink-jet
    4. thermal
    5. other
      a. daisy-wheel
      b. chain
  C. Plotters
  D. Voice Output

III. Future Developments

OBJECTIVES
The student should be able to:

1. Explain the difference between keyboard and direct-entry input devices and the POS terminal.

2. Describe the features of keyboards and the three types of terminals.

3. Describe the direct-entry devices used with microcomputers.

4. Explain output devices including monochrome, color monitors, and flat-panel displays.

5. Describe and contrast the various types of printers.

6. Describe the application of voice-output devices.

37

VOCABULARY

bar code reader	EGA	mouse	speech recognition
bidirectional	Enter	numeric key pad	SVGA
CGA	facsimile transmission	numeric keys	terminal
cursor control keys	machines	OCR	thermal printer
dedicated fax machines	fax boards	OMR	touch screen
digitizer	fax machine	pen-based computer	tractor feed
digitizing tablet	hardcopy	platform scanner	typewriter keys
direct entry	image scanner	POS terminal	VGA
direct imaging plotter	ink-jet	reader/sorter	virtual fax board
directional arrow keys	intelligent terminal	Return	voice-input
dot matrix printer	laser printer	smart terminal	voice-output
dumb terminal	light pen	softcopy	wand reader
		source document	XGA

INPUT: KEYBOARD versus DIRECT ENTRY (pages 86-87)

Input devices take data that people can read or understand and convert it to a form that can be used by the computer (electronic on and off signals).

Keyboard entry devices allow data to be input through a keyboard similar to a typewriter. Data is typically entered from a **source document**.

Direct entry employs devices (ie. wand reader or platform scanner) other than a keyboard to input computer readable data.

KEYBOARD ENTRY (pages 87-88) *TM 5.01*

Keyboards vary in size and shape depending on the intended purpose. Most keyboards of today's computer systems will have the following:

* **Typewriter keys** resemble the letters, numbers, punctuation marks, and most special characters found on a typewriter keyboard, including an **enter** or **return** key.

* **Function keys** labeled as "F1", "F2", and so on, through a sequence of ten or twelve keys, each may take on a special purpose or task depending on which application program is currently running. These keys can be programmed to do a variety of tasks meeting the specific needs of the user. Function keys save keystrokes and limit repetitive tasks.

* **Numeric keys** are on the top row of the typewriter keyboard and most computer keyboards also have a numeric key pad on the right hand side of the keyboard.

* The **directional arrow keys** are used for moving the cursor. Many keyboards have two sets of arrow keys: on the numeric key pad and a separate set that are solely direction keys.

* <u>Special-purpose keys</u> would include **Ctrl (control)**, **Del (delete)**, **Alt (alternate)**, etc.. Some of these keys can perform editing tasks (like Del) while others are only used in conjunction with other keys (like Ctrl and Alt) to perform tasks or special operations.

*Contrast the use of **terminals** with larger computers and a keyboard with a microcomputer.*

A **terminal** is an input/output device that includes a keyboard, a monitor, and a communications link into a CPU. The three types of terminals are:

* A <u>dumb terminal</u> does not have its own processor, thus, cannot process data independently. It is used solely as a means of inputting data and receiving information.

* A <u>smart terminal</u> has limited memory capacity to allow users to perform some editing or verification of data before it is sent to the CPU for processing.

* An <u>intelligent terminal</u> is a computer; meaning that it has a CPU, primary and secondary storage, and software for processing data. A microcomputer can be an intelligent terminal.

DIRECT ENTRY (pages 88-94) *TM 5.02*

Direct entry devices create machine-readable data on a medium that can be input directly into a CPU. This is a very efficient means of input that is economical and less prone to error compared to data that is key entered. Direct-entry devices are categorized into the three areas of pointing, scanning, and voice-input:

<u>Pointing Devices</u>

* A **mouse** which is a device for moving the cursor or pointer around the screen.

* A **touch screen** is a monitor screen covered with a plastic layer. Behind this layer of plastic are crisscrossed beams of infrared light. When the screen is touched the position of the contact is determined by the break in the coordinates of the infrared beams.

* A **digitizer** is a device used to convert an image into digital data that is input into the computer. The digitizer is moved or scanned over a drawing or photograph that will send the digital data to the screen, a printer, or to a disk for storage.

* A **light pen** is used with a special type of monitor that allows for the entering or modification of data that appears on the screen. When the light pen is placed against or near the screen's surface, it activates a photoelectric circuit.

* **Pen-based computing** is a small computer with a stylus to write directly on the display screen. This system works uses software to recognize a person's handwriting. The input can be stored as an image or with some systems can convert the handwriting into **typescript**.

Scanning Devices record images of text, drawings, and special symbols which are converted to digital form.

* An **image scanner (bit-mapping device)** converts images into electronic signals for processing and storage in the computer. The process identifies pictures or different typefaces by scanning the image with light and breaking it into light and dark dots.

* **Facsimile transmission machines (fax machines)** are an extremely popular office machine providing all the convenience of a copy machine but takes a step further by sending the copy electronically through the telephone lines to a receiving fax machine. *TM 5.03*

* **Bar-code readers** employ photoelectric scanners which read zebra-striped marks representing a product or identification value. This value is part of a standardized bar-code system being used in a particular application (ie. **Universal Product Code (UPC)** used in supermarkets).

* **Magnetic-ink character recognition (MICR)** is used by banks to read the numbers found at the bottom of check. A reader/sorter is the direct-entry device used to read the characters that are made of ink containing magnetized particles.

* **Optical-character recognition (OCR)** uses special characters read with a wand reader or some other type of OCR device. The characters have a specific formation that can not have any deviation if the OCR reader is to correctly read the character. This method of data entry is often used by retail stores and utility companies.

* **Optical-mark recognition (OMR)** senses the absence or presence of a mark (usually made with a pencil).

Voice-input devices (also known as **speech-recognition** or **voice-recognition devices**) converts human speech into digital code. The countless qualities making each individual's voice different, requires the system to be calibrated to the user's voice. This is accomplished by speaking into the device to store the unique speech patterns. These patterns are matched to the spoken data entered as input by the same user. Problems can occur if the user develops a cold. Some systems can recognize the spoken word of many people, however, the vocabulary is limited. The advantage of a voice-input system is that it frees the user's hands for other tasks.

Other Direct-Entry Devices

* A **point-of-sale terminal (POS)** has a keyboard, a screen, and a printer. They are used like a cash register in various types of stores. They often have a **bar code reader** or **scanner** that can read the zebra-striped Universal Product Code (**UPC**). This code can be matched with the product in the computer and create a receipt with the product name and price. It will also make adjustments to the inventory as the product is sold.

* A **touch-tone device** uses the telephone lines to send data to a computer. A **card dialer** can be used to determine an individual's credit card status by running the credit card through the dialer. Signals are sent via the telephone line to the computer and returns a status report that the user can read from the card dialer.

OUTPUT (pages 94-97)

The purpose of an output device to give the user feedback in an understandable form. Devices commonly used for output include monitors, printers, plotters, and voice.

MONITORS - may be classified by: resolution quality; single color (**monochrome**) or **color** display capability; and use with portable or larger computers.

Resolution is determined by the density of **pixels** (individual dots or picture elements) on the screen and the type of technology of the monitor.

* Larger computers, typically use **cathode-ray tube (CRT)** technology, while portable computers employ flat-panel display.

Today, a **monochrome** monitor (one color- usually amber, green, or white against a dark or solid background) is used principally with portable computers in **flat-panel technology**. A **flat-panel display** is classified into **liquid-crystal (LCD)**, **electroluminescent (EL)**, and **gas-plasma**.

* The **LCD** uses liquid crystal molecules having optical properties altered by an electric field.

* An **EL** is able to emit light when it is electrically charged.

* A **gas-plasma** display produces near CRT quality; however, it cannot run on batteries and does not show sharp contrast.

Color monitors for portable computers may be **passive-matrix** or **active-matrix** panels. Active-matrix panels are more expensive, but display more colors, faster and brighter than passive-matrix panels.

The most common color monitors use CRT technology. The technology has gone through the following stages: *TM 5.04*

* **CGA** (color graphics adapter), gives the computer color graphic capability. In a monochrome mode its resolution quality is 640 x 320 pixels. In a color mode, resolution for four colors is 320 x 200 pixels producing less defined text with a course grain.

* **EGA** (enhanced graphics adapter), has a resolution of 640 x 350 pixels supporting 16 colors. Purchasing this very popular board usually requires a monitor upgrade.

41

* **VGA** (video graphics adapter), in a text mode, this board has a resolution of 720 x 400 pixels. With 16 colors this board will produce resolution of 640 x 480 pixels.

* **Super VGA** displays up to 256 colors and has a minimum resolution of 800 x 600 pixels. This technology is used by highly skilled graphic designers and individuals who need the sharpest resolution and the most color available.

* **XGA** (extended graphics array) has a resolution up to 1024 x 768 pixels. It displays up to 256 colors under normal conditions. With special enhancements, it can display up to 65,536 colors. This monitor is becoming the standard for PS/2 486 processor technology.

PRINTERS (pages 97-102)

Printers used with microcomputers include dot-matrix, laser, ink-jet, and thermal.

* The **dot-matrix** printer forms its image using a matrix of pins traveling horizontally back and forth as the paper is fed through vertically. Each pin can form a dot on the paper. These dots are configured together to form images. The features of dot-matrix printers include: reliability; relatively fast printing; capability to print near letter-quality documents; ability to make a graphic image; and printing color using a multi-color ribbon. The dot-matrix printer is the most popular printer used with microcomputers.

* The **laser-printer** creates an image so sharp it has spawned the industry of desk-top publishing. Used with special software, the laser printer can merge text and graphics having a quality comparable to professional typesetters and graphic artist. The laser-printer bounces a laser beam on to a drum forming a "dotlike" image. This image is a magnetically charged "inklike" toner transferred from the drum to paper. A final process of heat makes the characters adhere to the paper. *TM 5.07*

* The **ink-jet** sprays droplets of ink producing a high quality image in a variety of colors. This type of printer allows the user to duplicate the color image appearing on the screen.

* **Thermal printers** use heat elements to produce images on heat-sensitive paper. They produce high quality color artwork and text at a low cost.

Other printer types include:

* The **daisy-wheel** printer has a type set for each character on the keyboard. A hammer strikes the type set to the ribbon against the paper to form the image. The daisy-wheel printer features very high quality print and the ability to exchange wheels for different fonts of print. Speed; inability to print quality graphics;, and initial cost (usually higher than the cost of a dot-matrix printer) are all disadvantages of the daisy-wheel printer.

* The **chain printer** is an expensive, high-speed (3000 lines/minute), and reliable printer. The microcomputer network has made this technology cost justifiable for the microcomputer environment. Several sets of characters are hooked together on a printing chain, which revolves in front of the ribbon and paper. Hammers aligned with each position strike the character as it passes by a particular position.

Some general qualities to note about microcomputer printers include:

* **Bidirectional** - print head printing as it moves in both directions.

* **Tractor feed** - reducing misalignment of continuous form paper.

* **Type styles** - fonts are changed by software and the right kind of printer hardware. Some (not all) printers have exchangeable printing elements to allow for a different type style.

* **Shared use** - the ability to have more than one computer share expensive resources. Dot-matrix and daisy-wheel printers are often used with a single microcomputer. Ink-jet, laser, and chain printers are often linked to several computers through a communications network.

* **Portability** - is another consideration when selecting a printer. Portable printers are more rugged, battery operated, weigh less than 7 pounds, and are typically dot-matrix or ink-jet.

PLOTTERS (page 102)

Plotters produce a type of hardcopy output intended for producing bar charts, maps, architectural drawings, and three dimensional illustrations. Some plotters also handle large size documents. They come in four types: pen, ink-jet, electrostatic, and direct image.

* **Pen** plotters include: the **flatbed (table plotter)** with stationary paper and moving pens drawing the image; and the **drum plotter** with pens moving horizontally and paper rolling vertically on a drum. The paper and pen move at the same time to make a curved line.

* **Ink-jet** plotters form images by spraying droplets of ink onto paper. They can quietly produce good quality color output relatively quickly. The major disadvantage is clogged ink-jets, requiring more maintenance.

* The **electrostatic plotter** uses charges making little dots on specially treated paper to produce an image. Electrostatic plotters produce high-resolution images in less time than conventional pen plotters.

* **Direct imaging** plotters (**thermal** use heat-sensitive paper and electrically heated pins to produce good high-quality two-color output.

VOICE-OUTPUT DEVICES (page 103)

Output vocalizing prerecorded sounds the computer activates to resemble human speech.

A LOOK AT THE FUTURE (page 103)

Input/output processes will undergo some significant transition as:

* portable computers become smaller and have wireless communication capability.
* keyboards are replaced with devices that convert handwritten text into electronic data.
* voice-recognition technology becomes more sophisticated.
* one-inch display screens are developed for hand-held computers.
* flat-panel, full-color screens replace CRTs.
* graphics become more lifelike (3-dimensional video holograms).
* microcomputers and television technologies merge allowing us to watch TV on our computer--but, also to freeze video images to create still images that can be stored.
* digital high-definition television (HDTV)

REVIEW QUESTIONS

True/False

T 1. Input devices translate symbols that people understand into symbols that computers can process.

F 2. A <u>plotter</u> is a device that can be used to trace or copy a drawing or photograph.

T 3. Banks use a method called magnetic-ink character recognition (MICR) to automatically read and sort checks.

F 4. Laser printers are highly reliable <u>but the quality of their output limits their use to rough drafts and in-house communications</u>.

T 5. Plotters are special-purpose drawing devices.

Multiple Choice

E 1. Esc, Ctrl, Del, and Ins are <u>special-purpose</u> keys.

B 2. A device that converts images on a page to electronic signals that can be stored in a computer: **Answer; scanner**

A 3. The type of portable color panel that can display more colors, faster, and brighter: **Answer; active-matrix**

E 4. The printer that produces very high quality images using heat elements on heat-sensitive paper: **Answer; thermal**

C 5. The plotter that creates images using heat-sensitive paper and electrically heated pins: **Answer; direct imaging**

Fill in the Blank

1. Another name for the mouse that has a ball that is controlled with the thumb is **trackball or rollerball**.

2. **Fax** machines are popular office machines because they can transfer documents at electronic speeds.

3. The **dot-matrix** printer is a reliable, inexpensive printer that forms letters by a series of small pins on a print head.

4. Many printers can print a line either right to left or left to right. This feature is called **bi-directional** printing.

5. **Voice-output** devices make sounds that resemble human speech.

Open Ended

1. What are the differences between keyboard entry and direct entry as forms of input?

   Data that is entered from a typewriter like keyboard is referred to as keyboard entry data. Data that is produced in a computer-processable form as it is entered into the computer is referred to as direct entry data.

2. What is a POS terminal? What are the two input devices on it that represent the two methods of inputting data?

   A point-of-sale terminal has a keyboard, a screen, and a printer. They are used like a cash register in various types of stores. They often have a bar code reader or scanner that can read the zebra-striped Universal Product Code. This code can be matched with the product in the computer and create a receipt with the product name and price.

3. Distinguish among the three kinds of terminals: dumb, smart, and intelligent.

   A dumb terminal does not have its own processor, thus, cannot process data independently. It is used solely as a means of inputting data and receiving information.

   A smart terminal has limited memory capacity to allow users to perform some editing or verification of data before it is sent to the CPU for processing.

   An intelligent terminal is a computer in its own right, meaning that it has a CPU, primary and secondary storage, and software for processing data. Usually a microcomputer serves as the intelligent terminal.

45

4. What are pixels? What do they have to do with screen resolution?

Resolution is determined by the density of pixels on the screen. A pixel is an individual dot or picture element when combined with other pixels form a screen image. A matrix of 200 row by 300 column dots is a medium resolution quality, 200 by 640 is considered a high resolution display.

5. Is voice output more difficult to engineer than voice input? If so, Why?

No. Synthesized speech activated by a computer has many applications and is much easier to use than voice-input because humans have a discriminating ability to understand the spoken word from a variety of sources. A computer has difficulty duplicating this human ability because of the countless variables that are involved when humans speak.

CHAPTER 6
SECONDARY STORAGE
Chapter at a Glance

I.   Direct Access Versus Sequential Access

II.   Four Kinds of Secondary Storage

    A. Diskettes
        1. direct access
        2. parts of a diskette
        3. care and treatment

    B. Hard Disk
        1. internal
        2. hard-disk cartridge
        3. hard-disk pack
        4. access time
            a. seek time
            b. head switching time
            c. rotational delay time
            d. data transfer time
        5. head crash
        6. data compression

    C. Optical Disks
        1. CD-ROM
        2. WORM
        3. reusable

    D. Magnetic Tape
        1. sequential access
        2. tape streamers
        3. tape reels
            a. IRG
            b. IBG
            c. tape libraries

III. A Look at the Future of Secondary Storage

OBJECTIVES

The student should be able to:

1. Contrast direct access and sequential access storage.

2. Describe how diskettes and disk drives work and how to take care of them.

3. Describe the following: internal hard disk; hard-disk cartridge; and hard-disk packs.

4. Describe ways to improve the hard-disk operations of: disk caching; data compression; and redundant arrays of inexpensive disks.

5. Discuss optical disks.

6. Describe magnetic tape streamers and magnetic tape reels.

VOCABULARY

access arm	drive B	magnetic tape streamer	seek
access time	drive A	magnetic tape drives	seek time
backup tape cartridge	drive gate	nonvolatile	sequential access
unit	erasable optical disk	optical disk	storage
CD-ROM	flexible disks	program disk	soft-sectored disks
data transfer time	floppies	read-only	supply reel
data compression	floppy disks	read-write heads	take-up reel
decompression	hard-disk packs	redundant arrays of	tape libraries
digital audiotape (DAT)	head crash	inexpensive disks	tracks
drives	head switching time	(RAIDS)	volatile
direct access storage	internal hard disk	rotational delay time	WORM
disk caching	jacket	search	write once
disks	magnetic tape units	sectors	write-enable ring
			write-protect notch

Identify the purpose of secondary storage and contrast the two approaches to external storage: sequential and direct access.

A disk unit (also known as a **random access** or **direct access**) is an **online system**. It is much faster than a sequential access system and allows the computer to move to a specific item of data for retrieval at any moment. A **sequential access system** uses a tape storage medium requiring the computer to reel through the file to find the desired data. This method takes much longer but has the benefits of providing unlimited storage capacity and more security because it is **offline**.

FOUR KINDS OF SECONDARY STORAGE (pages 110-111) *TM 6.01*

Secondary storage for a microcomputer may be on floppy disk, hard disk, optical disk or tape.

Floppy disks are 5 1/4-inch size or the 3 1/2-inch size and made of a **mylar** plastic, coated with a metallic substance (usually iron oxide). The disk drive arranges the disk's metallic surface into electromagnetic impulses representing an "on" or an "off" signal on the disk.

The main components of the **floppy drive** include: a **drive gate** and a **read/write head** which moves on an **access arm**. The arm moves back and forth over individual tracks in a **seek** operation. At the same time the spindle rotates the disk to the desired location to read or write the data (this is called the **search** operation).

For convenience and additional storage capacity, many systems have two floppy disk drive units. The units are identified as **drive A** (usually found on the left or top if there is more than one drive), and **drive B** (usually found on the right or bottom of drive A).

The **parts of a disk** include :
* **tracks** - concentric circles where data may be placed
* **sectors** - divide the tracks into pie-shaped sections
* **write-protect notch** - prevents data erasure by not allowing data to be written on a disk
* **data access area** - exposing floppy-disk surface to drive's read-write head

The various types of disk drives include: single sided, double sided, single density, double density, or even quad density. The disk label usually indicates the type of disk, such as "DS,DD" or "2S/2D" (for double sided, double density). The capacity of a disks will vary depending on its density and its size. However, size can be deceiving, typical a 5 1/4-inch floppy hold less than the 3 1/2-inch version of the same density and usable number of sides.

HARD DISKS (pages 115-118)

A hard disk is factory sealed having one or more metallic platters, an access arm, and read/write heads. The operation and size is much the same as a floppy disk drive unit (5 1/4-inch or 3 1/2-inch diameter disk). Because the integrity of the disk surface is greater (due to the lack of access and outside contaminants), a greater storage capacity is possible. In addition, the access time is faster and more reliable than a floppy disk system.

The tolerance between a hard disk system's read/write head and the disk is so thin that a particle of smoke would not fit between them. If the head touches the disk surface it could cause a **head crash**, ruining the unit. It is very important to know the care of your system, (especially when you plan to move it) this information should be in the owner's manual.

A **hard-disk cartridge** can be removed, allowing for unlimited storage capacity (limited only by the number of cartridges one makes available to the system) along with fast access.

A **hard-disk pack** is predominately used with mini and mainframe computers. It contains several platters stacked above one another. These platters are spaced to allow the access arm and the read/write heads (one set for the top side and one set for the bottom side) to move in and out. *TM 6.03 and TM 6.04*

Terms associated with disk technology include:

access time - time between the computer's request and the completed transfer of data
seek time - time it takes for the access arm to move into position over a track
switching time - activation speed fora particular read/write head
rotational delay time - time it takes for the disk to rotate under the read/write head
data transfer time - speed of data to transfer from the disk track to memory
performance enhancements - include disk caching, data compression, and RAIDS)

* **disk caching** - improves hard-disk performance by anticipating data needs.
* **data compression** and **decompression** - reduces the amount of space required to store data and programs
* **redundant arrays of inexpensive disks (RAIDS)** - expands external storage using networking and special software. Treats grouped disks as one large-capacity hard disk.

OPTICAL DISKS (pages 118-120) *TM 6.05*

An **optical disk** holds 650 megabytes of data, making an immense amount of information available to a microcomputer. An optical disk employs a laser beam which burns tiny pits representing data into the surface of a plastic or metal disk. The disk sizes vary in diameters of 3 1/2, 4 3/4, 5 1/4, 8, 12, and 14 inches. The kinds of optical disks available are:

CD-ROM (compact disk-read only memory) is a plastic disk with data represented as small pits in the disk surface. Data is imprinted on them by the manufacturer holding 540 to 738 MB of data. The user can only read this data off of the disk, data cannot be stored on the optical disk by the user.

WORM (write once, read many) is a metal-film disk surface recorded on by lasers. The user can write data on a surface area only once; it cannot be erased from the disk surface. The data written on this disk surface, does not deteriorate and can be read many times. This type of optical disk stores between 122 and 6400 MB of data.

Erasable Optical Disks is much like CD-ROM except it allows data to be written and erased from the disk surface. The predominant type is a **magneto-optical (MO)** disk drive which uses both magnetic and optical technologies. An erasable optical disk can store 281 to 320 MB of data.

MAGNETIC TAPE (pages 120-122)

Magnetic tape provides an excellent backup storage to a computer system's hard disk system. The two types of magnetic tape media are **magnetic tape streamers** and **magnetic tape reels**. In the event that a head crash should occur, a device called a **tape streamer** or **tape backup unit** can expediently duplicate the lost data off of a previously stored backup tape cartridge. It can store from 1 to 5 megabytes per minute, which is considerably faster than working with 40 - 50 floppy disks to backup the system.

SECONDARY STORAGE IN THE FUTURE (page 122)

Three storage technologies of the future which have promise to increase the storage capacity in more compact form are: **wet disks**; **glass disks**; and **holographic systems**.

* Wet disks replace the air cushion between the disk and the drive head with a liquid. This allows the drive head to get closer to the disk and read approximately twice the capacity of today's disk within the same storage space. This technology has an expected introduction date of 1996.

* Glass disks (while more expensive) can hold more data than the traditional hard disk made of aluminum. An advantage of this technology over wet disk technology is that glass disks can be used with traditional hard disk drives. Commercial versions are already on the market.

* **Holographic** storage (like those seen on a credit card) can potentially hold the equivalent of thousands of books in a three-dimensional "sugar cube" size of special material, retrievable in 1 second. This technology should be available within the next year.

REVIEW QUESTIONS

True/False

F   1.   Secondary storage holds information <u>within the CPU</u>.

T   2.   Floppy disks are also known as flexible disks and as floppies.

T   3.   Sectors are wedge-shaped sections on a disk.

T   4.   Cross formatting can cause problems when double-density disks are formatted at high density.

T   5.   Laser beams are used to record data on optical disks.

Multiple Choice

C   1.   Which of the following is exclusively a sequential access storage media? **Answer; magnetic tape**

A   2.   On a floppy-disk drive, data signals are transferred to the computer through: **Answer; read-write heads**

E   3.   The disk with the greatest capacity: **Answer; CD-ROM**

B   4.   The hard-disk type that has several platters aligned one above the other: **Answer; hard-disk pack**

B   5.   The method of improving hard-disk performance by anticipating data needs is: **Answer; disk caching**

Fill in the Blank

1.   The primary advantages of optical disks over the other kinds of external storage are direct access and **high capacity**.

2.   Data is recorded on a disk in rings called **tracks**.

3.   Internal hard disks have two advantages over floppy disks: **capacity** and speed.

4.   Data **transfer** time measures how long it takes to move data from the hard-disk track to memory.

5.   The two forms of tape storage are magnetic tape streamers and magnetic tape **reels**.

Open Ended

1.   Explain the difference between direct access storage and sequential access storage. Which is more apt to be identified with magnetic disk and which with magnetic tape?

Direct access storage is also known as random access storage because the data and information can be stored and later retrieved randomly. Disk storage technology is best suited for direct access storage.

A sequential access system stores the data sequentially in a numeric or alphabetic organization. Magnetic tape is most often used with sequential access. To access data, the computer must reel through the tape to find the desired data. This method takes much longer but has the added benefit of providing unlimited storage capacity.

2. What are the four kinds of secondary storage? What are their relative advantages and disadvantages?

Floppy diskette - Advantage: inexpensive; direct access
Disadvantage: low capacity (1.44mb); slow access

Hard disk - Advantage: fast; direct access
Disadvantage: Limited capacity for each disk not easily removed

Optical disk - Advantage: High capacity; direct access
Disadvantage: Slow access, predominately a read-only technology

Magnetic tape - Advantage: High capacity
Disadvantage: Slow; sequential access only

3. State the three primary rules about taking care of flexible diskettes.

1. Don't bend the diskettes.
2. Don't touch the inner surface of the disk.
3. Keep disks away from magnetic fields, extreme heat, and chemical solvents.

4. What is so disastrous about a head crash?

The a head crash occurs when the read/write heads touch the disk surface when it is in operation. This causes a loss of data or loss of access to the stored on the disk.

5. What are the three types of hard-disk drives? Discuss their differences and similarities.

An internal hard disk drive may have a capacity ranging form 60-500 MB. While this capacity may be adequate for the vast majority of applications it still is a fixed amount of storage. The hard disk is very reliable and has a much faster access time a floppy disk system.

A hard-disk cartridge has a removable cartridge that is a self-contained unit with as much as 40 megabytes of storage capacity. This provides a microcomputer system with unlimited fixed storage capacity.

A hard-disk pack consist of several platters aligned one on top of another. This gives a much greater storage capacity than a hard-disk can provide to the system. A microcomputer hard-disk has one or possibly two disk platters and one or two access arms.

CHAPTER 7
COMMUNICATIONS and CONNECTIVITY
Chapter at a Glance

I. Introduction to Communications Systems

II. Communications and Connectivity Options

   A. Connectivity
      1. expanded access
      2. multiple users

   B. Communications
      1. fax
      2. electronic bulletin boards
      3. electronic mail
         a. mailbox
         b. passwords
      4. voice message systems
      5. sharing resources
      6. databases
      7. commercial services
         a. teleshopping
         b. home banking
         c. investing
         d. travel reservations
      8. groupware

III. User Interface/Communications Hardware - Modems

   A. Types of signals
      1. analog
      2. digital

   B. Direct-connect modem
      1. external
      2. internal

IV. Communications Channels

   A. Telephone lines
   B. Coaxial cable
   C. Fiber-optic cable
   D. Microwave
   E. Satellites

V.   Data Transmission

   A. Bandwidth
       1. voiceband
       2. medium band
       3. broadband

   B. Serial transmission
       1. serial port
       2. RS-232C
   C. Parallel data transmission
   D. Direction of data transmission
       1. simplex
       2. half-duplex
       3. full-duplex

   E. Modes of transmitting data
       1. Asynchronous data communication
       2. Synchronous data communication

   F. Protocols and Parity

VI.   Network Configurations

   A. Definition of a network
   B. Star network
       1. host computer/file server
       2. polling
   C. Bus network
   D. Ring network
   E. Hierarchical

VII.   Network Types

   A. LAN (Local Area Network) - network gateway
   B. MAN (Metropolitan Area Network)
   C. WAN (Wide Area Network)

VIII.   Communications and the Future

   A. Integrated services digital network (ISDN)
   B. Terminal adapters
   C. Supernet
   D. Portable Office
   E. Downsized applications

OBJECTIVES

The student should be able to:

1. Describe communications resources available.

2. Describe communications hardware, such as types of modems.

3. Describe the cable and air communications channels.

4. Discuss bandwidth, serial versus parallel transmission, direction of flow, modes of transmission, and protocols.

5. Explain four communication network arrangements: star, bus, ring, and hierarchical.

6. Describe local area, metropolitan area and wide area networks.

VOCABULARY

analog signals	downloading	internal modem	satellites
a s y n c h r o n o u s transmission	E-mail	local area networks (LANs)	serial data transmission simplex communication
a s y n c h r o n o u s communications port	electronic mail electronic bulletin boards	medium band metropolitan area	s t a r networksynchronous
bandwidth	external modem	network (MAN)	transmission
baud rate	fax machines	microwaves	time-sharing system
broadband	fiber-optic cable	modulation	twisted pairs
bus network	full-duplex	network gateway	uploading
bus	communication	parallel data	user name
coaxial cable	groupware	transmission	v o i c e - m e s s a g i n g
data communications systems	half-duplex communication	password	systems
demodulation	hierarchical network	polling	voiceband
digital signals	hybrid network	protocol	wide area networks
		ring network	(WANs)
		RS-232C connector	wireless modem

COMMUNICATIONS and CONNECTIVITY OPTIONS (pages 128-134) *TM 7.01*

Define communications systems as a means of transmitting data over communications lines from one location to another and relate it to connectivity. Data communications is considered an essential business tool allowing people to share a most valuable resource "information".

Connectivity is the ability to connect a microcomputer to other computers and sources of information via the telephone or other communications channels. The concept of connectivity expands the definition of computer competence to knowing about larger computer systems as well as microcomputers and makes available the following options:

* **fax machines** sending and receiving data using a scan technology that converts the image to electronic signals. Microcomputers can use virtual fax (built-in facsimile circuit boards) to allow them to send and receive messages.

56

* **electronic bulletin boards** are open to anyone as a resource to access knowledge on virtually an endless list of subjects.

* **electronic mail (E-mail)** using a dedicated communications line, it resembles an electronic bulletin board but offers confidentiality to the user. Employing the use of a **password** an electronic message can be sent to mailbox for a specific person or several individuals to electronically "open" at their convenience. In addition, a user can check on the status of the message by knowing if and when the receiver accessed it.

* **voice-messaging systems** link telephones converting the human voice into digital bits. They resemble telephone answering machines and electronic mail systems. These systems are advantageous because they can receive large numbers of incoming calls and route them to the appropriate "**voice mail-boxes**". These mail-boxes can usually be accessed from any touch-tone telephone.

* **sharing resources** is an important option to the microcomputer user, because it lets them share expensive computer peripheral devices and other resources.

* multiple users, in different locations, accessing the same **database**.

* **commercial services** and **personal services** of **teleshopping** (shopping for products using a credit card number for cash and a home address for delivery of the product); **home banking** (paying bills, making loan payments, and fund transfers); **investing** (permits a user to get stock prices and even buy and sell shares of stock); making **travel reservations**; and many other possibilities microcomputer users can access from the convenience of their home or office.

* **groupware**, a new kind of software developed through established networks, allows two or more people on a network to work on the same information at the same time.

USER INTERFACE (pages 134-135) *TM 7.02 and 7.03*

Discuss how computer communications employ the use of a telephone.

The telephone transmits frequencies created by the human voice. An **analog signal** represents the range of frequencies the telephone requires for transmitting. Computers send and receive **digital signals** represented by the presence or absence of an electronic pulse. For the successful transmission of computer data through telephone lines, the digital signal must be converted to an analog signal.

A **modem (modulate-demodulate)** converts the signal during the communications process. The computer's signal is modulated (converting the digital signal to analog), transmitting the signal through the telephone line to the other modem that demodulates the signal (converts it from analog back to a digital signal). The speed of data transmission is measured in **baud rates**. One baud is equal to one bit per second (**bps**). The rates of transmission are typically speeds of 300, 1200, 2400, and 9600 baud. The speed and successful transmission of data is dependent on the modem, the telephone line, and the computer system.

A **direct-connect modem** connects the microcomputer directly to a telephone line without using a telephone receiver. This same telephone line can be used for both data and voice transmission, but not at the same time. The direct-connect modem can be an **external modem** (a separate device outside the computer) or an **internal modem** (a plug-in circuit board, connected to the mother board of the computer, with a telephone jack). Computer systems connected with coaxial cable or fiber-optic cable can transmit digital data directly through the channels without the use of a modem.

COMMUNICATIONS CHANNELS (pages 135-137) *TM 7.04*

Identify the five types of communications channels through which data may flow:

Most <u>telephone lines</u> are made of copper wires, called **twisted pairs**, bundled together to form a cable.

A <u>coaxial cable</u> is a single solid core cable replacing the multiple wire telephone lines. It permits a high-frequency transmission and is used for undersea telephone lines.

A <u>fiber-optic cable</u> transmits pulses of light through tubes of glass half the diameter of a human hair. They are lighter in weight, less expensive, and more reliable than coaxial cable. A fiber-optic cable is immune to electronic interference since the data travels on beams of light that are much faster than conductive wire.

A <u>microwave communications channel</u> transmits high-frequency radio waves traveling through the air in straight lines. The waves cannot bend, and must be relayed from antennas (also called **dishes**). *TM 7.05*

<u>Satellites</u> can also be used to bounce microwave signals around the world. These satellites are in a stationary orbit hovering approximately 22,000 miles above the earth.

DATA TRANSMISSION (page 137-140) *TM 7.06*

Discuss the considerations which must be made before successful communications can take place. Points to consider, include: speed or band-width, serial of parallel transmission, direction of flow, and protocols.

<u>Bandwidth</u> is the bits-per-second transmission rate capability of a channel. The speed of the transmission is related to the bandwidth type. Bandwidth may be of three types:

* **Voiceband** the bandwidth of a standard telephone, has a baud rate range of 110-9600 bps.

* **Medium band** is the bandwidth of special leased lines used mainly with mini and mainframe computers. It has a baud rate range of 9,600 - 256,000 bps.

* **Broadband** is used with microwave, satellite, coaxial cable, and fiber-optic channels. It is used with very high-speed computers whose processors communicate directly with each other. It has a baud rate range of 256,000 - 1 million bps.

Serial transmission has data flowing in a continuous stream of bits in a single file formation. This method is used in most data transmissions over telephone lines. A microcomputer's modem is usually connected to a **serial port** in the microcomputer. This port is also called an **RS-232C connector** or an **asynchronous communications port.**

Parallel data transmission has each bit in a byte flow through its own separate line simultaneously with the other bits (traveling through each of their respective lines) that make up the character. This is the standard method of sending data from the CPU to a parallel printer.

The **direction of data transmission** include **simplex, half-duplex,** and **full-duplex.**

* **Simplex** means data can only travel in one direction. It is not frequently used in today's data communications systems.
* **Half-duplex** allows data to flow in two directions, but not at the same time.
* **Full-duplex** is the fastest and most efficient direction of communication. It allows data to flow in both directions at the same time.

Modes of transmitting data include the rules established before data is transmitted between the sender and receiver for data communication. These rules, called **protocols**, help establish an environment for the successful transmission of data. *TM 7.07*

One set of protocols establishes if the transmission will be **asynchronous** or **synchronous.** Most microcomputers use **asynchronous data communications.** It is slower than synchronous transmissions, but more convenient to transmit data without tedious preparation and the need for careful synchronizing of the data as it is sent to the receiving computer.

Synchronous transmission is designed to send great quantities of data in larger units (usually several bytes) at a time. This mode of transmission is much faster but requires that the blocks of data be carefully sent at timed intervals.

NETWORK CONFIGURATION (pages 140-143)

Define computer network as the connection of two or more computer systems together as a telecommunications system. It allows the sharing of resources in the telecommunications system. These shared resources include hardware devices (printers, plotters, etc.), programs, and data. Terms associated with networks include:

* *Node - any device connected to a network.*
* *Client - a node using a network for processing or sharing of resources.*
* *Server - a node coordinating the communications and sharing of network resources.*
* *Client/server system - has several users and one server coordinating all activities.*
* *Peer-to-peer system -has several users all equally sharing the responsibility of coordinating network activities.*
* *Distributed processing - computing power is located and shared at different locations; this is common is decentralized organizations.*
* *Host computer - a large centralized computer, usually a mini- or mainframe computer.*

59

The four basic network arrangements are star, bus, ring, and hierarchical.

* A **star network** links a number of small computers and/or peripheral devices to a central unit. This central unit may be a large **host computer** or a **file server** (a hard disk storage device with a large capacity). All communications pass though the central unit that maintains control by means of **polling** (checking to see if a message is ready to be sent) each device in the network. The advantage of this network is time-sharing of resources. *TM 7.08*

* A **bus network** allows each device to handle its own communications control. All communications travel along a **bus** (common connecting cable to all the devices in the network). As a message passes through the bus, each device checks to see if the message is intended for it. This system is frequently used when the networked devices are few in number. *TM 7.09*

* A **ring network** is formed by having each device connected to two other devices eventually forming a circle or ring. Messages are passed around the ring until they reach the correct destination. The ring network makes a **distributed data processing system** for a decentralized organization possible. *TM 7.10*

* A **hierarchical network** consists of several computers linked to a central host computer, like the star network. Each one of these computers is a host to other smaller computers and peripheral devices. This **hybrid network** is useful in centralized organizations to share databases, processing power, and/or other output devices.

NETWORK TYPES (pages 131-133)

A <u>local area network</u> (LAN) connects devices close proximity. They can be linked by telephone, coaxial, or fiber-optic cable and often use a bus form of organization. An important feature of a LAN is a **network gateway** linking it to other LANs or larger networks. *TM 7.11*

A <u>metropolitan area network</u> (MAN)is a network between office buildings within a city. The cellular telephone has created some new applications utilizing a MAN.

A <u>wide area network</u> (WAN) covers a much larger geographic region possibly spanning the country or even the globe. A WAN will very likely use the microwave and satellite channels as well as the other data channel types. *TM 7.12*

COMMUNICATIONS AND THE FUTURE (page 129)

The possible improvements in communications hardware in the next few years will involve: modems, fax machines, file servers, and fiber-optic cables allowing us to have cheaper and faster communications.

60

The **Integrated Services Digital Network (ISDN)**, consisting of a set of technologies and international-exchange standards, will expand making today's telephone system completely digital.

Modems would be replaced by terminal adapters enabling the transmission of data at tremendously faster rates. It will also allow for data, fax, voice and video information to be transmitted at the same time.

The creation of a national data highway called **"Supernet"** (a $5-billion project mandated by an act signed by President Bush and given top priority by President Clinton) will support the transmission of live video, graphics, and data files in a much faster manner than is currently possible. It will allow individuals and organizations to have access to tremendous amounts of information located around the country and accessed via this national information highway.

The "standalone" computer (one not connected to a network) will no longer be a viable tool by itself.

The era of the portable office (hooking a portable computer and/or fax to cellular networks or radio networks) will make people on the go more efficient and productive.

The downsizing of applications (meaning microcomputers having capabilities of minicomputers and mainframes via networks) are now possible on networked-linked microcomputers.

REVIEW QUESTIONS
True/False

T   1.   A local area network connects two or more computers within a limited area, such as within the same building.

F   2.   CompuServ and Prodigy are two well-known <u>protocols</u>.

T   3.   Frequently, computer communications over telephone lines require a modem.

F   4.   In half-duplex communication, data flows in both directions <u>at the same time</u>.

F   5.   In a client/server, <u>each node on the network has equal responsibility</u> for coordinating the network's activities.

Multiple Choice

D   1.   A special sequence of numbers or letters that limits access to electronic mail boxes is a: **Answer; password**

C   2.   Transferring data from a larger computer to your microcomputer is called: **Answer; downloading**

C   3.   What communications channel transfers data as pulses of light? **Answer; fiber-optic cable**

A 4. Rules for exchanging data on a network: **Answer; protocols**

E 5. A system frequently used in decentralized organizations in which computing power is located and shared at different sites: **Answer; distributed**

Fill in the Blank

1. <u>Voice messaging</u> systems are computer systems linked to telephones that convert the human voice into digital bits.

2. Transferring data from your microcomputer to a minicomputer or mainframe is called <u>uploading</u>.

3. Because <u>microwaves</u> travel in straight lines through the air and cannot bend with the curvature of the Earth, they can transmit data only over short distances (<u>by themselves</u>).

4. A <u>peer-to-peer</u> system typically has several users who equally share the responsibility of coordinating the activities on a network.

5. <u>Wide area networks</u> are countrywide and worldwide networks that connect users over long distances.

Open Ended

1. What are electronic bulletin boards? How do they differ from electronic mail systems?

   Electronic bulletin boards allow individuals to share interest, hobbies, and information on virtually any subject via a communications channel connected to a computer. They are a public domain area of access which allow computer users to talk with one another using there computers.

   Electronic mail usually has special communications channels offering a more secure and confidential environment for users to communicate with one another. Electronic mail is often limited to the people within the same organization, but it can permit outsiders to access the system if it is desirable. Electronic mail affords the same convenience of real mail with some additional advantages. Electronic mail can be opened, discarded, stored electronically, printed to paper, distributed to an individual, and even mass mailed to many individuals.

2. List and describe the five kinds of communications channels.

   Telephone lines are usually made of copper wires, called twisted pairs, bundled together to form a cable.

   Coaxial cable is a single solid core cable replacing the multiple wire telephone lines. It permits a high-frequency transmission and is used for undersea telephone lines.

62

Fiber-optic cable transmits pulses of light through tubes of glass half the diameter of a human hair. They are lighter in weight, less expensive, and more reliable than coaxial cable. A fiber-optic cable is immune to electronic interference since the data travels on beams of light that are much faster than conductive wire.

Microwave communications channel transmits high-frequency radio waves traveling through the air in straight lines. The waves cannot bend, and must be relayed from antennas (also called dishes).

Satellites can also be used to bounce microwave signals around the world. These satellites are in a stationary orbit hovering approximately 22,000 miles above the earth.

3. What is the difference between a client/server system and a peer-to-peer system?

A client/server system has several users and one server coordinating all activities. A peer-to-peer system has several users all equally sharing the responsibility of coordinating network activities.

4. Describe the difference between simplex, half-duplex, and full-duplex communication.

Simplex means that data can only travel in one direction. It is not frequently used in today's data communications systems.

Half-duplex allows data to flow in two directions, but not at the same time.

Full-duplex is the fastest and most efficient direction of communication. It allows data to flow in both directions at the same time.

5. Discuss the four basic arrangements microcomputer communications networks may take.

The star network attaches all the computers and/or peripheral devices to a larger central host computer. This arrangement allows units attached to the network to share resources which include hardware, software, and data.

The ring network attaches units in the network from one unit to the next usually forming a circle or ring shaped network. There is no centralized computer. Instead, data is passed form one unit to the next until it reaches its destination.

A bus network requires that each device in the network to handle its own communications control. All communications travels along the same line until the destination unit picks it up upon recognizing it.

A hierarchical network consists of several computers linked to central host computer, like the star network. However, each one of these computers is a host to other smaller computers and peripheral devices.

CHAPTER 8
FILES and DATABASES
Chapter at a Glance

I. Files
    A. Data Organization
        1. characters
        2. fields
        3. records
        4. files

    B. Key Field

    C. Batch Processing versus Real-Time Processing
        1. batch processing
        2. real-time processing

    D. Master Files, Transaction Files and Types of File Organization
        1. Master files
            a. with sequential file organization
            b. with direct file organization
            c. with index-sequential file organization
        2. Transaction files
            a. with sequential file organization
            b. with direct file organization
            c. with index-sequential file organization

II. The Need for Databases
    A. Define database

    B. Need for databases
        1. sharing information
        2. security of the data
        3. data redundancy
        4. data integrity

    C. Software for a Database Management System
        1. define DBMS
        2. describe data dictionary
        3. purpose of a query language

III. DBMS Organizations
    A. Hierarchical database
    B. Network database
    C. Relational database

IV. The Types of Databases
    A. Individual database
    B. Shared database (or Company)
        1. common operational database
        2. common user database
    C. Distributed database
    D. Proprietary database

V. Database Uses and Issues
    A. Data for Strategic Uses
    B. Importance of Security
    C. The Database Administrator
    D. Processing Rights and Ethics

VI. Databases and the Future
    A. Specialty phone books
    B. Topologically Integrated Geographic Encoding and Reference system (TIGER)

OBJECTIVES

The student should be able to:

1. Describe how data is organized.

2. Understand the difference between batch and real-time processing.

3. Describe the difference between master files and transaction files.

4. Define and describe the three types of file organization.

5. Describe the advantages of a database.

6. Describe the two essential parts of a database management system (DBMS).

7. Describe three ways of organizing a DBMS.

8. Distinguish among individual, company, distributed, and proprietary databases.

9. Discuss some issues of productivity and security.

VOCABULARY

batch processing	data dictionary	index sequential file	pointers
child nodes	database	organization	processing rights
common user	administrator	key field	proprietary database
database	(DBA)	master file	query language
common operational	direct file	microcomputer	real-time processing
database	organization	database	relational database
company database	distributed database	network database	sequential file
computer virus	hashing	nodes	organization
	hierarchical database	parent node	transaction file

FILES (pages 152-156) *TM 8.01 and TM 8.02*

Students should know how files work by developing an understanding of data organization, key fields, batch versus real-time processing, master versus transaction files and file organization.

Data Organization is structured by the following:

* A **character** is a byte: a single letter, number, or special character found on the keyboard.

* A **field** is a set of related characters making a data item.

* A **record** is a collection of related fields, as they relate to one entity.

* A **file** is a collection of related records.

A **key field** contains data uniquely identifying a record (like a social security number).

Batch processing versus real-time processing relates to a storage system. Data is structured as a file and as a database. Data can be processed in two ways:

* With **batch processing**, data is collected for a given time period before it is processed. This time period may be a few hours or even weeks.

* **Real-time processing** (also called **transaction-oriented processing**) is increasing in use along with the capabilities of today's computer systems. The data is processed at the time the transaction occurs.

Master versus transaction files relates to the updating of files.

* A **master file** contains all current records up to the time it was last updated.

* A **transaction file** is made up of recent changes and/or new records in a file. A transaction file temporarily holds transactions until the data is processed into the master file.

Types of file organization include sequential, direct, or index sequential order.

* **Sequential files** store records in ascending or descending order by a key field. Magnetic tape is the medium often used with sequential files, but they can also be stored on a floppy or hard disk. **Advantages: good for frequent changes to the transaction file and infrequent changes to the master file.**

* **Direct files** do not require the records to be sorted in sequential order. A direct file assigns each record a key address where the data can be found on the disk. This is a very quick method for data interaction. **Advantages: quick data retrieval, but slow with the need for frequent transactions to the master file.**

* **Index sequential files** are a compromise between sequential and direct file organization methods. They store data sequentially and have an index for the data as well. The index is a key to groups of records holding the disk address where a group of records can be located. Index sequential files must be stored on a direct access storage medium. **Advantages: quick data retrieval, good for updating large groups of transactions**.

DATABASE (pages 156-158)

Discuss the tendency of organizations to have multiple files containing duplicate information pertaining to the same person or subject. As an item of data changes, this creates a need to make a change in all the separate data files. It is also desirable to interrelate data from multiple files. An integrated database offers the following advantages:

* **Sharing** information from one department to another in an organization.
* **Security** of the data can be maintained by giving users passwords and limiting access to only the particular data that is used by an employee.
* **Fewer files** are needed because the various departments of an organization can access one file. This limits **data redundancy**.
* **Data integrity** is maintained because as a change occurs in a record it only has to be corrected in one file.

Identify the purpose of software for a database management system (DBMS) is to create, modify, organize, access, and generate reports from a database. Special software is required and usually only operates in one of the three computer environments (micro-,mini, or mainframe). The DBMS software consists of a data dictionary and a query language.

* A **data dictionary** has a description of the data's structure used in the database. This would include the name, length, type of field (numeric, alphanumeric, alphabetic, etc.), and the identification of a key field. *TM 8.03*

* A **query language** accomplishes a means of access to the database. It is a "user friendly" language used to generate reports and many other activities concerning the data.

DBMS ORGANIZATION (pages 158-160)

Contrast the three organizational methods of structuring a database.

* The **hierarchical database** structures the fields or records as nodes--similar to the scheme used for creating a family tree. The nodes farther down the tree structure are subordinate to the ones above. To find a record, one must follow a path beginning with the node at the top of the hierarchy. Problems develop if the user is unfamiliar with the hierarchy structure, or if a parent node is erased deleting the path to all child nodes. *TM 8.04*

* A **network database** has a hierarchical arrangement of nodes. This scheme allows a child node to have more than one parent node, thus, a node may be reached by more than one path and possibly even sideways from nodes at the same level. *TM 8.05*

* A **relational database** is the most flexible organization structure. The data is stored in different tables of rows and columns and are found by means of indexes. A **table** is a **relation** resembling a file of information on the same subject. In the table, each row (also called a **tuple**) represents one record in the file and each column (also called an **attribute**) represents a field in the file. The advantage of a relational database is that it allows data to be added, deleted or modified very easily to the database. *TM 8.06*

TYPES OF DATABASES (pages 160-163)

Classify the databases into individual, company (or shared), distributed, and proprietary.

* The **individual database** (also called a microcomputer database) is a collection of integrated records useful to mainly one person.

* The **company database** (also called **shared**) is a collection of integrated databases useful mainly to one company. They can be further classified as a **common operational database** (concerned with company operations details) or a **common user database** (selected information from the common operational database and from proprietary databases used for decision making).

* The **distributed database** can be accessed from a variety of networks and does not require the data to be in one centralized location. Typically, data is located on different file servers connected to LANs or on hard disks connected to a centralized WAN mainframe.

* A **proprietary database** (also called information utility or data bank) is of enormous size and can cover a magnitude of subjects. These databases are offered to the public for a fee and include: **CompuServe, Dialog Information Services, Dow Jones News/Retrieval, Prodigy,** and **Chase Econometric Associates.**

DATABASE USES AND ISSUES (pages 163-164)

Identify the considerations a potential user should have regarding a database.

* **Data for Strategic Use** is a significant justification for creating and maintaining an organizational database. If designed correctly, an organizations's database can help users to stay current and assist them in decisions about the future by providing timely information. There are, also, many external databases (business directories, government demographics, business statistical information, periodical text and trade publications) organizations can access to assist in organizational planning and decision making.

* **Security** involves the protection of information, hardware, and software from unauthorized use and damage from intrusions, sabotage, and natural disasters such as fires or hurricanes. Types of security can range from placing guards at the entrance to the computer room and limiting access to authorized personnel; storing back-up tapes or disks of all valuable information in another location; putting equipment in fire- and earthquake-proof areas; and assigning passwords to employees.

Discuss the recent phenomenon of **computer viruses** *which have been a security problem for the entire computer industry.*

A computer virus has hidden instructions that "migrate" through networks and operating systems and become embedded in different programs and databases. They may lay dormant until a particular date or some data item happens to trigger them to destroy data to simply to display messages.

Discuss the individual means of protecting a computer system: a microcomputer user should make back-up copies of personal files and programs; an employee has an obligation to the employer to protect programs and sensitive information by being careful with computer passwords, access codes and diskettes.

* The **database administrator (DBA)** is a computer specialist charged with the responsibility of: determining the structure of the databases; evaluating the performance of the DBMS; determining who has access to what kind of data (known as **processing rights**); and of keeping the database safe from fire, sabotage, and other disasters.

A LOOK AT THE FUTURE (pages 164-165)

The collecting data, source automation devices, networks, and database software will be more sophisticated. Greater storage capacities and faster more powerful computers will all assist us in having the most up-to-date and useful information at our disposal. Improved technology make **specialty phone books** (holding corporate names, telephone numbers, etc.) and projects like **TIGER** (Topologically Integrated Geographic Encoding and Reference system) possible. This database project will contain 23 million street intersections coupled with statistics to provide a numerical or income profile of every block in the United States. **Privacy** and **security** issues will be a major concern in database technology.

Another development will be in **filtering technology** which is a means of sifting through mountains of data scanning for key words to provide specific information to a user. The end result, we should be better informed and making better decisions due to this technology.

REVIEW QUESTIONS
True/False

F   1. A record is a collection of related <u>files.</u>

F   2. In batch processing, data is processed <u>at the same time</u> the transaction occurs.

T   3. A data dictionary describes the structure of the data in a database.

T   4. A distributed database has data located in more than one location.

T   5. Processing rights are typically determined by the database administrator to specify which people have access to what kind of data.

Multiple Choice

D   1.   A collection of related fields: **Answer; record**

C   2.   A temporary file containing recent changes to records: **Answer; transaction**

A   3.   The database organization in which fields and records are structures in nodes with each child node having only one parent. **Answer; hierarchical**

E   4.   The type of database that is sometimes called an information utility or a data bank: **Answer; proprietary**

B   5.   Hidden instructions that "migrate" through networks and operating systems: **Answer; viruses**

Fill in the Blank

1.   The <u>key</u> uniquely identifies each record.

2.   <u>Indexed</u> file organization is good both for locating specific records and for updating all or a large part of an entire file.

3.   A database is a collection of **<u>integrated</u>** data.

4.   **<u>Relational</u>** databases are more flexible and easier to use than hierarchical and network databases.

5.   Large organizations employ database **<u>administrators</u>** to help determine database structures and evaluate database performance.are countrywide and worldwide networks that connect users over long distances.

Open Ended

1.   Describe how data is organized and give an example.

   The five levels of data organization are:

   A character (byte) - a single letter, number, or special character.

   A field   -   a set of related characters. It is an item of data such as a telephone number, street address, etc..

   A record   -   a collection of related fields. A group of data items that have a common relationship as a group.

   A file   -   collection of related records.

   A database   -   a collection of related files.

2. What are the differences between sequential, direct, and index sequential file organizations?

Sequential files store data in ascending or descending order by a key field. It is advantageous when frequent changes to the transaction file and infrequent changes to the master file occur.

Direct files do not require the records to be sorted in sequential order. A direct file assigns each record a key address where the data can be found on the disk. This is a very quick method for data interaction and data retrieval, but slow when the need for frequent transactions to the master file is necessary.

Index sequential files are a compromise between sequential and direct file organizations. Data is stored sequentially and has an index. The index is a key to groups of records holding the disk address where a group of records can be located. Index sequential files must be stored on a direct access storage medium. This method is advantageous for quick data retrieval and updating of large groups of transactions.

3. What are databases, and why are they needed?

A database is a collection of integrated data, meaning the data is organized as logically related files and records.

Organizations often have duplicate information pertaining to the same person or subject. A database can help eliminate much of this data redundancy. As an item of data changes, a need to change all related data files occurs. With a database it is possible to change the data by making the correction once and having it automatically update all files and to interrelate data from multiple files.

4. Discuss the three principal ways of organizing a database.

The hierarchical database has fields or records structured as nodes--similar to the scheme used for creating a family tree. The nodes farther down the tree structure are subordinate to the ones above. To find a record, a path is followed beginning with the node at the top of the hierarchy.

A network database has a hierarchical arrangement of nodes. This scheme allows a child node to have more than one parent node, thus, a node may be reached by more than one path and possibly even sideways from nodes at the same level.

A relational database is the most flexible with data stored in different tables of rows and columns and are found by means of indexes. A table is a relation that resembles a file of information on the same subject. In the table, each row (also called a tuple) represents one record in the file and each column (called an attribute) represents a field in the file. The advantages of a relational database is that it allows data to be added, deleted or modified very easily to the database.

71

5.   Describe each of the four types of database.

The individual database (also called a microcomputer database) is a collection of integrated records useful to mainly one person.

The company database (also called shared) is a collection of integrated databases useful mainly to one company. They can be further classified as a common operational database (concerned with company operations details) or a common user database (selected information from the common operational database and from proprietary databases used for decision making).

The distributed database can be accessed from a variety of networks and does not require that the data be in one centralized location. Typically, data is located on different file servers connected to LANs or on hard disks connected to a centralized WAN mainframe.

A proprietary database (also called information utility or data bank) is of enormous size and can cover a magnitude of subjects. These databases are offered to the public for a fee.

CHAPTER 9
INFORMATION SYSTEMS
Chapter at a Glance

I. The Information Revolution - "Supermicros"
   A. Better quality information
   B. Downsizing
      1. smaller hardware systems
         a. faster processing
         b. larger primary memory
         c. more powerful secondary storage
         d. easier access to larger databases
      2. smaller management staffs

II. The Information Flow of an Organization -(Organizational Structure)
   A. Functions (departments or divisions)
      1. accounting
      2. manufacturing
      3. marketing
      4. human resources
      5. research
   B. Management levels
      1. supervisors
      2. middle management
      3. top management
   C. Information flow

III. Levels of Computer-based Information Systems

   A. Transaction processing system
      1. creates databases of routine activities and employees hired
      2. sales order processing
      3. accounts receivable
      4. accounts payable
      5. payroll
      6. purchasing
      7. inventory
      8. general ledger
         a. income statements
         b. balance sheets
   B. Management information systems (MIS)
      1. scheduled reports
      2. exception reports
      3. predictive reports
      4. demand reports

C. Decision support system (DSS)
   1. interactive
   2. parts of a DSS
      a. user
      b. software system
      c. data
         1. internal
         2. external
      d. decision models
         1. strategic
         2. tactical
         3. operational

IV. Executive Information Systems (Executive Support Systems)
   A. User friendly
   B. Summarized reports
   C. Internal and external resources

V. Information Systems of the Future
   A. Conference room microcomputers
   B. Use of laptop and palmtop EISs

OBJECTIVES

The student should be able to:

1. Explain how changing technology has made the microcomputer a resource that can use information systems.

2. Explain how organizations can be structured according to five functions and three management levels.

3. Describe how information flows in an organization.

4. Distinguish among a transaction processing system, a management information system, and a decision support system.

5. Describe what an executive information system is.

VOCABULARY

accounts payable	exception reports	interactive	periodic reports
accounts receivable	executive information	inventory	purchasing
decision support system	systems (EISs)	management	sales order processing
(DSS)	executive support	information system	supervisors
decision models	systems (ESSs)	(MIS)	top-level managers
demand reports	general ledger	middle-level managers	transaction processing
downsizing	information system	payroll	system
			transactions

74

THE INFORMATION REVOLUTION - "SUPERMICROS" (pages 170-172)

Discuss how the term supermicro is applied in today's business community.

To the user, this new technology means larger memory, increased processing speeds, the handling of large programs, greater amounts of data, and more powerful DBMS software. In addition, high volume storage is possible using optical disks and using disk packs accessed through LANs. Another result of this technology is **downsizing**--smaller hardware systems and smaller management staffs both accomplishing more.

HOW INFORMATION FLOWS in an ORGANIZATION (pages 172-175)

Discuss how an organization is structured by two aspects: functions and management levels.

* Typical **functions** found in many organizations include accounting, manufacturing, marketing, personnel, and research. *TM 9.01*

* Management levels are divided into: **lower management (operational)**, responsible for supervision of employees who actually produce the goods or services; **middle management (tactical)**, supervises lower-level managers and implements long term goals of the organization; and **top management (strategic planning)**, determines the direction and needs of the organization for the future. *TM 9.02*

The **flow of information** in an organization is different at each level of management. Lower management needs detailed, day-to-day information. Middle management require summarized information (from other departments, and from both upper and lower management), such as weekly or monthly reports. Top management is provided with even more summarized information (from middle and lower level management) and the need for information outside the organization to forecast and plan long-range organizational goals. *TM 9.03*

THE LEVELS OF COMPUTER-BASED INFORMATION SYSTEMS (pages 176-177)

The three levels of computer-based information systems are **transaction processing system, management information system, and decision support system.**

TRANSACTION PROCESSING SYSTEMS (pages 177-178): *TM 9.04 and TM 9.05*

A **Transaction Processing System (data processing system)** records day-to-day transactions and is used by lower management to create a database to support an MIS and a DSS. These transactions are the basis for an accounting system consisting of the following six activities:

* **Sales order processing** records and assists with customer orders of the organization's products or services.

* **Accounts receivable** keeps track of what customers have paid or how much they owe to the organization.

* **Accounts payable** keeps track of the money the organization owes to its suppliers for materials and services.

* **Payroll** keeps track of each employee's compensation for services that is determined by the kind of job and hours worked.

* **General ledger** keeps track of summaries of all the above activities. **Income statements** and **balance sheets** can be generated from the general ledger.

MANAGEMENT INFORMATION SYSTEMS (pages 178-180) *TM 9.06*

A <u>Management Information System</u> (MIS) summarizes the daily transaction data in a structured form for middle level management. A key point is that a data processing system creates databases, an MIS uses databases generated by the various departments. To do this, an MIS requires a DBMS that integrates these databases. An MIS generates reports following a set format and always show the same kinds of content. These reports are categorized into four types:

* **Periodic** reports are produced at regular intervals such as daily, weekly monthly, or yearly.

* **Exception reports** are designed to call attention to an unusual event. These events might include excessive overtime, or production that is behind schedule, or past due accounts.

* **Demand reports** are produced at the request of a manager, possibly to investigate information obtained from an exception or scheduled report.

DECISION SUPPORT SYSTEMS (pages 180-181)

A **Decision Support System** (DSS) produces flexible, on-demand reports for managers to assist them in making decisions.

This system may utilize outside databases as well the databases within the organization. This type of system is **interactive** (immediate communication between the user and the computer system) and usually displays the results on the screen. Since the users of the DSS are managers and not programmers, the system must be user friendly. A decision support system consists of the following four **decision models**:

* **the user** is someone who has to make decisions.

* **the software system** is a user friendly and often a menu-driven program.

* **the data** includes **internal** and **external data**.

* **the decision model(s)** are based on statistical packages, simulations, long-range, plans and other concepts giving the DSS its analytical capabilities. The **operational, tactical,** and **strategic models** are specifically designed for each of the respective levels.

EXECUTIVE INFORMATION SYSTEM (pages 181-182) *TM 9.07*

Executive information systems (EIS) (executive support systems (ESS) are sophisticated software bringing together data from an organization's databases in a meaningful format.

An ESS is designed to be user friendly so that a top executive with little spare time does not have to devote much effort to learning the system. Information is often displayed in condensed form and in bold graphics. It often contains electronic mail setups allowing managers to communicate directly with other executives.

In addition, an EIS can retrieve information from outside databases to help executives be competitive and keep up with events happening in their respective industries.

EXECUTIVE INFORMATION SYSTEMS OF THE FUTURE (page 182)

Executive Information Systems of today are relatively simplistic. As the computer sophistication level of executives increases, the executive end-user will have expectations for more powerful EIS with many more options. Conference rooms with microcomputers will be communicating with corporate computers around the world.

By the mid 1990s, observers believe that executive will use laptop EIS to acquire information from virtually anywhere. Executives will be able to assess their EIS as they travel and deliver management presentations while attending distant business meetings.

REVIEW QUESTIONS
True/False

F   1.   Moving applications <u>from</u> microcomputers <u>to</u> minicomputers and mainframes is called downsizing.

T   2.   The production department takes in raw materials and puts people to work to turn out finished goods (or services).

T   3.   In smaller organizations such titles as vice president of marketing and director of human resources are often combined.

T   4.   CEO stands for chief executive officer.

F   5.   <u>Decision support systems</u> summarize the detailed data of the transaction processing system in standard reports.

Multiple Choice

B   1.   The key technology advance supporting downsizing that describes the importance of microcomputers replacing terminals: **Answer; easier access to large databases**

D   2.   This department finds and hires people and handles such matters as sick leave and retirement benefits: **Answer; human resources**

C   3.   The level of manager who deals with control and planning: **Answer; middle management**

A   4.   The level of managers whose information is primarily vertical: **Answer; supervisors**

E   5.   The computer-based information system that provides a flexible tool for analysis: **Answer; decision support system**

Fill in the Blank

1.   An information system is a collection of hardware, software, **people**, procedures, and data.

2.   The **research** department relates new discoveries and does product development.

3.   **Top-level** managers are concerned with long-range planning.

4.   **Transaction processing** systems record day-to-day activities such as customer orders and inventory levels.

5.   **Executive** information systems are specially designed, simplified systems for top-level executives.

Open Ended

1.   What are the five departments found in medium-sized and large organizations? Discuss the function of each department.

Typical departments found in many organizations include accounting, marketing manufacturing, personnel, and research.

The accounting department keeps track of all financial activities, pays bills, takes in money owed, writes paychecks, and organizes financial statements.

The marketing department advertises, promotes, and sells the products or services.

The production department makes the product by taking in raw materials and putting people to work to produce finished goods or services.

The human resources department finds and hires people, handles sick leave, retirement and matters concerning the employees.

The research department performs research to develop new or improved products.

2.   What are the three levels of management? What are the responsibilities of managers at each level?

Management levels are divided into: supervisors (operational), middle management (tactical), and top management (strategic planning).

Supervisors manage and monitor the day-to-day events along with employees who actually produce the goods or services.

Middle management supervises lower-level managers and implements long term (tactical) goals of the organization.

Top management (strategic planning) determines the direction and needs of the organization for the future.

3. Explain the differences between the three types of reports produced by a management information system.

    Periodic reports are produced at regular intervals such as daily, weekly monthly, or yearly.

    Exception reports are designed to call attention to unusual event. These events might include excessive overtime, or production that is behind schedule, or possibly past due accounts.

    Demand reports are produced at the request of a manager, possibly to investigate information obtained from an exception or scheduled report.

4. Discuss the three types of decision models used in a DSS.

    The operational models help lower-level managers accomplish the day-to-day activities of the organization.

    The tactical models help middle-level managers control the work of the organization.

    The strategic models assist top-level managers in long-range planning and other concepts that are the responsibility of managers at the top-level.

5. Explain what an executive information system is. Give an example.

    Executive information systems (EIS) are also known as executive support systems (ESS) consisting of sophisticated software bringing together data from an organization's databases in a meaningful format. It is user friendly to permit a firm's top executives to gain more direct access to information about the company's performance and often contains electronic mail setups allowing managers to communicate directly with other executives. In addition, an EIS can be organized to retrieve information from databases outside the company. Information is often displayed in condensed form and in bold graphics.

CHAPTER 10
SYSTEMS ANALYSIS AND DESIGN
Chapter at a Glance

I. Systems Analysis and Design
   A. Definition of information system
   B. Systems life cycle
      1. preliminary investigation
         a. defining problem
         b. alternative solutions
      2. systems analysis
         a. data gathering to study present system
            1. interviews
            2. questionnaires
            3. review of existing manuals
            4. review of organizational charts
            5. review of existing forms
         b. analyze data
      3. systems design
         a. designing alternative systems
            1. economic feasibility
            2. technical feasibility
            3. operational feasibility
         b. selecting the best system
            1. organizational fit
            2. system flexibility
            3. security of system
            4. benefits versus costs
      4. systems development
         a. software development
            1. off-the-shelf
            2. custom designed
         b. acquiring hardware
            1. kind of equipment
            2. location of installation
         c. testing the new system
      5. implementation (conversion)
         a. direct approach
         b. parallel approach
         c. pilot approach
         d. phased approach
         e. training personnel
      6. maintenance

II. Prototyping

Objectives

The student should be able to:

1. Describe the six phrases of the systems life cycle.

2. Discuss how problems or needs are identified during the preliminary investigation.

3. Explain how the current system is studied and new requirements are specified during the systems analysis phase.

4. Describe how a new or alternate information system is designed in the systems design phase.

5. Explain how new hardware and software are acquired, developed, and tested in the systems development phase.

6. Discuss how a new information system is installed and users are trained in the systems implementation phase.

7. Describe the systems maintenance, systems audit, and ongoing evaluation to see if a new system is doing what it is supposed to.

8. Understand prototyping.

VOCABULARY

automated design tools	data flow diagrams	preliminary investigation	systems audit
CASE tools	decision table	prototyping	systems life cycle
checklist	direct approach	system	systems analyst
computer-aided software engineering tools	grid chart	system flowcharts	systems analysis
	organization chart	systems analysis and design	systems design
	parallel approach		systems development
	phased approach		systems implementation
conversion	pilot approach	systems maintenance	top-down analysis methodology

SYSTEMS ANALYSIS and DESIGN (pages 188-190) *TM 10.01*

A **system** is a set of activities and procedures organized to accomplish a task or goal. An **information system** consists of computer hardware, software, people, and procedures designed to produce essential information for running an organization.

The **systems analysis and design process** is intended to develop a successful system. It has six steps, performed by an analyst: preliminary investigation, systems analysis, systems design, systems development, systems implementation, and systems maintenance.

PHASE 1: PRELIMINARY INVESTIGATION (pages 190-192) *TM 10.02*

The systems analyst is concerned with three tasks: defining the problem, suggesting alternative solutions, and preparing a report to help management make informed decisions.

PHASE 2: ANALYSIS (pages 192-197)

The present system is studied and new requirements are specified. This requires data to be gathered, the analyzing of this data, and a report that summarizes the information gathered.

* **Gathering data** can be accomplished by reviewing current written documents of the organization's systems, interviewing employees regarding the organization and its systems, conducting surveys using questionnaires. Included in the written documents would be the **organizational chart** which should be an indication about the flow of information within the organization. *TM 10.02*

* **Analyzing data** usually includes a set of tools that are used to determine why certain steps and procedures are followed. These tools include **data flow diagrams, system flowcharts, grid charts, decision tables, checklists, top-down analysis methodology, HIPO charts,** and **automated design tools.** *TM 10.03, TM 10.04, TM 10.05 and TM 10.06*

* The **systems analysis report** is written for upper management. It describes the current information system, the requirements for a new system, and a schedule for development of the new system.

PHASE 3: DESIGN (pages 197-198)

In **designing the alternative systems,** the analyst must consider:

* the **economic feasibility** (does the system cost too much for what it provides)
* the **technical feasibility** (availability of hardware, software, and trained people)
* the **operational feasibility** (will the system have the support individuals involved with it)

Selecting the best system means considering:

* the system fit to the organization.
* the flexibility of the system to be modified for future needs.
* security against unauthorized use.
* whether the benefits out weigh the costs.

Writing the systems design report takes all the above into consideration and summarizes it for higher management. It usually concludes by recommending one of the alternatives.

PHASE 4: DEVELOPMENT (pages 198-199) *TM 10.07*

The steps of systems development are: <u>developing software</u> by purchasing it off-the-shelf or having it custom-designed; <u>acquiring hardware</u> by identifying the kind of equipment and the location of installation (it may not mean that new computer equipment must be purchased); <u>testing the new system</u> is initiated after the software and hardware are installed and the training has started. Test data, simulating real transactions, are processed into information and evaluated for the correct results.

PHASE 5: IMPLEMENTATION (pages 199-201)

Employees are trained to operate the new information system and it is installed using one of the following conversion approaches:

The **direct approach** abandons the old system and starts fresh with the new. This can be very risky if the new system develops problems.

The **parallel approach** operates both the old and the new at the same time until the new system proves reliable. This can be expensive.

The **pilot approach** is implemented in only one part of the organization. When the system proves successful, it is implemented for the entire organization.

The **phased approach** implements parts of the new system gradually replacing the old system.

PHASE 6: MAINTENANCE (pages 201-202)

Systems maintenance is an ongoing phase where the system is continually evaluated and updated to meet organizational requirements.

PROTOTYPING (page 202)

Prototyping is a faster alternative to the six phase systems analysis and design approach. A model is developed for users to try before the system is implemented. It can be an expedient method of determining if a system will work. However, it is very risky because the system may be changed or installed without giving consideration to all the costs and needs of the total organization.

THE SYSTEMS LIFE CYCLE IN THE FUTURE (pages 202-203)

The systems life cycle can be a very lengthy process. The pace of business and competition makes it a necessity to shorten development life cycles. A method called **rapid applications development (RAD)** is intended to reduce the systems development life cycle. RAD uses powerful development software (like CASE), small teams, and trained people to produce applications much faster and with higher-quality results than the traditional systems life cycle.

REVIEW QUESTIONS
True/False

T   1.   Systems analysis and design is a way to reduce the chance of creating an ineffective information system.

F   2.   In large organizations, the person who uses the systems life cycle the most is called a <u>database administrator</u>.

F   3.   Defining the problem is a task in <u>Phase 2, design</u>.

F   4.   Software is either purchased or developed in the <u>implementation phase</u>.

T   5.   In pilot conversion, one part of the organization initially tries out the new system.

Multiple Choice

B   1.   A collection of hardware, software, people, procedures, and data: **Answer; system**

A   2.   This phase in the systems life cycle focuses on evaluating and determining the need for a new information system: **Answer; preliminary investigation**

D   3.   Phase 2, analysis, involves gathering data, analyzing the data, and: **Answer; documenting the systems analysis stage**

B   4.   The evaluation of economic, technical, and operational feasibility is made during this phase: **Answer; systems design**

E   5.   The final step in Phase 4, development, is: **Answer; testing the new system**

Fill in the Blank

1.   The six phase problem-solving procedure for systems analysis and design is the <u>systems analysis and design</u>.

2.   Defining the problem, suggesting alternative systems, and preparing a short report are all parts of <u>preliminary investigation</u>.

3.   <u>Data flow</u> diagrams trace data from its origination through processing, storage, and output.

4.   Once the new system is operational, a <u>system audit</u> is performed to compare the original design specifications with the actual system.

5.   A <u>prototype</u> is a model of a system.

Open Ended

1.   What is the purpose of systems analysis and design? Who is involved with this process?

> **Developing a successful system is essential to allow the organization to achieve its goals. While there is not any fool proof means of developing a system there is a process that can be followed that will increase the chances for success. The six steps of the systems analysis and design process are performed by the systems analyst — the individual responsible for systems development decisions.**

2.   What are the six phases in the systems life cycle? Briefly describe each phase.

> *   **Preliminary investigation - the information problems or needs are identified.**
> *   **Systems analysis - the present system is studied in depth and new requirements are specified.**

* Systems design - a new or alternative information system is designed.
* Systems development - new hardware and software are acquired, developed, and tested.
* Systems implementation - the new information system is installed and adapted to the new system, and people are trained to use it.
* Systems maintenance - an ongoing phase, the system is periodically evaluated and updated as needed.

3.   Describe top-down analysis methodology.

The top-down analysis methodology is used to identify the top-level component of a system. This component is then broken into smaller components that make each component easier to analyze and to resolve.

4.   Explain the three steps in Phase 4, systems development.

Systems development is the fourth phase where new hardware and software are acquired, developed and tested. The three steps of systems development are: developing software, acquiring hardware, and testing the new system.

The software development occurs by purchasing it off-the-shelf or custom-designed.

Acquiring hardware requires identification of equipment and the location of installation. It may not mean that new computer equipment must be purchased.

Testing the new system is initiated after the software and hardware are installed and the training has started. Test data simulating real transactions are processed into information and evaluated for the correct results.

5.   Describe the four possible ways of implementing a system. Which one would you recommend?

The direct approach abandons the old system and starts fresh with the new. This can be very risky if the new system develops problems.

The parallel approach operates both the old and the new at the same time until the new system proves reliable. This can be expensive.

The pilot approach is implemented in only one part of the organization. When the system proves successful, it is implemented for the entire organization.

The phased approach implements parts of the new system gradually over time replacing the old system.

Student recommendations may vary.

CHAPTER 11
PROGRAMMING AND LANGUAGES
Chapter at a Glance

I. Programs and Programming
  A. Program specification
  B. Program design
      1. top-down design
      2. pseudocode
      3. program flowcharts
      4. structured programming using logic structures

  C. Program code
  D. Program test
      1. types of errors
          a. syntax
          b. logic
      2. debugging tools and procedures
          a. desk checking the program
          b. manual testing with sample data
          c. structured walkthrough
          d. attempt at translation
          e. computer testing with sample data

  E. Program documentation
      1. program flowcharts
      2. structure charts
      3. pseudocode
      4. other written descriptions and procedures

  F. Program maintenance

II. Five Generations of Programming Languages
  A. Machine language
  B. Assembly language
  C. Procedural languages
      1. translators
      2. compilers

  D. Problem-oriented languages
      1. application software - "What is wanted"
      2. Lotus, dBase IV, and others
      3. query language
      4. applications generator
  E. Natural languages

86

Objectives

The student should be able to:

1. Understand the six steps of programming.

2. Describe Step 1, the problem specification.

3. Describe Step 2, program design, and the program design tools of top-down program design, pseudocode, flowcharts, and logic structures.

4. Explain Step 3, coding the program.

5. Describe Step 4, testing the program, and the tools for correcting programs.

6. Discuss Step 5, documenting the program.

7. Discuss Step 6, maintaining the program.

8. Explain the five generations of programming languages.

VOCABULARY

Ada	FORTRAN	object-oriented	programming
applications	generations of	programming (OOP)	pseudocode
generator	programming languages	Pascal	query languages
assembly language	IF-THEN-ELSE	portable	RPG
BASIC	structure	procedural languages	selection structure
C	interpreter	program flowcharts	sequence structure
COBOL	levels of programming	program specification	software development
coding	languages	program definition	structured
compiler	logic structures	program modules	programming
debugging	logic error	program maintenance	techniques
desk checking	loop structure	program analysis	syntax error
DO WHILE structure	machine language	program design	top-down program
DO UNTIL structure	modules	program-oriented	design
documentation	natural languages	languages	

PROGRAMS and PROGRAMMING (pages 208-209) *TM 11.01*

A program is a problem-solving procedure in the form of step-by-step instructions written in a programming language. Programming consists of the following six step approach for creating a list of instructions that a computer needs to accomplish a task:

* program specification
* program design
* program code
* program test
* program documentation
* program maintenance

STEP 1: PROGRAM SPECIFICATION (pages 210-211)

The program specification (also called **program definition or program analysis**) requires the programmer to determine the program's objectives, the desired output, the necessary input data, and the processing necessary to turn input data into the desired output. Five tasks are specified when following this procedure:

* determining program objectives
* determining the desired output
* determining the input data
* determining the processing requirements
* determining the program's specifications

STEP 2: PROGRAM DESIGN (pages 212-218) *TM 11.02*

A **structured programming approach** involves **top-down program design, pseudocode**, and **flowcharts** all employing **logic structures**.

Top-down program design requires the programmer to determine the program's processing steps after identifying the desired output and required input. Each processing step is in the form of a module which is a logically related program statement designed to accomplish one function. A module may be broken into smaller submodules which complete tasks needed to accomplish the primary function of the module. The rules of top-down design specify each module to have only one entry and one exit point, have a single function, and limit the program instructions to 50 lines of code or less. *TM 11.03*

Pseudocode a narrative form of the program's logic. It is an outline form of the program that is to be written. *TM 11.04*

Program flowcharts graphically represent the detailed sequence of programming steps necessary to solve the problem. It is a visual presentation of the program's logic. *TM 11.05*

Logic structures are used in the development of structured programs. They include:

* **Sequence structure** means that one program statement follows another. *TM 11.06*

* The **selection structure (IF-THEN-ELSE** or **decision structure)** makes a decision and determines one of two paths to be followed in the program code. *TM 11.07*

* The **loop structure** describes a process (sequence of instructions) that may be repeated when a certain condition exists. This control structure is also called **iteration**. It has two variations: **DO UNTIL** and **DO WHILE**. *TM 11.08*

Object Oriented Programming (OOP)improves efficiency of programming by organizing a program into objects containing data and processing operations to perform a task. These objects can be reused as self-contained components in other programs.

CASE (computer-aided software engineering) tools provide some automation and assistance to the program design process, including coding and testing.

STEP 3: PROGRAM CODE (pages 195-196) *TM 11.09*

The programmer translates the program code into a specific computer language. Selecting the best language to match the needs of the organization, is a very important decision. A maintainable **structured program** should be written using the top-down design approach.

STEP 4: PROGRAM TEST (pages 219-220)

Debugging tests the program to eliminate errors. It involves the execution of the program code and correcting the parts not working correctly. The two types of errors found in a program are **syntax** (errors in the rules of the language) and **logic** (errors in the required steps to complete the program's purpose). A logic error is usually much more difficult to find than a syntax error. Tools used to find and remove errors include:

* **Desk checking** a printout of the program looking for both types of errors on a line by line basis, while sitting at a desk.

* **Manual testing with sample data** processed by the programmer not using a computer.

* **Attempt at translation** involves executing the program through a translator or compiler to convert the code to machine language. If a syntax error is detected, the translating program will identify it. A compiler program will produce a list of syntax errors.

* **Testing sample data on the computer** can be attempted after all the syntax errors are removed. Sample data is used to test the program for logic errors.

STEP 5: PROGRAM DOCUMENTATION (pages 220-221)

Documentation consists of the program flowcharts, structure charts, pseudocode, and other written descriptions and procedures found both in the actual program code and on separate forms used as a program reference. The process of developing documentation occurs throughout the entire program development process. It is not a step that occurs only at the end of the programming process. Documentation is important for people that may be involved with the program, including: **users**; **operators**; and **programmers**.

STEP 6: PROGRAM MAINTENANCE (pages 221-222) *TM 11.10*

The final step of the software development is maintenance (ensures that current programs are operating efficiently, effectively, and error free. Maintenance activities are categorized as:

* **operations** - locating and correcting operational errors, making programs easier to use and standardizing software. Employing structured programming techniques, keeps the above activities to a minimum.

* **changing needs** - all organizations change and programs must change with them to address the new requirements of the organization.

FIVE GENERATIONS of PROGRAMMING LANGUAGES (pages 222-225) *TM 11.11*

Programming languages can be classified in a range from low to high level. The low level language is more cryptic and closer to the language the computer uses (0s and 1s).

The high level languages are closer to the English language. As hardware and software technology has improved, languages have become more English-like. There are five generations of computer language each achieving a higher level from the previous generation.

Machine Language (pages 222-223)

The **first generation language** communicates with the computer in its most primitive form. The characters (bytes) consist of bits in the form of 0s and 1s. As we have discussed before, these values represent on and off signals to the computer.

Assembly Language (page 223)

This **second generation language** uses abbreviations to represent the 0s and 1s. This level language is still considered low and very cryptic to most people.

Procedural Languages (pages 223-224)

Third generation languages are procedural and more like our own language. Procedural languages require training to use to solve general problems. Three very popular procedural languages are **BASIC, COBOL,** and **Pascal**. A procedural language requires program code to be translated into machine language for the computer program execution. The translation process is accomplished with **compilers** and **interpreters**.

A **compiler** converts the entire program's **source code** (code written by the programmer) into **object code** (code that is in machine language) at one time and checks for syntax errors.

Once a clean compile (program without errors) is produced, the object code can be saved and used later. COBOL and FORTRAN are examples of compiler languages. A compiler language can run faster than an interpreter once the object code is saved.

An **interpreter** converts one procedural language statement at a time into machine language as it is being executed interactively. If a syntax error is detected, the program's execution is halted. No object code is saved. BASIC is an example of a language using an interpreter. The advantage of an interpreter is that it can be useful in interactive programming.

The principal procedural languages used currently include: **BASIC, Pascal, C, COBOL, FORTRAN, Ada,** and **RPG**.

Problem-Oriented Languages (pages 224-225)

Fourth generation languages are problem oriented and designed to solve specific problems. They allow the user to describe "what is wanted" rather than "how to do it". Many problem-oriented languages consist of application software like LOTUS 1-2-3 or dBASE IV. They also include query languages and application generators.

A **query language** enables users to use easily understood commands to search a database.

An **applications generator** contains program modules with logically related preprogrammed statements to accomplish various tasks. The user simply selects the appropriate module for the task to be accomplished and the application generator develops it into a program.

Natural Languages (page 225)

Fifth generation languages consists of natural languages in the developing stage to provide people with a more human ("natural") connection to the computer.

PROGRAMMING IN THE FUTURE (page 202)

Professional programmers are constantly looking for ways to make their work easier, faster and more reliable. Some recent improvements for programmers include:

OOP (object-oriented programming languages) differ from conventional programming languages in that they use and manipulate **objects**. These objects can be graphic symbols, modules or blocks of programming code, or data. OOP languages will be a significant part of programming in this decade for two reasons:

1. They are well suited for designing and using graphical user interfaces.
2. They are highly modular, allowing programmers to isolate, combine, and reuse programming code very efficiently.

REVIEW QUESTIONS

True/False

T   1.   A program is a list of instructions for the computer to follow to accomplish the task of processing data into information.

F   2.   All documentation is performed in the <u>last step in the programming</u>.

F   3.   CASE stands for computer <u>association of scientific engineers</u>.

T   4.   A translator converts a programming language into machine language.

F   5.   Assembly is in the <u>first</u> generation of programming languages.

Multiple Choice

A   1.   Another name for applications software is: **Answer; applications programs**

C   2.   The structured programming technique that graphically presents the detailed steps needed to solve the problem: **Answer; flowcharts**

B   3.   The last thing to do before leaving the program design step: **Answer; document**

D   4.   The last step in programming: **Answer; maintenance**

B   5.   Translator that converts procedural languages one statement at a time into machine code before it is to be executed: **Answer; interpreter**

Fill in the Blank

1.   In program specifications, you should specify **outputs** before inputs.

2.   The logic structure **IF-THEN-ELSE** is used when a decision must be made.

3.   **Debugging** is another name for testing the program.

4.   Seventy-five percent of software costs can be attributed to program **maintenance**

5.   **COBOL** is the most frequently used language in business programming.

Open Ended

1.   Describe the six steps involved in programming.

Step 1: Program specification - (also called program definition or program analysis) usually requires the programmer to determine the program's objectives, the desired output, the necessary input data, and the processing necessary to turn input data into the desired output.

Step 2: Program design - A structured approach should be used to develop custom-made software involving top-down program design, flowcharts, and pseudocode.

Step 3: Program Code - The programmer writes the program code in a specific computer language. A structured program should be written using top-down design.

Step 4: Program test - Means to test the program and eliminate the errors by the execution of the program code and correcting the parts that do not work.

Step 5: Program documentation - by having program flowcharts, structure charts, pseudocode, and other written descriptions and procedures found both in the actual program code and on separate forms used as a program reference. The process of developing documentation occurs throughout the entire program development process.

Step 6: Program maintenance - Programmers update software to correct errors, to improve usability, to standardize, and to adjust to organizational changes.

2.   Identify and give an example for each of the three logic structures.

Three logic structures used in program coding are:

*   **sequence - one programming statement following another.**
*   **selection - occurring when a decision is made and the outcome of the decision determines which of two paths to follow.**
*   **loop - is the repeating of the program or of statements within the program.**

3.   List and discuss the five generations of programming languages?

First Generation - machine language
Second Generation - assembly language
Third Generation - procedural language
Fourth Generation - problem-oriented language
Fifth Generation - natural language

4.   Explain the difference between a compiler and an interpreter.

An interpreter translates one line of code into machine language at a time as the program is executed. If a syntax error is detected, the execution stops.

A compiler program translates all program code into machine language at once and stores it in a file, if syntax errors are found a list will be produced to help the programmer debug the program. Execution happens after a clean compile is made.

5.   Discuss the principal advantage of natural languages if researchers are successful in developing them?

It is the intent of the researchers to enable the computer to "learn" (to remember information and improve upon it).

CHAPTER 12
APPLICATIONS SOFTWARE: POWER TOOLS
Chapter at a Glance

I. Personal Information Managers (PIM)
    A. Notepad
    B. Appointment calendar (with alarm)
    C. Telephone directory
    D. Memory-resident programs

II. Project Management Software

III. Desktop Publishing
    A. Required hardware and software
    B. Quality of output
    C. Style sheets
    D. Page description languages

IV. Hypertext and Multimedia

V. CAD/CAM
    A. Computer aided design program (CAD)
    B. Computer aided design and drafting program (CADD)
    C. Computer aided manufacturing (CAM)

VI. Artificial Intelligence
    A. Robotics
    B. Knowledge-based and Expert Systems
    C. Artificial Reality

VII. A Look to the Future

Objectives

The student should be able to:

1. Describe personal information managers.

2. Discuss project management software.

3. Explain what desktop publishing is.

4. Describe new media: hypertext and multimedia.

5. Describe CAD/CAM software.

6. Explain artificial intelligence, robotics, knowledge-based system and expert systems, and virtual reality.

VOCABULARY

artificial reality
artificial intelligence (AI)
computer-aided manufacturing
 (CAM)
computer-aided design (CAD)
computer-aided design
 and drafting (CADD)
expert systems
Gantt chart

hypermedia
hypertext
memory-resident programs
multimedia
page description languages
personal information managers
 (PIMs)
PERT (Program Evaluation
 Review Technique) chart

project
project management software
robotics
robots
shells
style sheet
virtual reality
virtual environments

PERSONAL INFORMATION MANAGERS (pages 232-233) *TM 12.01*

PIM software provides tools which many professionals use to assist them with time-management and organizational tasks. The tools include an appointment calendar (with alarm), Rolodex files, address books, index cards, wall charts, notepad, personal telephone directory, and Post-it notes. Personal information managers are called **memory-resident programs** because they stay in primary storage at the same time with an application.

PROJECT MANAGEMENT SOFTWARE (pages 233-234) *TM 12.02 and TM 12.03*

Projects are one-time operations involving several tasks to be completed by a stated time. **Project management software** is designed to assist users in planning, scheduling, and controlling the people, resources, and costs within the time schedule. Project management software might display the schedule beginning and ending dates using:

* **Gantt charts** of bars and lines, indicating a time schedule measured in a time unit.

* Program Evaluation Review Technique (**PERT**) **chart** show the timing of a project and the relationship among the tasks represented by lines connecting boxes stating the tasks.

DESKTOP PUBLISHING (pages 234-237)

Desktop publishing is the process of using a microcomputer, laser printer, and software to mix text and graphics for producing near professional quality forms and publications. Newsletters, forms, catalogs, brochures, posters, menus, and advertisements are all examples of output produced by desktop publishing.

The software allows the user to select a variety of type styles in a text format along with graphic files to design a desired publication format. A **style sheet** is defined to determine the basic appearance of single or multiple pages. The number of columns per page, the size and type style of text and headings, the width of lines and boxes, and the alignment of the text with the graphics can all be specified in a style sheet. Using **page description languages**, a composed document is transmitted to an output device.

Hypertext is software allowing one to connect a text file with a graphics file. It stores information as nodes, each of which has an individual label. These separate nodes are retrieved and displayed on a monitor as windows showing the connections between the various pieces of information. Apple's Macintosh software **HyperCard** has been the catalyst for generating the interest in this information management, and programming tool.

Multimedia (also called **hypermedia**) is much more elaborate than hypertext. **Multimedia** can link information, including text, graphics, animation, video, music, and voice. CD-ROM and videocassette tapes play a major role in this technology.

CAD/CAM (pages 241-242)

Discuss computer-aided design/computer aided manufacturing as two separate entities: the first is used for designing products and the other is used for manufacturing products.

* A **computer-aided design (CAD)** program manipulates images on a screen and allows one to create three-dimensional images that can be rotated to see all sides. A variation of CAD is **computer-aided design and drafting (CADD)** program. A CADD program consists of graphic elements including straight lines, arcs, and circles used to create an image. Most CADD programs only work in two dimensions (some can work in three dimensions) where the user edits drawings by moving images, changing shapes, and rotating objects. Some CADD programs have drawings layered like acetate overlays.

* **Computer-aided manufacturing (CAM)** describes programs that control automated factory equipment including machine tools and robots.

ARTIFICIAL INTELLIGENCE (pages 242-246)

The goal of **artificial intelligence** is to help people be more productive, not to replace human intelligence. Computers have used calculating power very successfully to solve structured problems. However, unstructured problems have typically required individuals with intuition, reasoning, and memory to reach a solution.

Artificial intelligence (**AI**) is attempting to develop systems to mimic human thought processes and actions, including reasoning, learning from past actions, and simulation of human senses such as vision and touch. Several tools emulate problem solving and information processing have been developed with practical applications for business, medicine, law, and many other fields. Artificial intelligence is presently categorized into:

<u>Robotics</u> concerned with developing machines that can be programmed and reprogrammed to perform several repeated and/or routine tasks. There are various types of robots including:

- **Industrial robots** used in factories to perform assembly-line tasks.
- **Perception systems** that imitate some of the human senses. *TM 12.06*

- **Mobile robots** that act as transporters to carry mail, supplies, equipment, etc. on a preprogrammed route around a business or office complex.

<u>Knowledge-Based Systems</u> use a collection of facts and widely accepted rules people have developed over time as they pertain to various situations and tasks. The programs of a knowledge-based system helps users to make decisions and accomplish specific tasks much like an operator's manual instructs one on how to use a lawn mower. An **expert system** is a more sophisticated knowledge-based system. The programs of an expert system retain and emulate the human experts skilled in a particular field. An expert system differs from knowledge-based systems in three ways: *TM 12.07*

1. They are based on true expertise, involving highly specialized knowledge.
2. They take several months or even years to develop.
3. They consist of several hundred or even thousands of rules.

Expert systems are used in many fields, including medicine, geology, chemistry, agriculture, robot repair, and military science. They have primarily been operating in a larger computer environment, but some are now available for the microcomputer.

<u>Virtual reality</u> (**Artificial reality** or **virtual environments**) has a user wear headgear and gloves connected to a computer with software that translates data into images. The headgear has earphones and three-dimensional stereoscopic screens. The glove has sensors that collect data about hand movements. When coupled with the software, this sensory equipment allows the user to experience alternative realities to the physical world. Applications for this technology include recreation, and more importantly simulation exercises for such things as surgical procedures, flying, spaceship repair, or nuclear disaster cleanup. *TM 12.08*

A LOOK AT THE FUTURE (page 247)

This will have a profound affect on individuals and their careers as it relates to the computing resources available to them through **"downsizing"**, meaning microcomputers will perform the tasks that could previously only be done on mainframes. .

In addition, we should see a broadening of scope of applications meaning computers will integrate even more with our homes, careers, workplace, and our personal lives. Examples of this integration include: **pen-based computers** with handwriting-recognition; televisions equipped with CD players enabling viewers to navigate by sight and sound through atlases and encyclopedias; and **information appliances** which bundle a computer, telephone, fax machine, photocopier, color printer, laser discs, and CD's into one intelligent machine.

There are and will continue to be attempts to go beyond artificial intelligence to something called **artificial life**. Researchers are trying to develop programs that learn and develop on their own. Computers can be used to simulate living systems and to make computerized environments where simulated organisms eat, reproduce and die. The result of these explorations may produce defenses against computer viruses, human health problems, and possibly numerous societal problems that we face into the twenty-first century.

REVIEW QUESTIONS

True/False

T   1.   PIMs typically include electronic calendars, to-do lists, address books, and notepads.

F   2.   <u>Desktop publishing software</u> helps you to plan, schedule, and control the people, resources, and costs of a project.

F   3.   In hypertext, a <u>stack</u> in the basic filing unit.

F   4.   Multimedia sales are expected to <u>remain constant</u> for the next few years.

T   5.   Expert systems are programs that give advice to individuals who would otherwise rely on human experts.

Multiple Choice

E   1.   A one-time operation composed of several tasks that must be completed during a stated period: **Answer; project**

D   2.   The applications software that allows you to mix text and graphics to create documents of nearly professional quality: **Answer; desktop publishing**

C   3.   The application that can link all sorts of media into one form of presentation: **Answer; multimedia**

B   4.   Clothing, furniture, industrial products, and just about anything else can be designed using _____ software: **Answer; CAD**

A   5.   An area of artificial intelligence that simulates certain experiences using special headgear, gloves, and software that translates data into images: **Answer; virtual reality**

Fill in the Blank

1.   Lotus Organizer is an example of a <u>**personal information manager**</u>.

2.   In desktop publishing, a <u>style sheet</u> helps you to create the basic appearance of single or multiple pages.

3.   Linking text, graphics, animation, video, music, and voice into one presentation can be done using <u>multimedia</u>.

4.   Unlike most assembly-line machines, <u>**robots**</u> can be reprogrammed to do more than one task.

5.   Expert system <u>shells</u> are special programs that allow a person to custom-build an expert system.

98

Open Ended

1. What does a Personal information manager do? What are they used for?

    This software provides the professional time management and organization tools including an appointment calendar (with alarm), Rolodex files, address books, index cards, wall charts, notepad, personal telephone directory, and Post-it notes. Personal information managers are called memory-resident programs because they stay in primary storage at the same time with an application.

2. Explain what project management software does. Give an example of how one might be used.

    It is designed to assist users in planning, scheduling, and controlling the people, resources, and costs within the time schedule. Project management software might display the schedule beginning and ending dates using Gantt charts and PERT charts. It would likely be used to show the scheduled beginning and ending dates for a particular task such as a contractor building a housing development.

3. What does a desktop publishing program let you do? Describe what a page description language does.

    It allows one to use a microcomputer, laser printer, and software to mix text and graphics for the purpose of producing near professional quality forms and publications. Newsletters, forms, catalogs, brochures, posters, menus, and advertisements are all possible examples of output that can be produced by desktop publishing.

    A page description languages, sends instructions to an output device (usually a laser printer). These instructions determine the basic appearance of the output including: number of columns per page, the size and type style of text and headings, the width of lines and boxes, and the alignment of the text with the graphics.

4. Explain how multimedia works.

    Multimedia (also called hypermedia) can link information, including text, graphics, animation, video, music, and voice. It employs CD-ROM, video cameras, speakers, television monitors, and videocassette tapes to produce output.

5. What are the three areas of artificial intelligence?

    Robotics, Knowledge-Based Systems, and Virtual Reality

CHAPTER 13
WORKPLACE ISSUES: ERGONOMICS, ETHICS, COMPUTER CRIME and SECURITY
Chapter at a Glance

I. Ergonomics
    A. Physical Health
    B. Mental Health
    C. Design with people in mind

II. Ethics - Privacy, Accuracy, Property, Access
    A. Use of large databases
    B. Use of electronic networks
    C. The major laws on privacy
        1. Fair Credit Reporting Act (1970)
        2. Freedom of Information Act (1970)
        3. Privacy Act (1974)
        4. Right to Financial Privacy Act (1979)
        5. Computer Fraud and Abuse Act (1986)
        6. Electronic Communications Privacy Act (1986)
        7. Video Privacy Protection Act (1988)
        8. Computer Matching and Privacy Protection Act (1988)

III. Computer Crime
    A. Computer criminals
        1. employees
        2. outside users
        3. "hackers" and "crackers"
        4. organized crime
    B. Computer crime
        1. damage and theft
        2. unauthorized copying
        3. manipulation
    C. Other hazards
        1. natural disasters
        2. civil strife and terrorism
        3. technological failures
        4. human error

IV. Security
    A. Restricting access
    B. Anticipating disasters
    C. Backing up data

V. A Look at the Future

OBJECTIVES

The student should be able to:

1. Describe ergonomics and how it helps avoid physical and mental risks.

2. Discuss the four ethical issues: privacy, accuracy, property, and access.

3. Discuss the ethical issues raised by the presence of large databases and electronic networks.

4. List the major laws on privacy.

5. Explain the effects of computer crimes, including the spreading of computer viruses.

6. Describe other hazards to the computer.

7. Discuss security measures that may be taken.

VOCABULARY

access
accuracy
bacteria
biometrics
carpal tunnel syndrome
cold sites
computer crime
Computer Matching and
 Privacy Protection Act of
 1988
Computer Fraud and Abuse
 Act of 1986
Computer Fraud and Abuse
 Act of 1986
cracker
cumulative trauma disorders

disaster recovery plan
Electronic Communications
 Privacy Act of 1986
ergonomics
ethics
Fair Credit Reporting Act of
 1970
Freedom of Information Act
 of 1970
hacker
hot sites
physical security
privacy
Privacy Act of 1974
property
repetitive motion injury

repetitive strain injury (RSI)
Right to Financial Privacy Act
 of 1979
security
software piracy
Software Copyright Act of
 1980
spike
surge protector
Trojan horse program
Video Privacy Protection Act
of 1988
viruses
voltage surge
worm

ERGONOMICS (pages 252-255) *TM 13.01*

Discuss how each new technological "advancement", is be measured with time and experience the degree the technology has made an improvement or possibly a detriment to the world.

Ergonomics is the study of human factors related to computers and technology. This science is also concerned with designing technology to increase productivity and avoid health risks.

Physical health studies discovered negative outcomes related to the use of computers, including: eyestrain, headaches, back pain, neck pain, repetitive strain injury (RSI), carpal tunnel syndrome, and electromagnetic fields (EMF) links to pregnancy miscarriages and cancers. In each of these instances, ergonomic studies have designed systems or made suggestions to minimize the degree of risk to physical health.

Mental health studies show computers can have an irritating affect on people, including: creating a noisy work environment, equipment too sophisticated or difficult to use and stress from excessive electronic monitoring from an employer. Studies have also indicated greater instances of boredom, higher tension, extreme anxiety, depression, anger, and severe fatigue.

Design with People in Mind - Manufacturers have recently started a trend to strip down products to make them less complicated. This is in response to consumer surveys indicating a desire for "plug and play" equipment. The computer industry is attempting to make computers easier to use with more menus, windows, icons, and pictures.

ETHICS (pages 255-259) *TM 13.02*

Privacy is the right to keep personal information secure. The ability of individuals to maintain privacy is very difficult considering the amount and type of information collected about each of us, including: *what we buy, when we buy it, how much we buy, the price we pay, our names, addresses, phone numbers, medical histories, and the list goes on and on.*

We should be concerned with:
* **what information is spread**
* **who is spreading it and by what means it is distributed without our consent**
* **spread of inaccurate information.**

Issues arising from the use of electronic mail are fundamental to our individual freedoms, including: **eavesdropping on electronic mail and freedom of speech against censorship in the use of electronic mail or network services.**

The **major laws** governing privacy matters include:

The **Fair Credit Reporting Act of 1970** is to keep inaccuracies out of credit bureau files and prevent credit agencies from allowing unauthorized accessing of records. Consumers can review and correct their records and are to be notified of inquires from insurance companies or employers. Credit agencies may share records with anyone deemed as having a "legitimate business need".

The **Freedom of Information Act of 1970** entitles individuals access to records held by government agencies. Portions of the records may be deleted for national security reasons.

The **Privacy Act of 1974** limits the manner federal agencies may share information about American citizens. Information collected for one purpose cannot be used for another purpose.

The **Right to Financial Privacy Act of 1979** sets strict procedures in examining customer records in banks by federal agencies.

Electronic Communications Privacy Act of 1986 protects the privacy of users on public electronic-mail systems. It does not cover communication with an organization's internal electronic communications.

The **Computer Fraud and Abuse Act of 1986** permits prosecution for unauthorized access to computers and databases.

The **Video Privacy Protection Act of 1988** prevents retailers from selling or disclosing video-rental records without the customer's consent or a court order.

The **Computer Matching and Privacy Protection Act of 1988** has rules federal agencies must use to match computer data to a person's eligibility for federal benefits or recovering delinquent debts.

Privacy is still an **ethical issue**, especially for nongovernment organizations not covered by existing laws. It is encouraging to see a number of information-collecting businesses adopting the **Code of Fair Information Practice** recommended in 1977 by a committee established by former Secretary of Health, Education, and Welfare, Elliott Richardson. *TM 13.03*

COMPUTER CRIME (pages 260-263)

The major threats to a computer system, include: criminal acts, natural hazards, human error, technological failure, civil strife, and terrorism.

Any of these threats can cause major problems for an individual, business, or organization if data, programs, or hardware is lost or permanently destroyed.

A **computer crime** is an illegal action using computer technology. Computer criminals are of four types: **employees, outside users, "hackers" and "crackers", and organized crime**.

Employees make up the largest group of computer criminal. They have the easiest access to computers, software, and data. Their actions include physically stealing equipment and/or software or unauthorized use of information, electronic funds, or computer time. Sometimes they do other damage as an act of resentment or revenge.

Outside users may include suppliers or clients to an organization that have access to a company's computer system. This group poses a threat to the organization and it's computer system in a variety of ways.

"Hackers" are people who gain unauthorized access to a computer system for the fun or challenge of it. **"Crackers"** do the same thing for malicious purposes, such as: stealing information, or placing a destructive computer program into the system.

Organized crime uses computers for illegal purposes, including: inventory of stolen goods, drugs, and gambling debts. In addition, counterfeiters and forgers use microcomputers and printers to produce documents like checks and driver's licenses.

Computer Crime (the criminal action on a computer system) takes many forms including; **damage, theft of hardware, piracy, and unauthorized use.**

A **trojan horse program** is a type of virus with lines of code that attaches to legitimate software, designed to destroy or modify software programs and data. *TM 13.04*

A **virus** "migrates through networks and operating systems attaching themselves to different programs and databases. As a user accesses a computer system with a virus, it attaches itself to the users program files later stored on a floppy disk of hard disk. As long as the virus goes undetected in a computer system, it will continue to infect every program coming into contact with it.

A variation of a virus is a **worm** or **bacteria**, which fills a computer system with self-replicating information slowing the computer system or locking it up so it is unable to perform any other tasks. Once the virus is in a system it may lay dormant until a particular date or some data item happens to trigger the instructions to destroy data or to simply display messages on the screen. It is difficult to protect a system from viruses. *TM 13.05*

Detection programs exist but not all viruses can be detected, since new viruses are being constantly developed. The best safeguard is for the user to know the origin of the software being installed in the computer and to be cautious when using electronic bulletin boards.

Theft can be the physical stealing of hardware, software, or data. It can also be what is often termed "white-collar crime" which is the theft of information from a computer system to be used in a variety of ways.

Piracy is a form of theft. A person who buys a software program (or at least the license to use it) has the right to copy the program for backup purposes. However, an individual may not sell or give away any copy unless the software licensing agreement expressly identifies the use of the software program in this manner. Penalties for violation of the **Software Copyright Act** are monetary damages to the developer of the program and possibly prison.

Manipulation involves unauthorized accessing of a computer system and modifying data, programs, or just leaving a "harmless" message. This action is against the law. In fact, the **Computer Fraud and Abuse Act of 1986** makes it a crime for unauthorized persons to even view data. Provisions of the law allow sentencing of offenders up to 20 years in prison and fined up to $100,000.

Other Hazards to computers include:
* natural disasters of flood, fire, wind, lightening, earthquakes, etc..
* civil strife and terrorism.
* technological failures involving hardware or software not working as intended, electrical outages, voltage surges, or voltage spikes.
* human errors in data entry, programming, faulty design, procedures, etc.

SECURITY (pages 263-264)

Security is concerned with protecting information hardware, and software from all the above threats. Measures should be taken to protect the system from unauthorized use, damage, sabotage, and natural disasters. A good security system should include:

Restricted access to the system both physically and electronically. Physical security includes locks on buildings, rooms, and cabinets to protect from outsiders and also environmental protection against natural disasters. Electronic security involves the use of passwords, dial-back systems, and possibly **biometrics** (the science of measuring individual body characteristics to uniquely identify an authorized individual to the system. This type of security also called **data security** is concerned with protecting software and data from unauthorized tampering and damage.

Development of a **disaster recovery plan** describing the ways to continue operation in the event of a computer system failure. Part of a disaster recovery plan might include a cooperative arrangement with another company to share equipment in the event of a disaster. Some organizations create emergency facilities in the likelihood of a disaster. A **hot site** would be fully equipped to handle the computing needs of an organization. A **cold site** is an empty shell where hardware must be installed. Paramount to any security system or plan is the routine **backup of data**.

Security for microcomputers include:

* avoidance of extreme environmental conditions like temperature, water, smoke, food and drink, and electricity (use a surge protector).

* guarding the computer from theft or use with locks and passwords to gain physical or electronic access to the computer system.

* guarding programs and data by storing them securely. Making backup copies of both data and programs and storing them at another location.

A LOOK AT THE FUTURE (pages 264-265)

Technology and people who learn to apply technology in "creative" ways are always ahead of existing social and political institutions. Listed in this chapter were several laws designed to protect us against abuses and infringements of our basic rights and freedoms. Laws have been passed, however, many of these laws are not keeping pace with the technology. As a member of a society, we have to be living at a higher level ethically and morally above the standards our laws presently govern. Teaching our youth by example and being role models for what we want our society to become will help us take advantage and thrive on what technology offers to us.

REVIEW QUESTIONS

True/False

F   1.   Most people who use computers are midlevel managers.

T   2.   EMF stands for electromagnetic field.

F 3. <u>Our legal system</u> is the essential element used to control computers today.

T 4. Over 20 percent of business search through employees' electronic messages and computer files.

F 5. A <u>Trojan horse</u> is a virus that keeps replicating itself until the computer system's operations are slowed or stopped.

Multiple Choice

C 1. The study of human factors related to computers: **Answer; ergonomics**

B 2. A repetitive strain injury that causes damage to nerves and tendons in hands: **Answer; carpal tunnel syndrome**

E 3. The ethical issue that deals with the responsibility to control the availability of data: **Answer; access**

D 4. The largest category of computer criminals: **Answer; employees**

A 5. Restricting access, anticipating disasters, and making backup copies of data are all aspects of: **Answer; security**

Fill in the Blank

1. <u>Noninterlaced</u> is a type of monitor that does not flicker.

2. The new word **technostress** is used to describe harmful stress associated with computer use.

3. Computer **ethics** are guidelines for the morally acceptable use of computers in our society.

4. People who gain unauthorized access to a computer system for fun and challenge are called **hackers**.

5. <u>Software piracy</u> is the unauthorized copying of programs for personal gain.

Open Ended

1. What kind of activities can you perform to avoid computer-related eyestrain, headaches, and back and neck pains?

Eye-strain can be minimized by taking periodic breaks away from the VDT; placing screens away from windows and bright lights, using anti-glare shields; having the screen 3-4 times brighter than surrounding room light; keeping materials and the screen at the same distance from your eyes.

Back and neck pain can be avoided by adjusting equipment in comfortable positions including the keyboard, screen, chair, and document holders.

2. Describe some mental health problems associated with frequent computer use.

    Computers can have an irritating affect on people in a variety of ways, including: creating a noisy work environment, equipment too sophisticated or difficult to use and stress from excessive electronic monitoring from an employer.

3. What are four types of computer criminals?

    Employees, outside users, "hackers" and "crackers", and organized crime

4. What are computer ethics? What are the four major issues?

    They are guidelines for the morally acceptable use of computers in our society. The four primary issues are: privacy; accuracy; property; and access.

5. Define security. Name three ways of protecting the security of computers.

    Security is concerned with protecting information hardware, and software. Methods Measures of protecting security include:
    Restricted access to the system both physically and electronically.

    Development of a disaster recovery plan describing the ways to continue operation in the event of a computer system failure.

    A system or plan to routinely backup data and programs.

CHAPTER 14
YOUR FUTURE:
USING INFORMATION TECHNOLOGY
Chapter at a Glance

I.   Being a Winner in the Information Revolution
    A. People capable of using technology
    B. Demonstrating confidence to learn and manage technology
    C. Developing an *individual* strategy to be technologically competitive

II. Technology and Organizations
    A. New products
    B. New enterprises
    C. New customer and supplier relationships

III. Technology and People
    A. Cynical
    B. Naive
    C. Frustration

IV. Staying Current with Technology to be a Winner
    A. Keep current in your field or profession
    B. Keep current with technology
        1. trade journals
        2. professional associations
    C. Develop and cultivate professional contacts
    D. Develop specialized and generalized skills
    E. Be alert to organizational change
    F. Look for innovative applications of the technology

Objectives

The student should be able to:

1.   Explain why it's important to have an individual strategy in order to be a "winner" in the information age.

2.   Describe how technology is changing the nature of competition.

3.   Discuss three ways people may react to new technology.

4.   Describe how you can use your computer to stay current and to take charge of your career.

New technology requires people who are capable of using and working with it. This requires not only an ability, but an attitude on the part of the user that demonstrates confidence to learn and to manage the new technology. The key is how to integrate the technology with the people who use it. Learning the most current technology and using its tools to your advantage helps one to become a winner in the information revolution. Develop an **individual** strategy to deal with change and to be technologically competitive.

TECHNOLOGY and ORGANIZATIONS (pages 271-272)

Prompt the students to discuss the trends they see to apply technology to organizations.

To inspire the students' discussion, review some of the current technological trends, including:

* more **powerful processors** and **operating systems** permitting multitasking capability with a microcomputer.

* **powerful laptops** cutting the ties holding the user close to an electrical outlet.

* **graphics and desktop publishing** making more useful machines for graphics applications and publications.

* **scanners** can "read" existing documents which speeds up input, reduces errors, allows graphic and text images, and can be transmitted to another computer.

* **voice recognition** frees the users hands for more important activities other than typing.
* **better printers** many of which can produce near professional quality images and publications, some even in color.

* **workstations, terminals, and microcomputers** that are cheaper and take up less space.
* **micro to mainframe communications** are being improved by new operating systems and application software programs that give the microcomputer user capabilities previously reserved only for mainframe computer users.

* **cellular phone networks** that can be connected with modems and microcomputers are providing new opportunities for doing business.

* **communications standards** that will help relieve the "connectivity" problems associated with incompatible systems. These standards are important for providing the services of **facsimile transmission, electronic mail, automatic appointment scheduler, telecommuting,** and **teleconferencing.**

* **hypertext** enabling people to join text and graphics.

* **multimedia joining** pictures, music, animation and video sequences as well as words and numbers.

* **access** to huge volumes of data made possible with the improved direct access storage devices, magnetic disk packs, optical disks and DBMS software.

The above list of technological changes have altered the nature of competition by creating new products, new enterprises, new customers and supplier relationships.

New enterprises develop everyday as people find applications for both new and old goods and services that have a new perspective due to the changing technology.

New customer supplier relationships can be developed if people and organizations take advantage of information technology. Applying the laws of supply and demand to the instant information at their disposal can be a very prosperous application for those who are enterprising.

The method of doing business may drastically be altered by **natural-language processing, artificial intelligence, robots, artificial reality,** and **knowledge-based and expert systems.**

The trends listed above are a summary of many of the technological advances that have been covered through the book. These items are not specifically covered in Chapter 14. However, it provides the instructor a means to summarize some of the high points of the book.

TECHNOLOGY and PEOPLE (pages 272-273)

The success of an individual and possibly of an organization depends on the reaction or attitude toward technology. It is suggested that the reaction can be categorized as cynical, naive, and/or frustrated.

The **cynic** believes that the use of a microcomputer is overrated. Learning and training requires too much time. Managers may say that it is necessary for them to understand about word processors and spreadsheets, but the operation of these applications is to be accomplished by clerical workers.

The **naive** believe that computers can solve almost any problem and put too much confidence into computers.

The **frustrated** is a very busy worker who hates to take time to learn about microcomputers. Thus, frustration is the result of committing some time but not enough time to learn how to use the system well. This may describe the majority of people.

Progressive organizations are using the technology of the information age. If an individual desires to increase the chances for success in today's business world, the following ideas may provide sound advice:

Stay current with your field by learning how to apply the current technology to the task of improving one's particular area of expertise.

Stay current with technology by reading trade journals and affiliations with professional associations. In addition, there are several magazines which can keep people abreast of the latest technology.

Develop professional contacts by being a member of a professional organization and maintaining contact with the individuals through telephone, letter, and personal engagements. These interactions can be very useful for knowing what others are doing in your profession and it can also be a source for new job opportunities.

Develop specialty skills as well as general skills to help you grow as a well rounded individual. Look for ways to adapt skills to new job opportunities.

Be alert for organizational change by using formal and informal lines of communication. Be alert to new innovations, hiring practices, layoffs, mergers, automation, etc. within the organization.

Look for innovative opportunities by finding ways to improve the way you do your job and making yourself more efficient. Discuss your ideas with someone that will see that you get the credit you deserve. Present your ideas in terms of saving money rather than improving information.

A LOOK TO THE FUTURE: THE REST of YOUR LIFE (page 277)

Live for today by acting on the opportunities and prevailing technology of the moment. Concentrate on establishing daily goals and strive to achieve them. Develop you r computer competency by applying it to your daily situation and taking control of the new tools available to you.

REVIEW QUESTIONS
True/False

T   1. Most businesses are making formal plans to track and to implement technology into their competitive strategies.

F   2. Businesses <u>never</u> allow customers access to their information systems.

F   3. In all fields, successful professionals have to be <u>experts</u> in their own fields as well as <u>in computer technology</u>.

T 4. *Infoworld, PC World, and MacWorld* are magazines that specifically cover microcomputers and information.

T 5. The office grapevine can be a good source to alert you to organizational changes.

Multiple Choice

D 1. The real issue with new technology is: **Answer; how to integrate with people**

B 2. By giving their customers access to their package tracking information system, Federal Express is developing new: **Answer; desktop publishing**

C 3. The type of person who underestimates the difficulty of changing computer systems or of generating information is **Answer; naïve**

A 4. By staying in touch with others in your field, you are: **Answer; developing professional contacts**

E 5. A good approach to present your innovative ideas is to present them: **Answer; in terms of saving money**

Fill in the Blank

1. ATM cards, home banking, and programs to analyze cursive writing are examples of how some banks are looking to use technology in their competitive **strategies**.

2. The person who thinks that microcomputers are overrated can be classified as a **cynic**.

3. Reading trade journals about the use of technology is a good way to stay **current**.

4. **Grapevine** is another name for the informal lines of communication within an organization.

5. Being computer-competent means taking **positive** control.

Open Ended

1. How do you become and stay a winner in the information age?

New technology requires people capable of using and working with it. It requires ability and an attitude on the part of the user that demonstrates confidence to learn and to manage the new technology. The key is how to integrate the technology with the people who use it. Learning the most current technology and using its tools to your advantage helps one to become a winner in the information revolution.

2.   Give an example of how technology can change the nature of competition.

Being competitive in the information age has taken on an entirely new definition because of any number of developments in our technology. Individual's in today's business world have the technological capability to do business virtually anywhere in the world.

Telecommunications allows us to communicate and transact business over very long distances. We can use fax machines to send and receive legal documents, a video conferencing allows us the capability to participate in a business meeting with the participants scattered in several different locations.

Hardware and especially software developments have given enormous computing power to end users with little computer experience. Natural-language processing, knowledge-based and expert systems have allowed us to build on past knowledge to a magnitude that has never been reached before. Huge databases can be built to allow business people access to information that is current and up the moment.

Technology can alter the nature of competition by creating new products, new enterprises, new customers and supplier relationships.

3.   What are three responses of attitudes that people in organizations are apt to have when confronted by new technology?

The success of an individual and possibly of an organization depends on the reaction or attitude toward technology. It is suggested that the reaction can be categorized as cynical, naive, and/or frustrated.

The cynic believes the use of a microcomputer is overrated. Learning and training requires too much time. Managers may say it is necessary for them to understand about word processors and spreadsheets, but the operation of these applications is to be accomplished by clerical workers.

The naive believe computers can solve almost any problem and put too much confidence into computers.

The frustrated is a very busy worker who hates to take time to learn about microcomputers. Thus, frustration is the result of committing some time but not enough time to learn how to use the system well. This may describe the majority of people.

4.   Name six strategies individuals should follow in order to be successful in the information age.

Progressive organizations are using the technology of the information age. If an individual desires to increase the chances for success in today's business world, the following ideas may provide sound advice:

Stay current with your field by learning how to apply the current technology to the task of improving one's particular area of expertise.

Stay current with technology by reading trade journals and affiliations with professional associations. In addition, there are several magazines which can keep people abreast of the latest technology.

Develop professional contacts by being a member of a professional organization and maintaining contact with the individuals through telephone, letter, and direct contact.

Develop specialty skills as well as general skills to help you grow as a well rounded individual. Look for ways to adapt skills to new job opportunities.

Be alert for organizational change by using formal and informal lines of communication. Be alert to new innovations, hiring practices, layoffs, mergers, automation, etc. within the organization.

Look for innovative opportunities by finding ways to improve the way you do your job and making yourself more efficient. Discuss your ideas with someone that will see that you get the credit you deserve. Present your ideas in terms of saving money rather than improving information.

5.   What periodicals might you read in order to keep current on changes in microcomputer technology?

There is a wide variety of professional journals and periodicals concerned with the application of computers and technology to the business world and for personal use. Some examples of popular magazines are Personal Computing, InfoWorld, PC World, MacWorld, and Byte. General business periodicals include Business Week, Fortune, Inc., and The Wall Street Journal to name just a few that carry technology related articles on a regular basis.

Types of Computers

Type	Description
Microcomputers	Desktop, also known as personal computers, widely used and number increasing fast
Minicomputers	Medium-sized, also known as midrange, used by medium-sized organizations and departments within larger organizations
Mainframes	Large computers for large organizations
Supercomputers	High-capacity machines for specialized uses like research

TM 1-1

Text Reference: Top Left Figure

FIVE PARTS OF AN INFORMATION SYSTEM

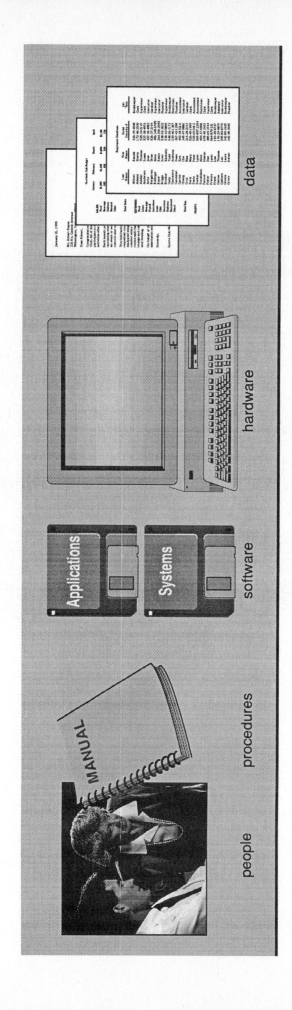

people   procedures   software   hardware   data

TM 1-2

Text Reference: Figure 1-3

MICROCOMPUTER HARDWARE COMPONENTS

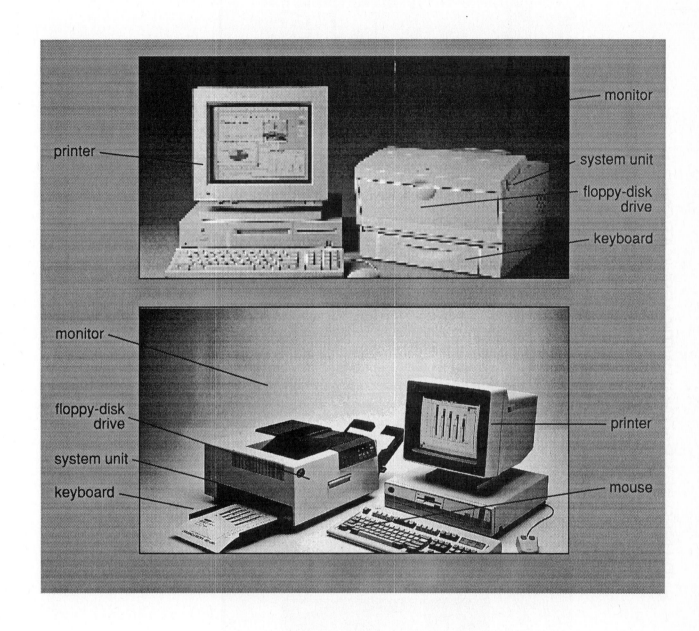

TM 1-3

Text Reference: Figure 1-4

END-USER INTERACTION WITH APPLICATIONS

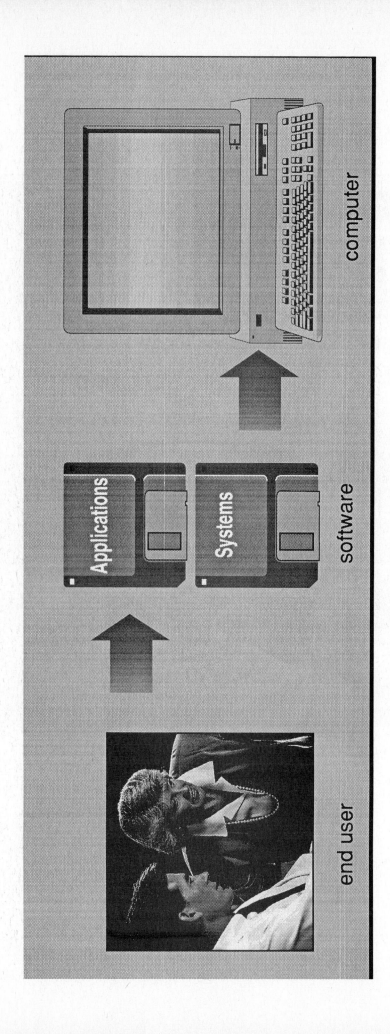

TM 1.4

Text Reference: Figure 1-5

PULL-DOWN MENU

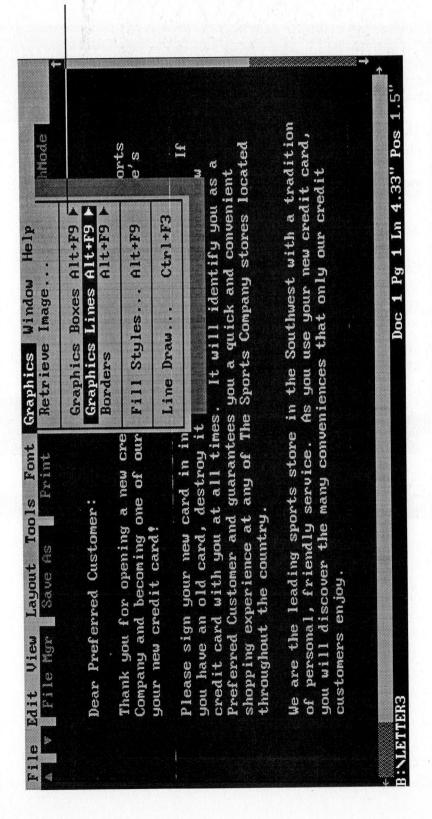

pull-down menu

TM 2-1

Text Reference: Figure 2-2

HELP SCREEN

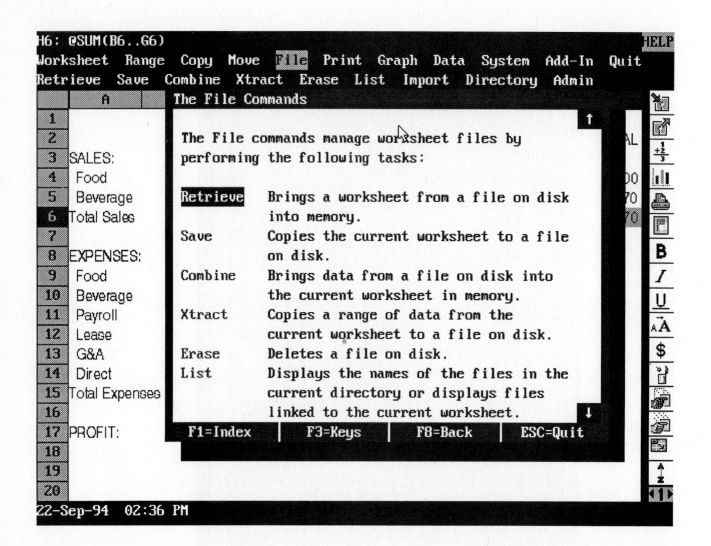

TM 2-2

Text Reference: Figure 2-3

SPREADSHEET

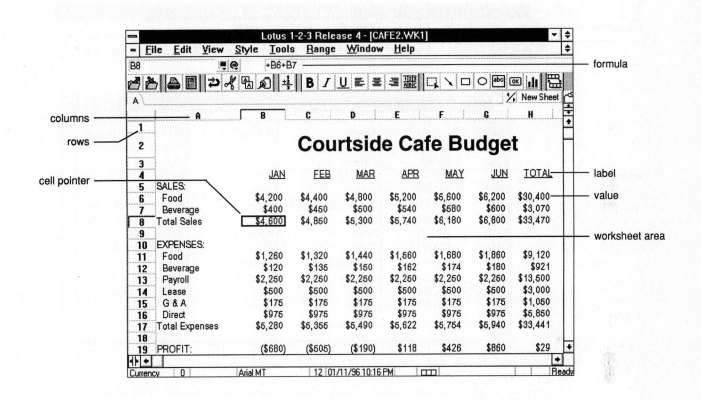

TM 2-3

Text Reference: Figure 2-7

DATABASE

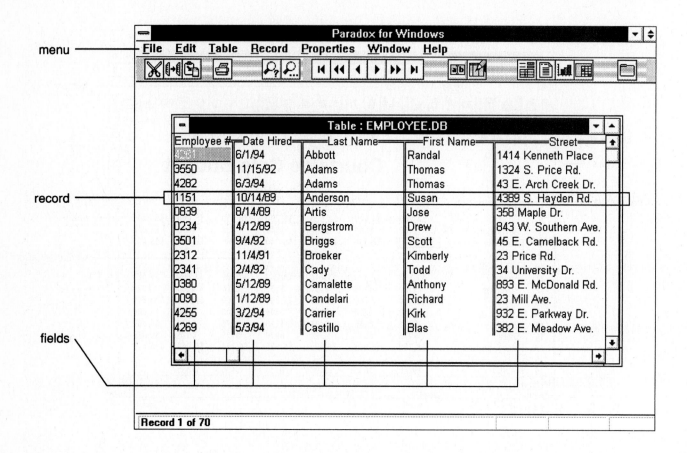

TM 2-4

Text Reference: Figure 2-8

ANALYTICAL GRAPHING

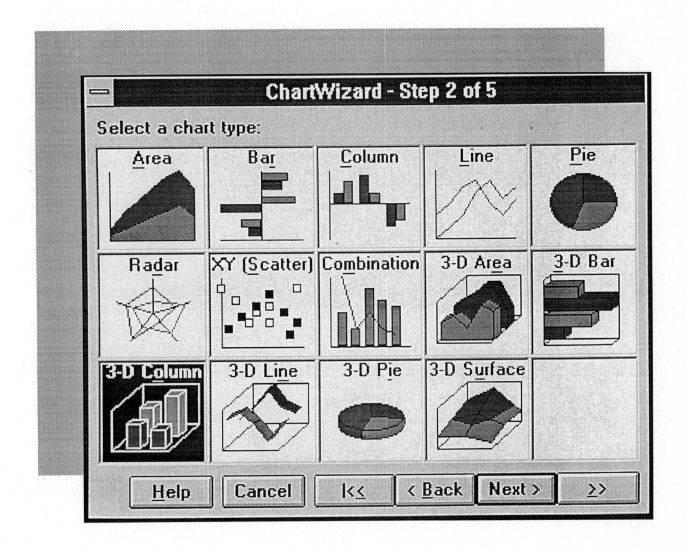

TM 2-5

Text Reference: Figure 2-10

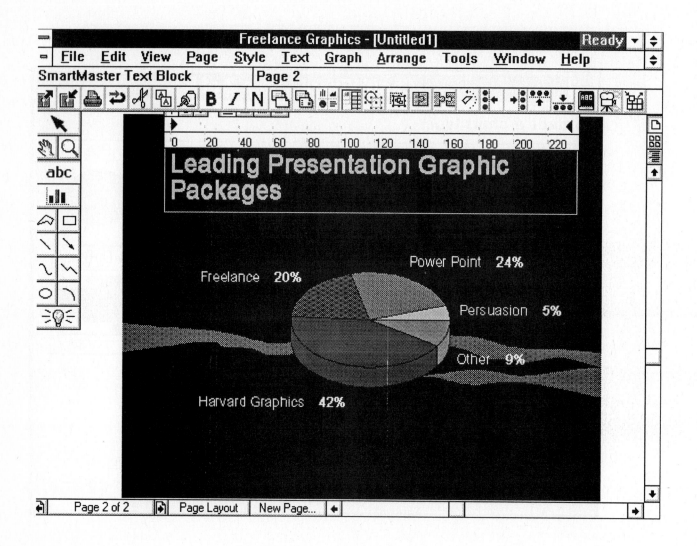

TM 2-6

Text Reference: Figure 2-11

BASIC APPLICATION SOFTWARE TOOLS

Basic Tools

Application	Popular packages
Word processors	WordPerfect, AmiPro, Word, MacWrite
Spreadsheets	Lotus 1-2-3, Excel, Quattro Pro
Database managers	dBASE, Paradox, Access, FoxPro
Presentation graphics	Harvard Graphics, Persuasion, Power Point, Freelance
Drawing programs	Adobe Illustrator, Aldus Freehand, Micrografx Designer
Communications	ProComm, Smartcom, Crosstalk
Integrated	Microsoft Works, Lotus Works, Symphony, Framework
Software suites	Microsoft Office, Lotus SmartSuite

TM 2-7

Text Reference: Figure 2-16

MS-DOS 6.0 SHELL

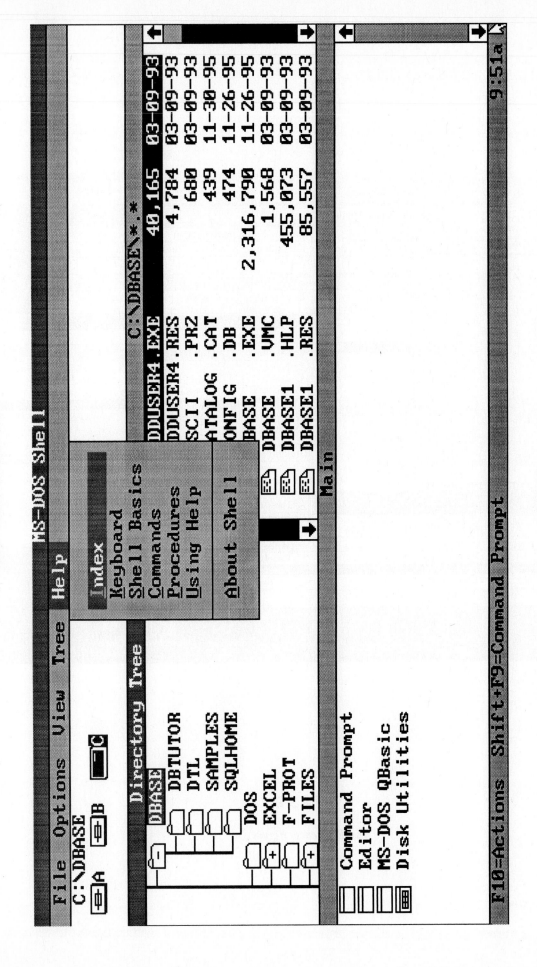

TM 3-1

Text Reference: Figure 3-5

WINDOWS (GRAPHICAL USER INTERFACE)

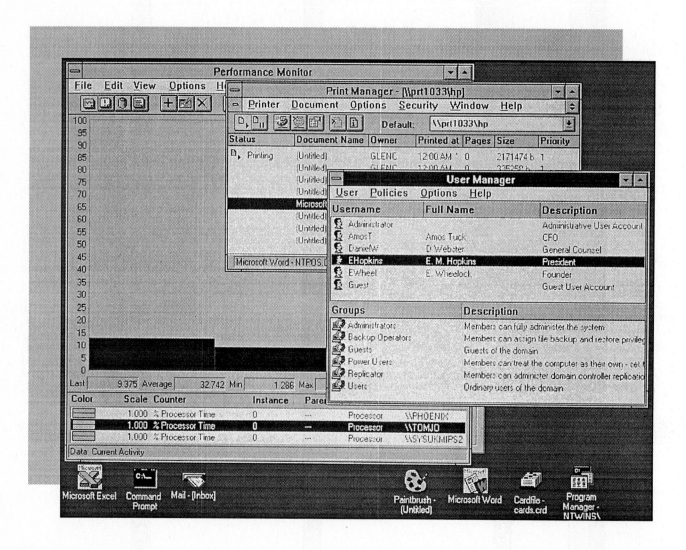

TM 3-2

Text Reference: Figure 3-6

OS/2 (VERSION 2.0) MENUS

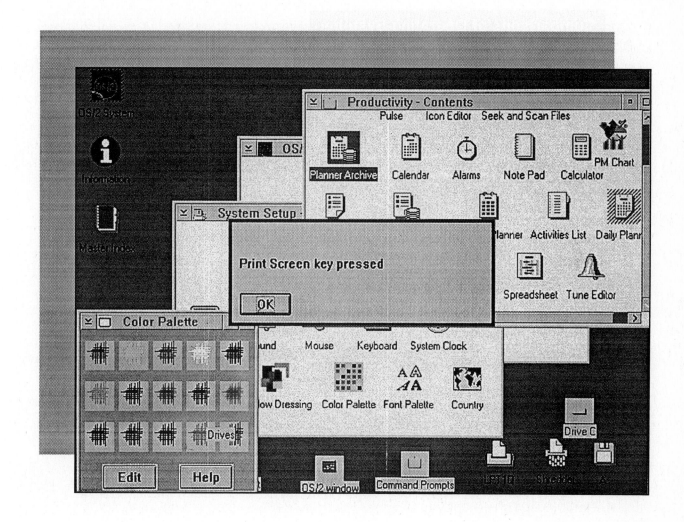

TM 3-3

Text Reference: Figure 3-7

COMPARING OPERATING SYSTEMS

Comparisons of Operating Systems

Operating system	Advantages	Disadvantages
DOS	Many existing users, microcomputers, and applications	Limited memory; single tasking only; character-based interface
DOS with Windows	Multitasking; dynamic data exchange; graphical user interface; more memory	System requirements; occasional unrecoverable errors; limited network capabilities
Windows NT	Multitasking; graphical user interface; more memory; networking capabilities; flexibility; multiprocessing, multiuser	Few users; few applications; system requirements
OS/2	Multitasking; graphical user interface; more memory; flexibility; common user interface	Few users; few applications; system requirements
Macintosh	Ease of use; quality graphics; graphical user interface; multitasking; communication among programs	Market perception; compatibility
Unix	Multitasking; multiprocessing; multiuser; networking capabilities	Limited business applications; no standard version; difficult to learn

TM 3-4

Text Reference: Figure 3-9

THE FOUR TYPES OF COMPUTER SYSTEMS

Types of Computers

Type of Computer	Size	Applications
Microcomputer	Palm-sized to desktop	Wide range of tasks, from basic tools to scientific and engineering applications
Minicomputer	Desk-sized	General-purpose and special-purpose tasks, including distributed data, processing applications, and medium to large database operations
Mainframe	Automobile-sized	General-purpose tasks on a larger scale, such as large to very large database operations
Supercomputer	Room-sized	Large, special-purpose tasks, such as worldwide weather forecasting

TM 4-1

Text Reference: Figure 4-10

HOW THE CPU AND MEMORY WORK

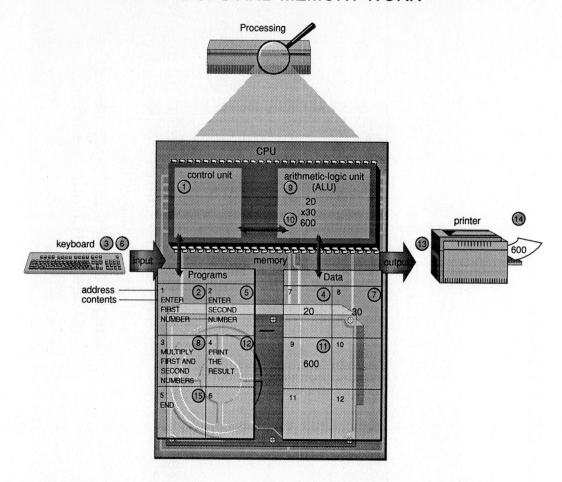

(1) The control unit recognizes that the entire program has been loaded into memory. It begins to execute the first step in the program.

(2) The program tells the user, ENTER FIRST NUMBER.

(3) The user types the number *20* on the keyboard. An electronic signal is sent to the CPU.

(4) The control unit recognizes this signal and routes the signal to an address in memory—address 7.

(5) After completing the above program instruction, the next program instruction tells the user, ENTER SECOND NUMBER.

(6) The user types the number *30* on the keyboard. An electronic signal is sent to the CPU.

(7) The control unit recognizes this signal and routes it to memory address 8.

(8) The next program instruction is executed: MULTIPLY FIRST AND SECOND NUMBERS.

(9) To execute this instruction, the control unit informs the arithmetic-logic unit (ALU) that two numbers are coming and that the ALU is to multiply them. The control unit next sends the ALU a copy of the contents of address 7 (*20*) and then sends a copy of the contents of address 8 (*30*).

(10) The ALU performs the multiplication: *20 x 30 = 600.*

(11) The control unit sends a copy of the multiplied results (*600*) back to memory, to address 9.

(12) The next program instruction is executed: PRINT THE RESULT.

(13) To execute this instruction, the control unit sends the contents of address 9 (*600*) to the printer.

(14) The printer prints the value *600.*

(15) The final instruction is executed: END. The program is complete.

TM 4-2

Text Reference: Figure 4-12

BITS AND BYTES

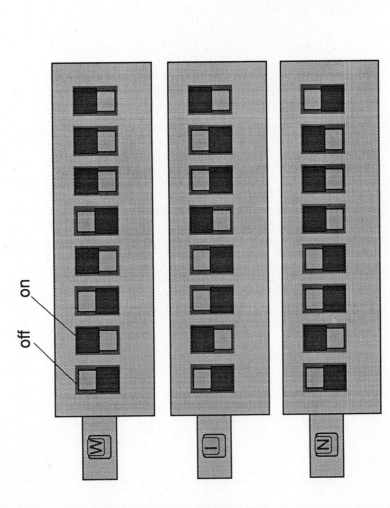

off
on

Memory Capacity

Kilobyte:	one thousand bytes
Megabyte:	one million bytes
Gigabyte:	one billion bytes
Terabyte:	one trillion bytes

TM 4-3

Text Reference: Figure 4-13 & 4-14

BINARY CODING SCHEMES

Binary Codes		
Character	ASCII	EBCDIC
A	0100 0001	1100 0001
B	0100 0010	1100 0010
C	0100 0011	1100 0011
D	0100 0100	1100 0100
E	0100 0101	1100 0101
F	0100 0110	1100 0110
G	0100 0111	1100 0111
H	0100 1000	1100 1000
I	0100 1001	1100 1001
J	0100 1010	1101 0001
K	0100 1011	1101 0010
L	0100 1100	1101 0011
M	0100 1101	1101 0100
N	0100 1110	1101 0101
O	0100 1111	1101 0110
P	0101 0000	1101 0111
Q	0101 0001	1101 1000
R	0101 0010	1101 1001
S	0101 0011	1110 0010
T	0101 0100	1110 0011
U	0101 0101	1110 0100
V	0101 0110	1110 0101
W	0101 0111	1110 0110
X	0101 1000	1110 0111
Y	0101 1001	1110 1000
Z	0101 1010	1110 1001
0	0011 0000	1111 0000
1	0011 0001	1111 0001
2	0011 0010	1111 0010
3	0011 0011	1111 0011
4	0011 0100	1111 0100
5	0011 0101	1111 0101
6	0011 0110	1111 0110
7	0011 0111	1111 0111
8	0011 1000	1111 1000
9	0011 1001	1111 1001

TM 4-4

Text Reference: Figure 4-15

PARITY BIT

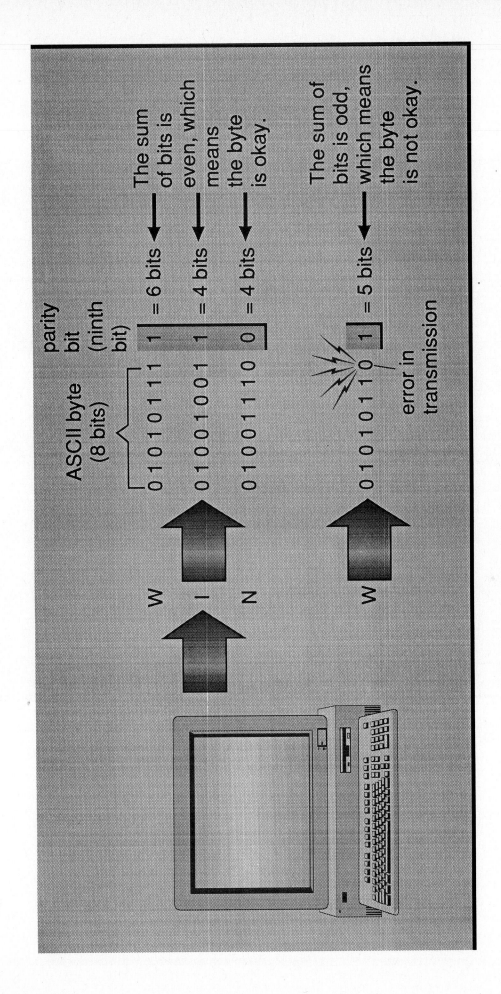

Text Reference: Figure 4-16

THE MICROCOMPUTER SYSTEM BOARD

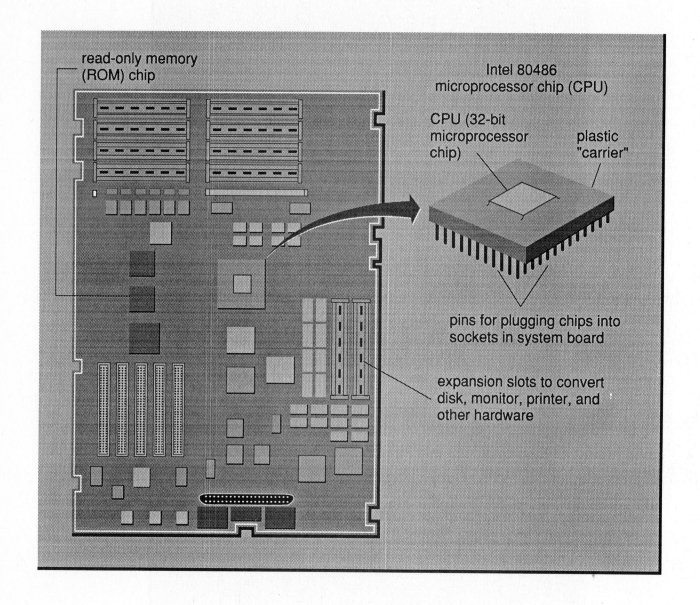

read-only memory
(ROM) chip

Intel 80486
microprocessor chip (CPU)

CPU (32-bit
microprocessor
chip)

plastic
"carrier"

pins for plugging chips into
sockets in system board

expansion slots to convert
disk, monitor, printer, and
other hardware

TM 4-6

Text Reference: Figure 4-17

MICROPROCESSOR CHIPS

Microprocessor Chips

Microprocessor		Application	Users
Intel	80386	Windows, OS/2, basic tools, desktop publishing	Single user, office staff, home office user
	80486	All of the above, Unix, multimedia	All of the above, multiusers
	Pentium	All of the above, virtual reality, communications	All of the above, specialists
Motorola	68030	Macintosh operating system, basic tools, desktop publishing, CAD/CAM	Single user, students, home office user, graphic designers
	68040	All of the above, multimedia	All of the above, multimedia
	Power PC	All of the above, virtual reality, communications	All of the above, specialists

TM 4-7

Text Reference: Figure 4-18

TYPES OF RAM

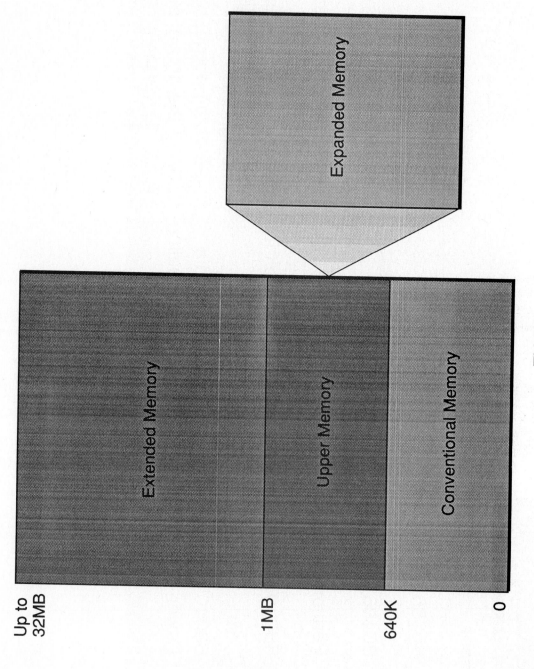

Up to 32MB — Extended Memory

1MB — Upper Memory

640K — Conventional Memory

0

Expanded Memory

TM 4-8

Text Reference: Figure 4-21

IBM PS/2 KEYBOARD

special-purpose keys

function keys

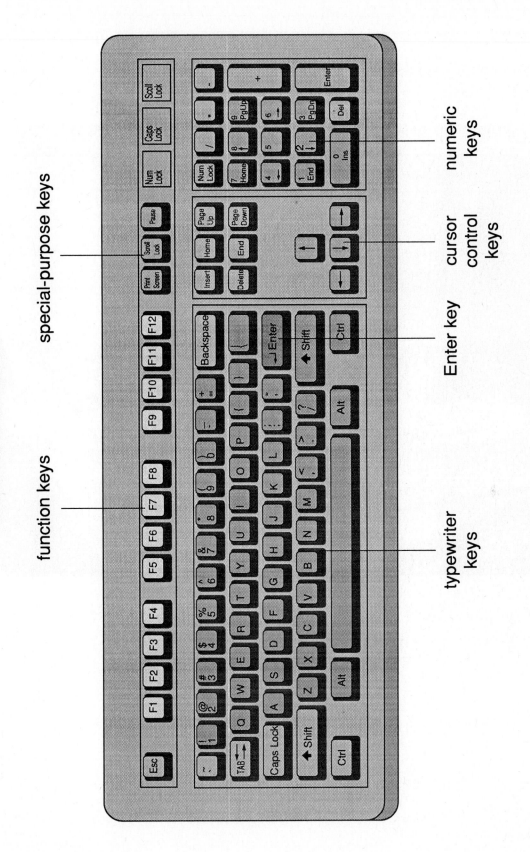

typewriter keys

Enter key

cursor control keys

numeric keys

TM 5-1

Text Reference: Figure 5-2

IMAGE SCANNER

TM 5-2

Text Reference: Figure 5-9

FAX MACHINE

TM 5-3

Text Reference: Figure 5-10

COLOR MONITORS

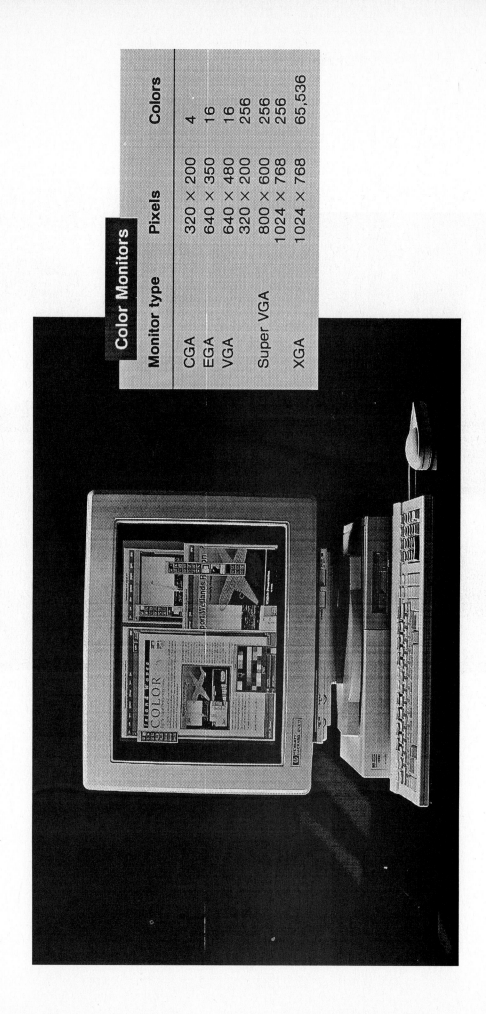

Color Monitors

Monitor type	Pixels	Colors
CGA	320 × 200	4
EGA	640 × 350	16
VGA	640 × 480	16
	320 × 200	256
Super VGA	800 × 600	256
	1024 × 768	256
XGA	1024 × 768	65,536

TM 5-4

Text Reference: Figure 5-16

TYPES OF PRINTERS

Printers

Printer	Characteristics	Typical use
Dot-matrix	Reliable, inexpensive; forms text and graphics by pixels; some color printing	In-house communications
Laser	Very high quality; forms text and graphics by pixels, using photocopying process	Desktop publishing, external documents
Ink-jet	High color quality; sprays drops of ink on paper	Advertising pieces
Thermal	Very high quality; uses heat elements on special paper	Art and design work

TM 5-5

Text Reference: Figure 5-17

DOT MATRIX PRINTER

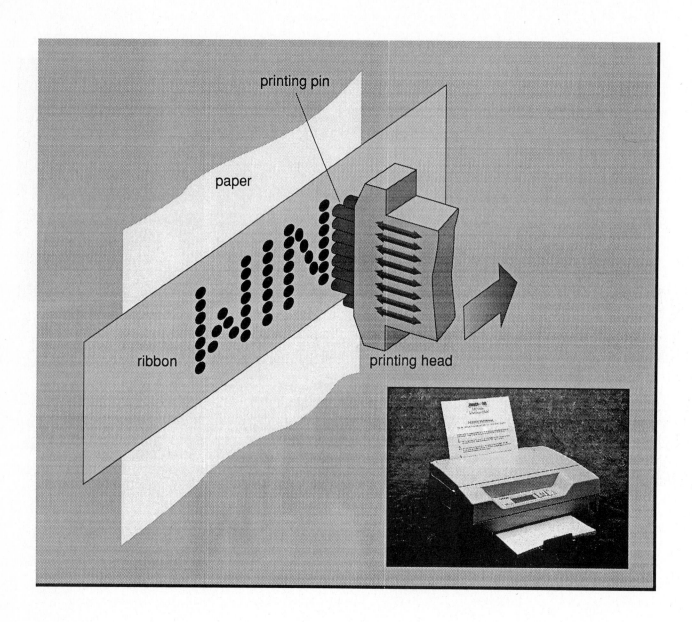

TM 5-6

Text Reference: Figure 5-18

LASER PRINTER

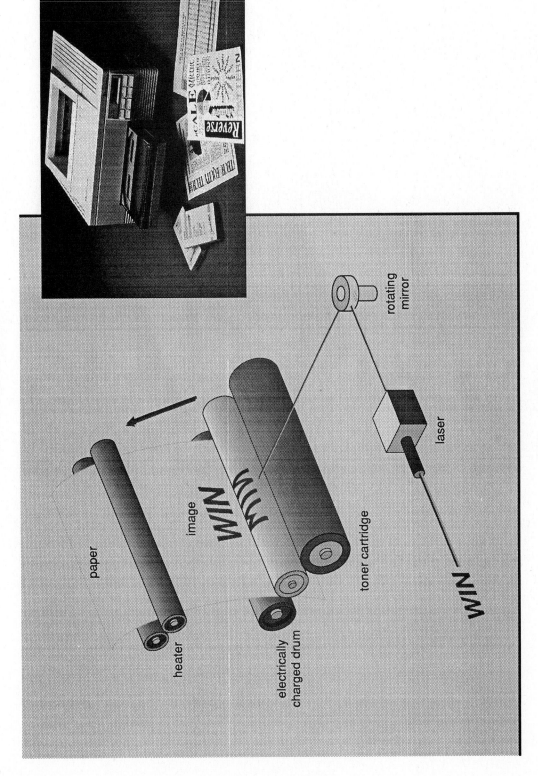

TM 5-7

Text Reference: Figure 5-19

FOUR KINDS OF EXTERNAL STORAGE

Four Kinds of External Storage

External storage	Major advantages	Major disadvantages
Floppy disk	Inexpensive, direct access	Low capacity, slow access
Hard disk	Fast, direct access	Limited capacity
Optical disk	High capacity, direct access	Slow access
Magnetic tape	High capacity	Slow sequential access

TM 6-1

Text Reference: Figure 6-1

READING AND WRITING DATA ON A DISK

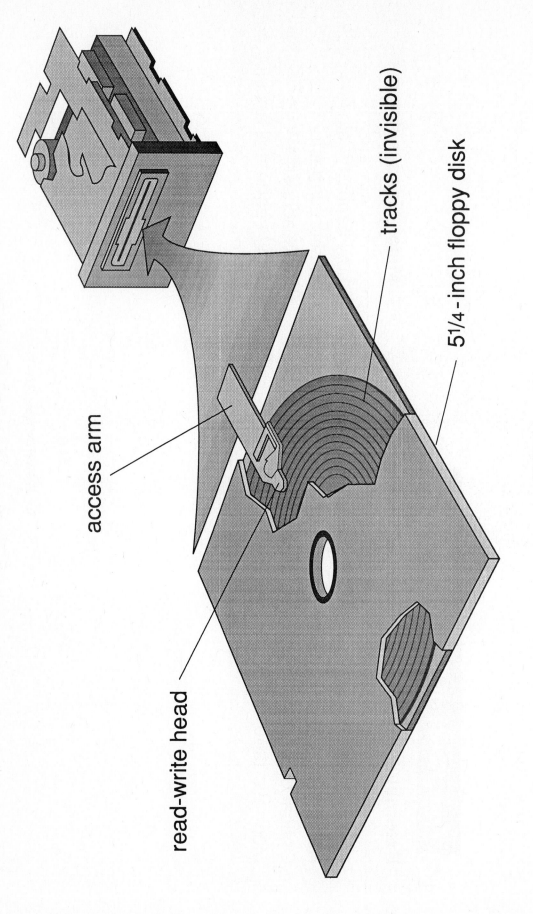

read-write head

access arm

tracks (invisible)

5¼ - inch floppy disk

TM 6-2

Text Reference: Figure 6-6

DISK PACK OPERATION

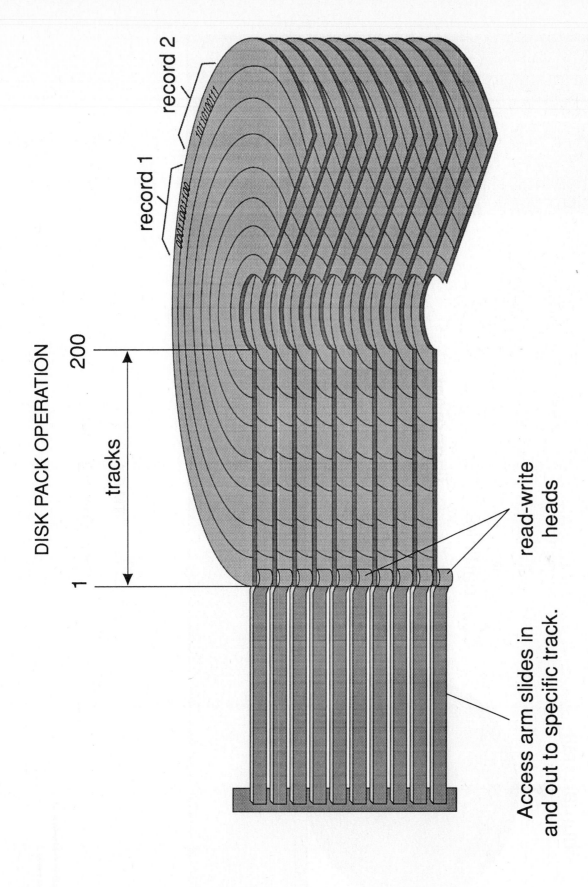

record 1

record 2

200

tracks

1

read-write heads

Access arm slides in and out to specific track.

TM 6-3

Text Reference: Figure 6-14

DISK HEAD CLEARANCE

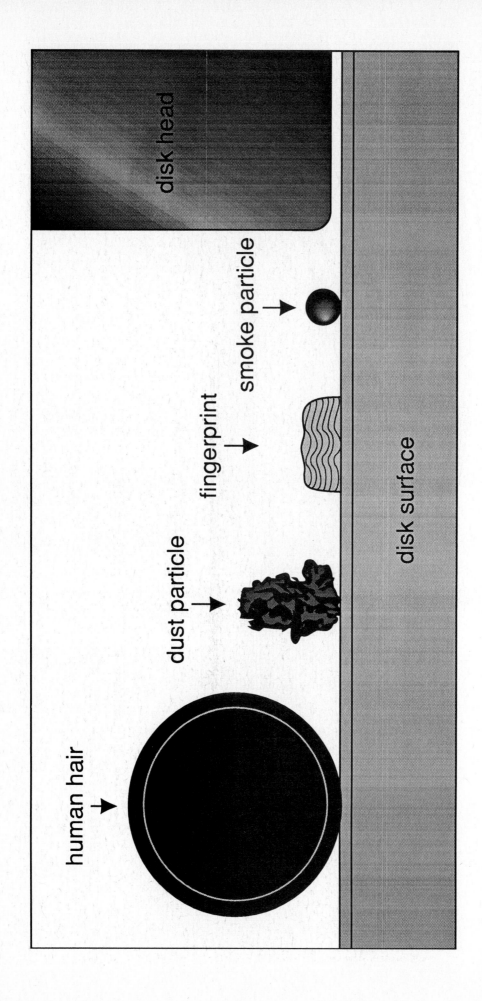

disk head

smoke particle

fingerprint

dust particle

human hair

disk surface

TM 6-4

Text Reference: Figure 6-15

SECONDARY STORAGE CAPACITIES

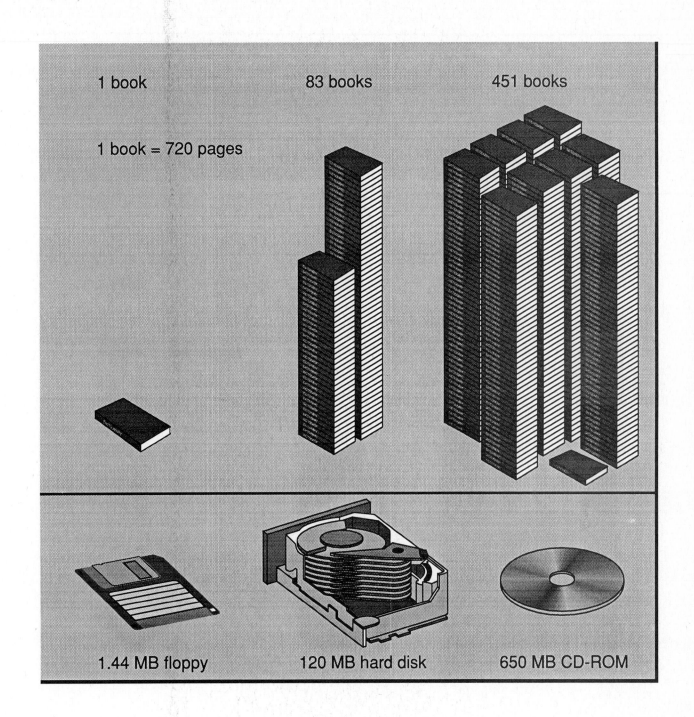

1 book

83 books

451 books

1 book = 720 pages

1.44 MB floppy

120 MB hard disk

650 MB CD-ROM

TM 6-5

Text Reference: Figure 6-17

CONNECTIVITY

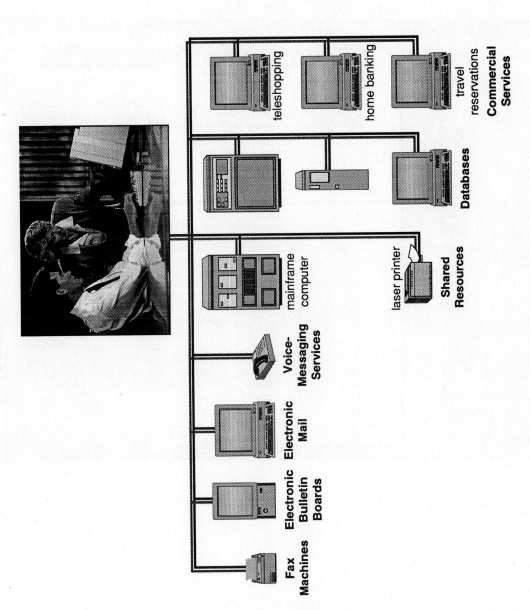

Fax Machines

Electronic Bulletin Boards

Electronic Mail

Voice-Messaging Services

mainframe computer

laser printer

Shared Resources

Databases

teleshopping

home banking

travel reservations

Commercial Services

TM 7-1

Text Reference: Figure 7-1

GROUPWARE

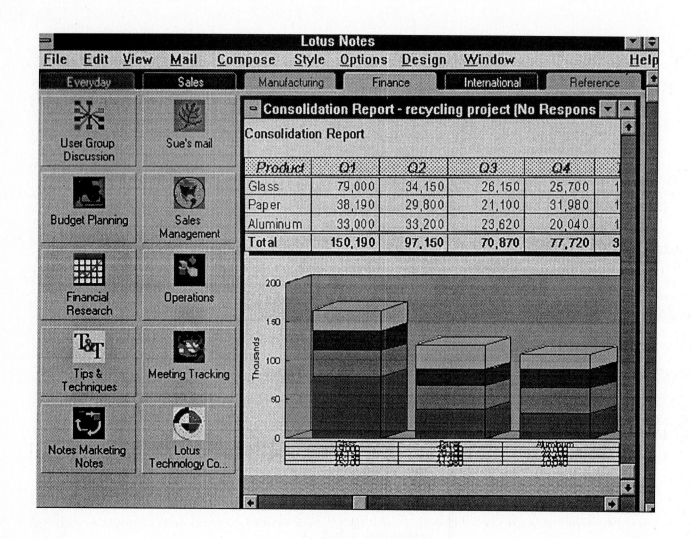

TM 7-2

Text Reference: Figure 7-5

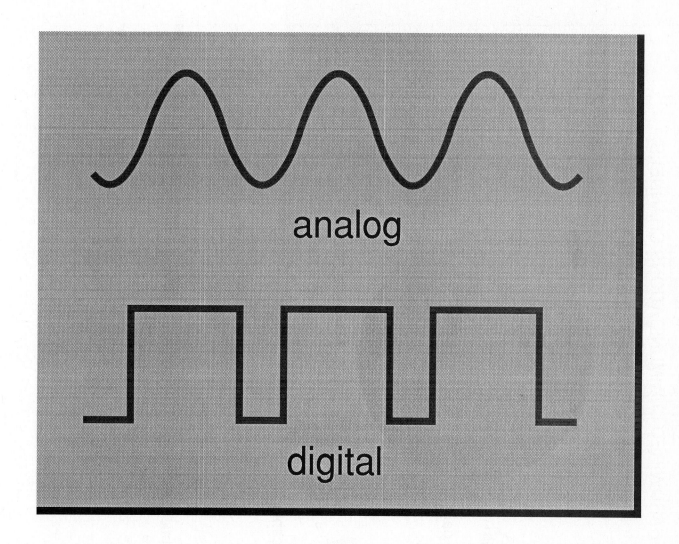

analog

digital

TM 7-3

Text Reference: Figure 7-6

HARDWIRED COMMUNICATIONS CHANNELS

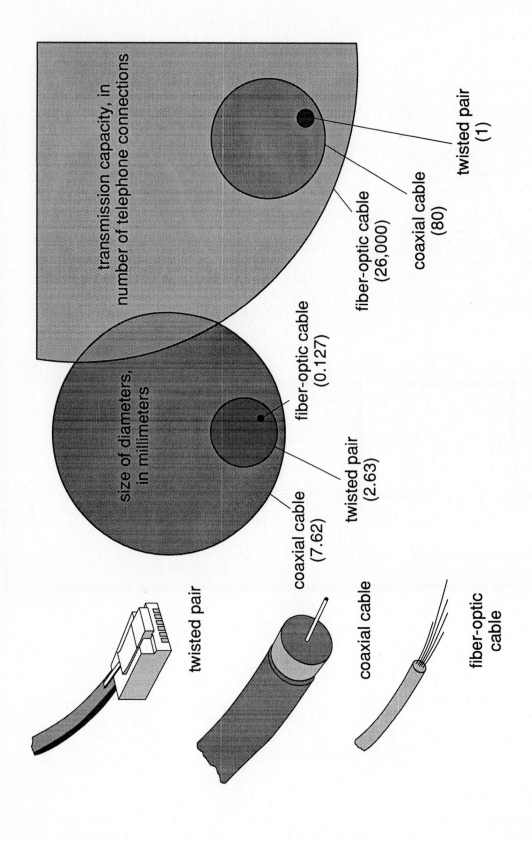

transmission capacity, in number of telephone connections

fiber-optic cable (26,000)

coaxial cable (80)

twisted pair (1)

size of diameters, in millimeters

fiber-optic cable (0.127)

coaxial cable (7.62)

twisted pair (2.63)

twisted pair

coaxial cable

fiber-optic cable

TM 7-4

Text Reference: Figure 7-10

MICROWAVE & SATELLITE TRANSMISSION

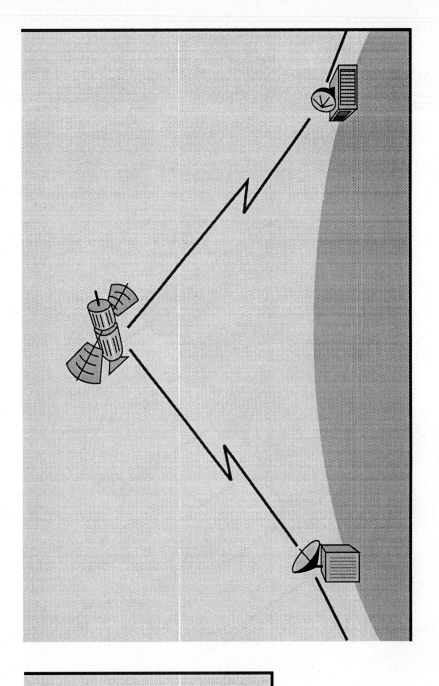

TM 7-5

Text Reference: Figure7-11 & 7-12

DATA TRANSMISSION

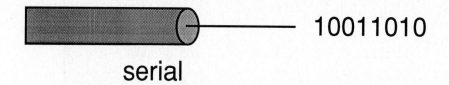

10011010

serial

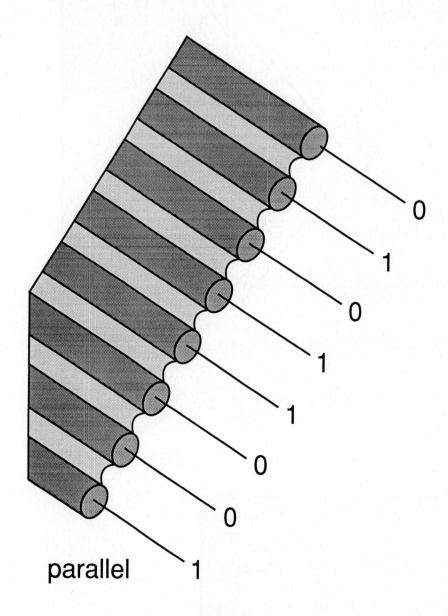

0

1

0

1

1

0

0

parallel   1

TM 7-6

Text Reference: Figure 7-13

MODES OF TRANSMISSION

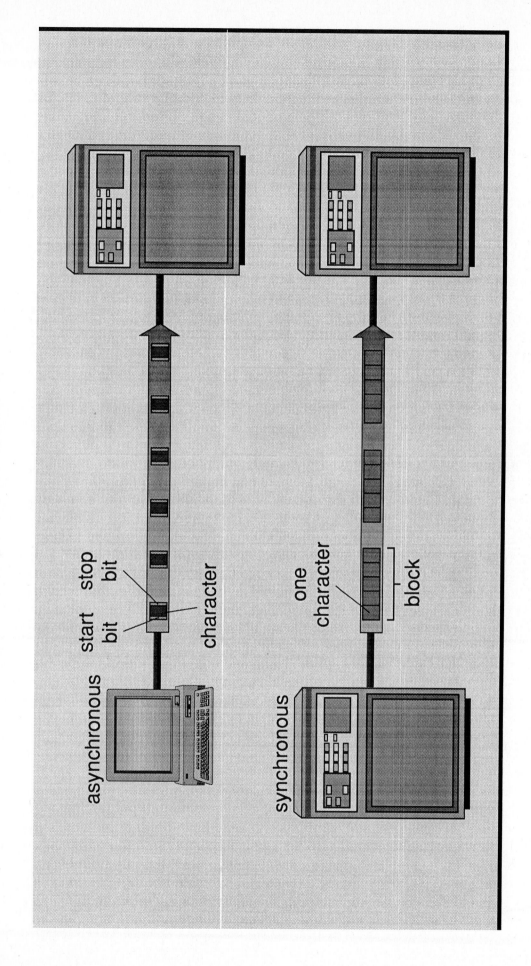

TM 7-7

Text Reference: Figure 7-15

STAR NETWORK

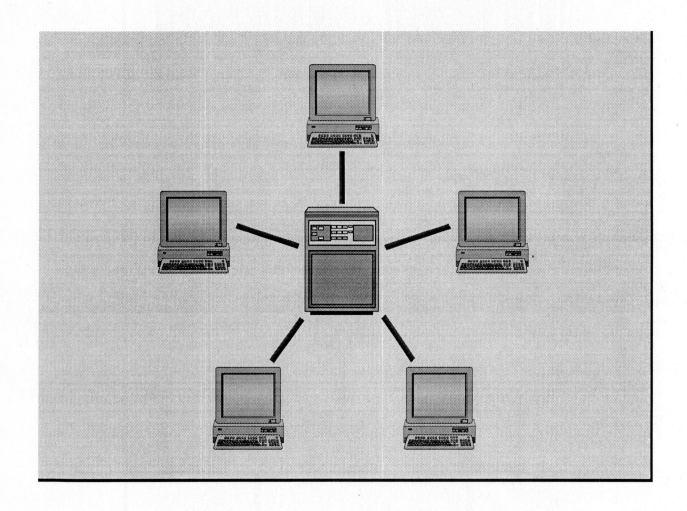

TM 7-8

Text Reference: Figure 7-16

BUS NETWORK

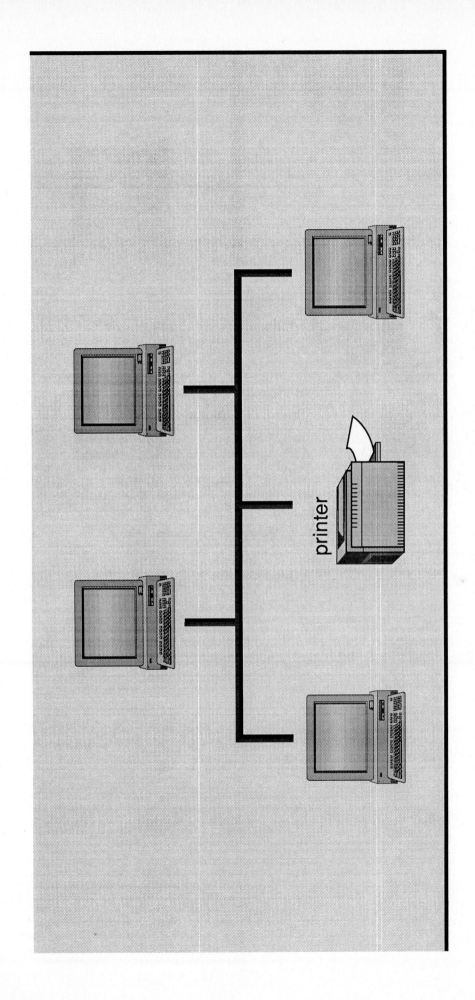

printer

TM 7-9

Text Reference: Figure 7-17

RING NETWORK

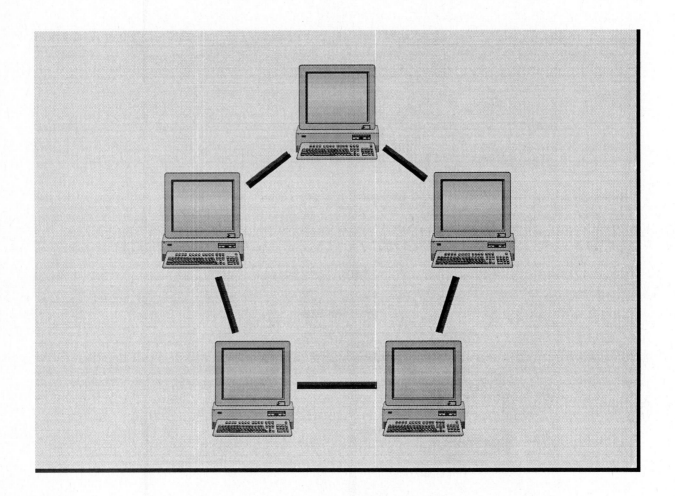

TM 7-10

Text Reference: Figure 7-18

LOCAL AREA NETWORKS

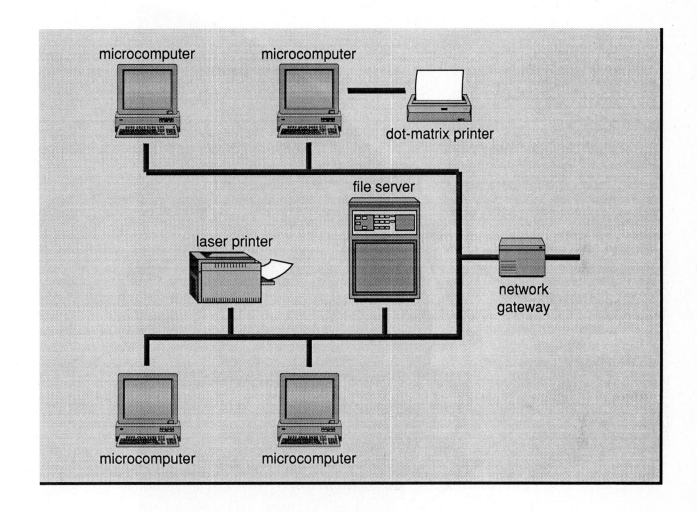

TM 7-11

Text Reference: Figure 7-20

WIDE AREA NETWORKS

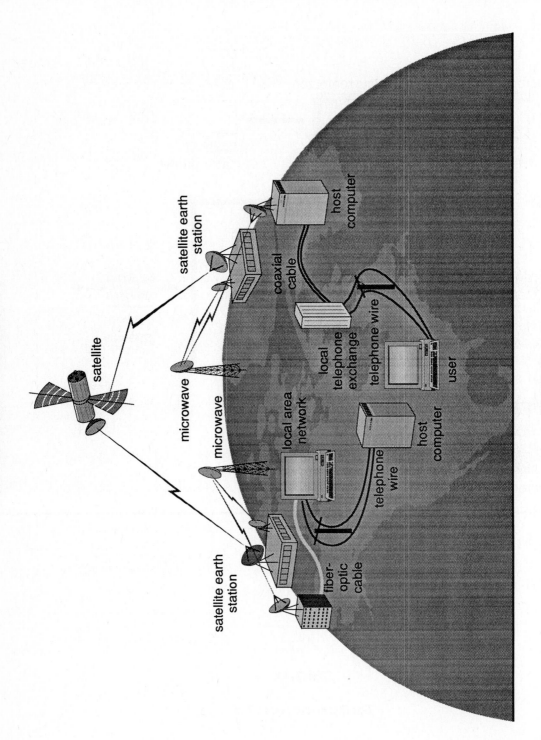

- satellite
- satellite earth station
- satellite earth station
- microwave
- microwave
- coaxial cable
- host computer
- local telephone exchange
- telephone wire
- user
- local area network
- host computer
- telephone wire
- fiber-optic cable

TM 7-12

Text Reference: Figure 7-22

HOW DATA IS ORGANIZED

Employee Database

Last Name	First Name	Social Security #	Job Title
Abbott	Randal	526-39-4548	Bookkeeper
Adams	Sherry	172-46-2530	Clerk
Addair	Thomas	525-34-2147	Supervisor
Anderson	Susan	527-38-4976	Clerk
Artis	Jose	427-36-4982	Instructor
Bergstrom	Drew	526-37-2194	Gardner
Bollinger	Alice	456-34-6789	Supervisor
Boyer	Kevin	264-36-2955	Instructor
Briggs	Scott	538-92-3832	Plumber
Broeker	Kimberly	538-43-9895	Supervisor
Cady	Todd	548-26-3172	Bookkeeper
Camalette	Anthony	239-46-1387	Electrician
Candelari	Dean	367-42-1298	Plumber
Carrier	Kirk	492-38-5216	Accountant
Chang	Che	345-47-9886	Instructor
Cruz	Blas	216-28-2193	Gardner
Darst	Mary	526-49-1999	Clerk
Davis	Peter	525-69-0412	Accountant
Decker	Lynn	565-87-2354	Accountant
Donaldson	Alice	494-37-6958	Electrician
Farmer	Sharon	678-45-3432	Clerk
Fisher	Dan	485-69-3744	Supervisor
Francis	Lynn	564-87-9231	Clerk
Frank	Lisa	183-49-8747	Bookkeeper
Gaines	Thomas	176-29-9879	Assistant
Gathers	Len	295-89-8775	Instructor
Givens	Laura	342-89-3435	Bookkeeper
Grove	Robert	342-48-3940	Plumber

file

record

key field

character   field

TM 8-1

Text Reference: Figure 8-1

TYPES OF FILE ORGANIZATION

File Organization

Type	Advantages	Disadvantages
Sequential	Efficient access to all or large part of records, cost	Slow access to specific records
Direct	Fast access to specific records	Inefficient access to all or large part of records, cost
Index sequential	Faster than sequential, more efficient than direct	Not quite as efficient as sequential, not quite as fast as direct, cost

TM 8-2

Text Reference: Figure 8-5

DATA DICTIONARY

Layout   Organize   Append   Go To   Exit   10:08:42 a

Bytes remaining: 3849

Num	Field Name	Field Type	Width	Dec	Index
1	CLIENT_ID	Character	6		Y
2	CLIENT	Character	30		Y
3	LASTNAME	Character	15		N
4	FIRSTNAME	Character	15		N
5	ADDRESS	Character	30		N
6	CITY	Character	20		N
7	STATE	Character	2		N
8	ZIP	Character	10		N
9	PHONE	Character	13		N
10	CLIEN_HIST	Memo	10		N

Database‖C:\dbase\samples\CLIENT ‖Field 1/10 ‖   ExclLock‖
Enter the field name. Insert/Delete field:Ctrl-N/Ctrl-U
Field names begin with a letter and may contain letters, digits and underscores

TM 8-3

Text Reference: Figure 8-6

HIERARCHICAL DATABASE

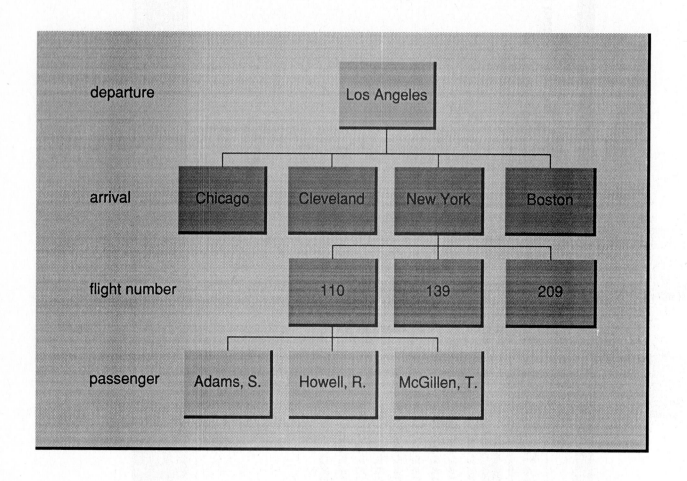

TM 8-4

Text Reference: Figure 8-7

THE NETWORK DATABASE

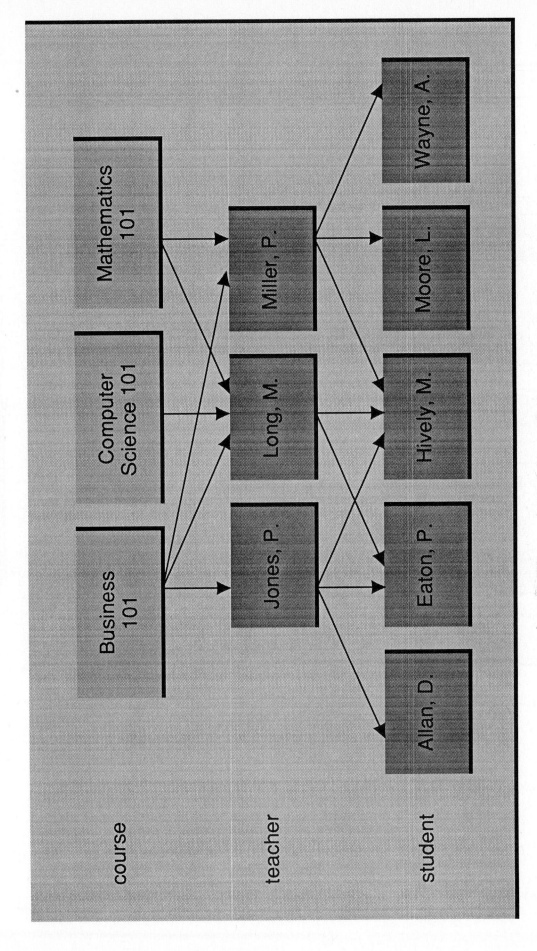

TM 8-5

Text Reference: Figure 8-8

THE RELATIONAL DATABASE

License plate/citations pair

License plate no.	Citation no. & violation
ABC 123	00300 Park in bus zone 17811 Double parking

key fields linked

License plate/owner pair

License plate no.	Owner name & address
ABC 123	Benedict, Arnold 10032 Park Lane San Jose, CA 95127
ABC 124	Hale, Nathan 779 Loma Verde Ave. San Jose, CA 95117

key fields linked

Driver's license no./citations pair

Drivers license no.	Citation no. & violation
F00827	10023 Illegal left turn Paid 24368 Speeding Unpaid

key fields linked

Driver's license no. /owner pair

Driver's license no.	Owner name & address
F00827	Benedict, Arnold 10032 Park Lane San Jose, CA 95127
D12372	Benedict, Charles B. 771 Randall Ave. Palo Alto, CA 94305

TM 8-6

Text Reference: Figure 8-9

FIVE FUNCTIONS OF AN ORGANIZATION

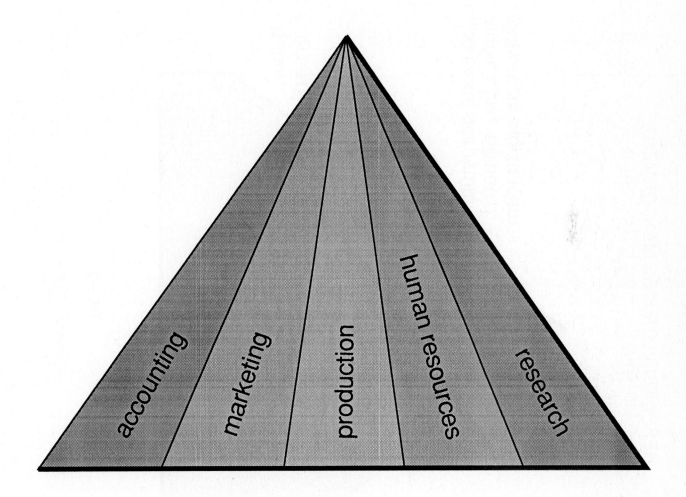

TM 9-1

Text Reference: Figure 9-2

RESPONSIBILITIES OF MANAGEMENT

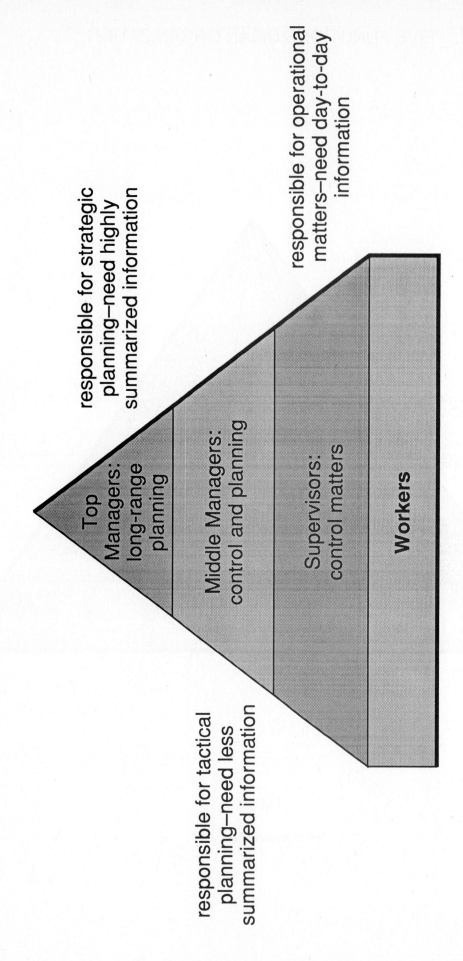

responsible for strategic planning—need highly summarized information

responsible for operational matters—need day-to-day information

Top Managers: long-range planning

Middle Managers: control and planning

Supervisors: control matters

Workers

responsible for tactical planning—need less summarized information

TM 9-2

Text Reference: Figure 9-5

FLOW OF INFORMATION IN AN ORGANIZATION

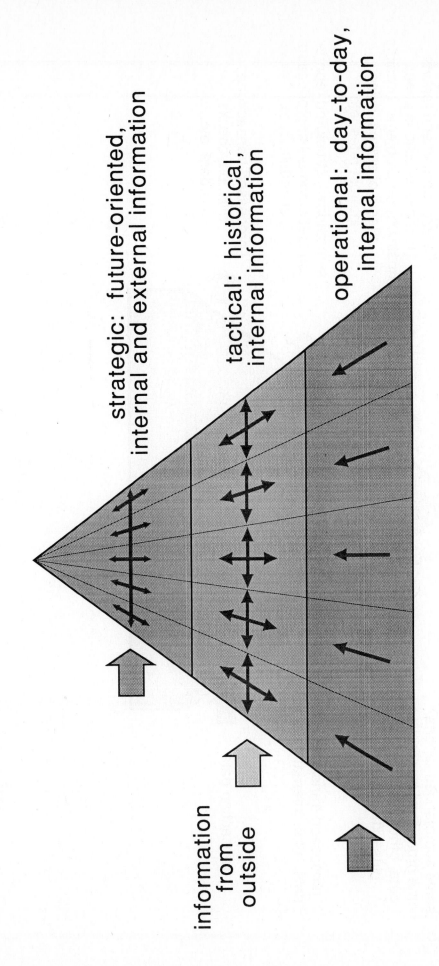

strategic: future-oriented,
internal and external information

tactical: historical,
internal information

operational: day-to-day,
internal information

information
from
outside

TM 9-3

Text Reference: Figure 9-6

THREE LEVELS OF INFORMATION SYSTEMS

Inputs

some summarized reports, some processed transaction data, other internal data plus external data

processed transaction data, other internal data

transaction data

Outputs

flexible, on-demand reports to make decisions about unstructured problems: possible effects of strikes, rising interest rates, etc.

summarized, structured reports: budget summaries, production schedules, etc.

processed transactions: bills, paychecks, orders, etc.

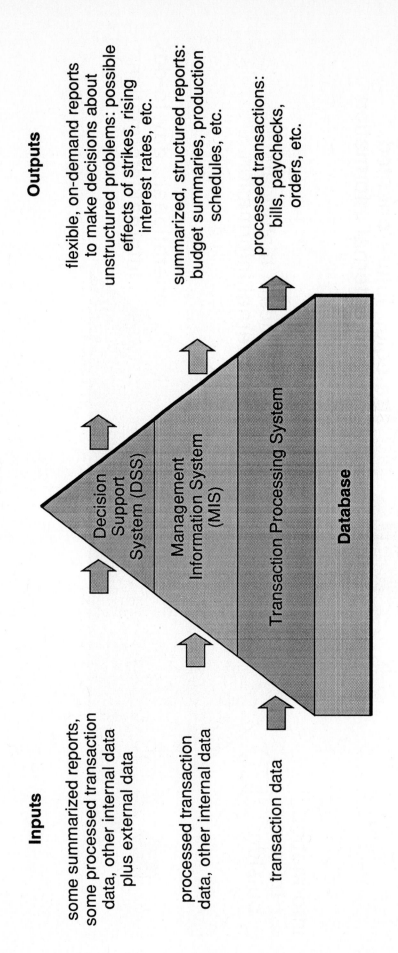

Decision Support System (DSS)

Management Information System (MIS)

Transaction Processing System

Database

TM 9-4

Text Reference: Figure 9-8

TRANSACTION PROCESSING SYSTEMS

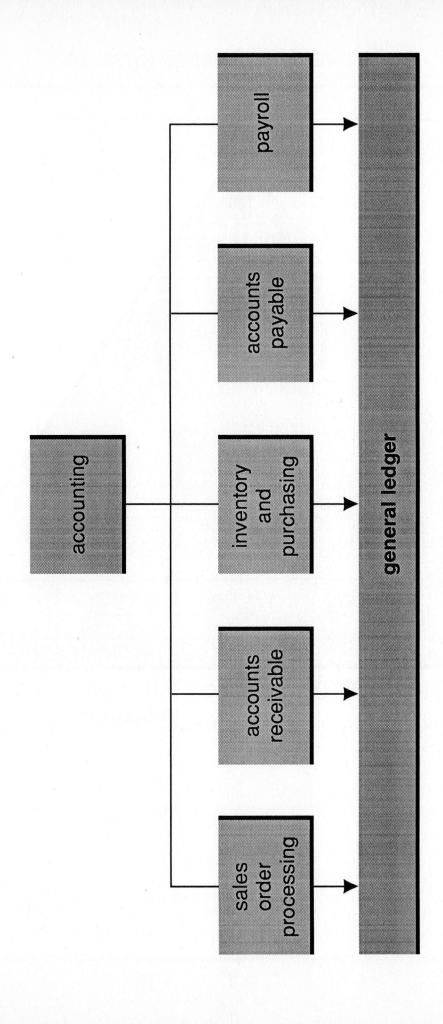

TM 9-5

Text Reference: Figure 9-9

MANAGEMENT INFORMATION SYSTEMS

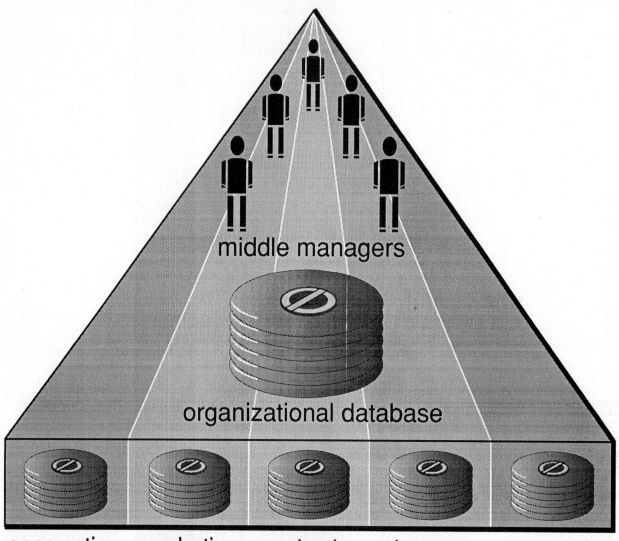

middle managers

organizational database

accounting marketing production human resources research

TM 9-6

Text Reference: Figure 9-11

TM 9-7

Text Reference: Figure 9-13

SYSTEMS ANALYSIS AND DESIGN

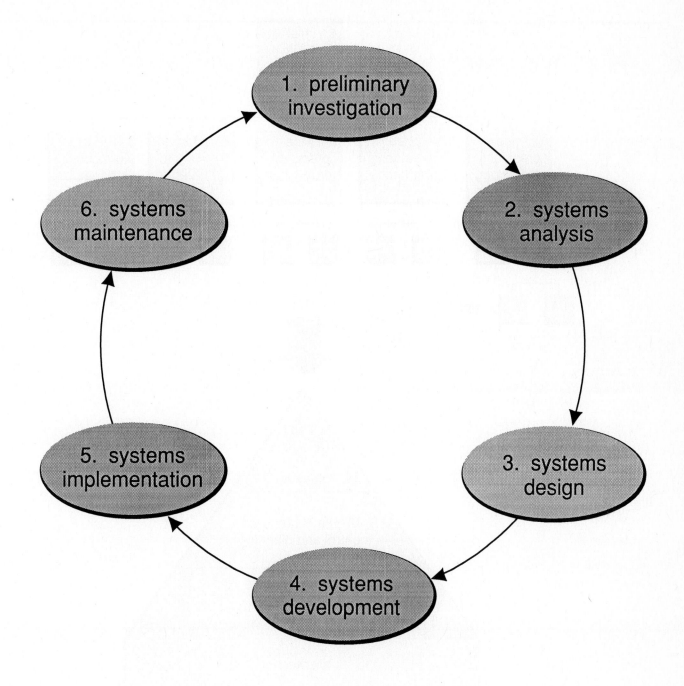

TM 10-1

Text Reference: Figure 10-1

AN ORGANIZATIONAL CHART

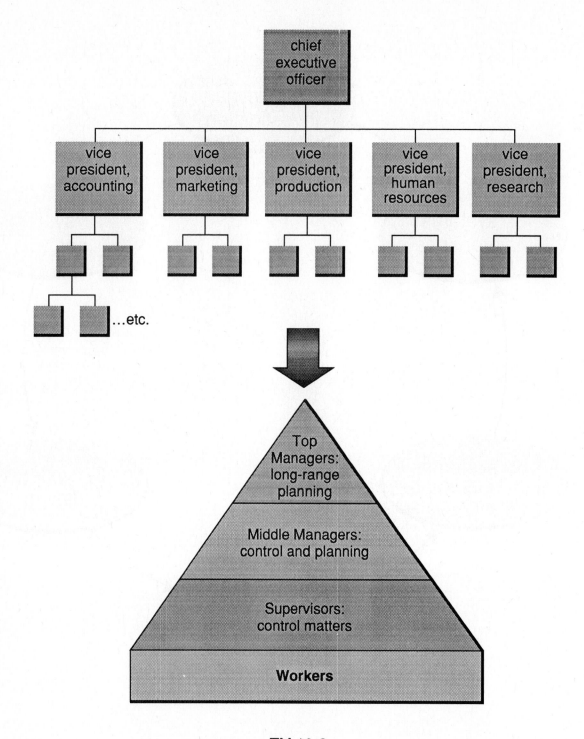

TM 10-2

Text Reference: Figure 10-4

GRID CHART

Forms (input)	Reports (output)		
	Report A	Report B	Report C
form 1	✓		✓
form 2	✓	✓	
form 3			✓
form 4			✓

TM 10-3

Text Reference: Figure 10-5

DECISION TABLE

Decision rules

Conditions	1	2	3	4	5	6	7	8
if. . . .	Y	Y	Y	Y	N	N	N	N
And if. . . .	Y	N	Y	N	Y	Y	N	N
And if. . . .	Y	Y	N	N	Y	N	Y	N
Actions Then do. . . .	✓							
Then do. . . .		✓	✓	✓	✓			
Then do. . . .						✓	✓	✓

TM 10-4

Text Reference: Figure 10-6

SYSTEM FLOWCHART

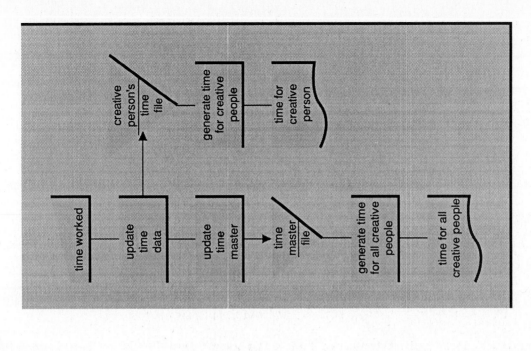

TM 10-5

Text Reference: Figure 10-7 & 10-8

DATA FLOW DIAGRAM

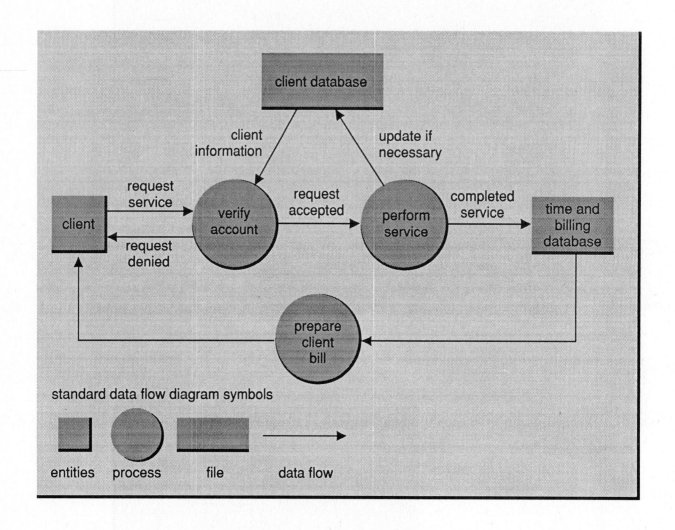

TM 10-6

Text Reference: Figure 10-9

SYSTEMS DEVELOPMENT LIFE CYCLE

Systems Development Life Cycle

Phase	Activity
1. Preliminary investigation	Define problem Suggest alternatives Prepare short report
2. Systems analysis	Gather data Analyze data Document
3. Systems design	Design alternatives Select best alternative Write report
4. Systems development	Develop software Acquire hardware Test system
5. Systems implementation	Convert Train
6. Systems maintenance	Perform system audit Evaluate periodically

TM 10-7

Text Reference: Figure 10-15

PROGRAMMING IN THE SYSTEMS LIFE CYCLE

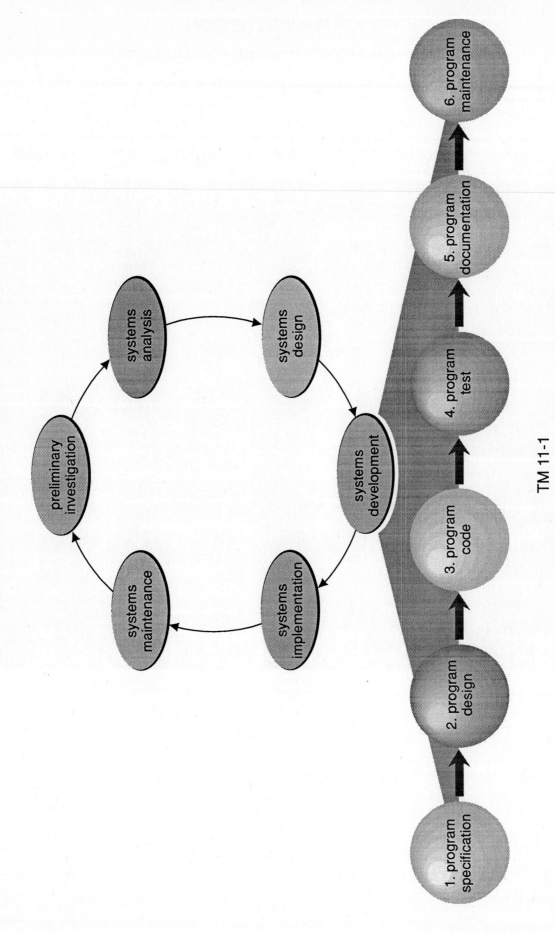

TM 11-1

Text Reference: Figure 11-1

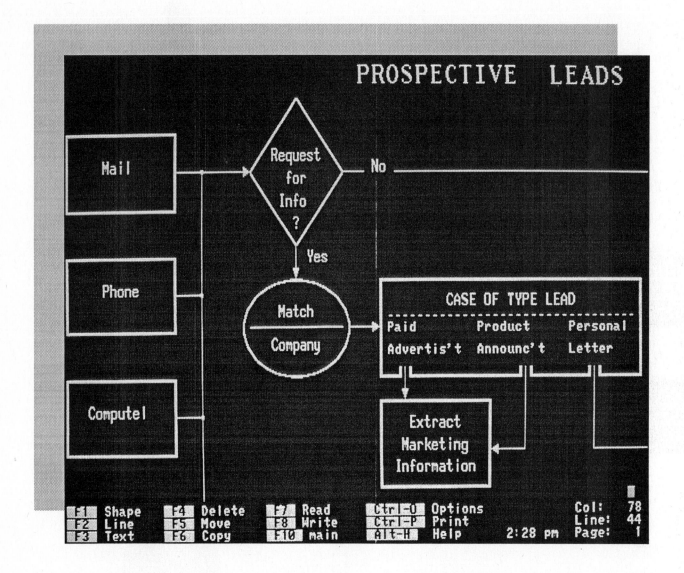

TM 11-2

Text Reference: Figure 11-5

TOP-DOWN PROGRAM DESIGN

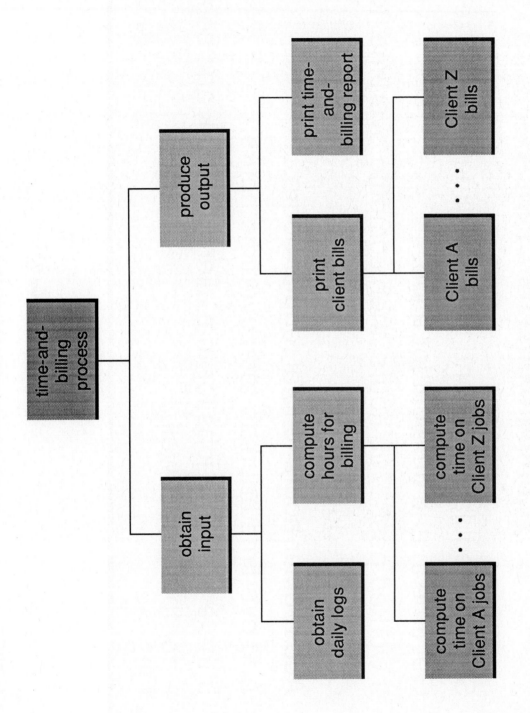

TM 11-3

Text Reference: Figure 11-6

Compute time for Client A

Set total regular hours and total overtime hours to zero.

Get time in and time out for a job.

If worked past 1700 hours, then compute overtime hours.

Compute regular hours.

Add regular hours to total regular hours.

Add overtime hours to total overtime hours.

If there are more jobs for that client, go back and compute for that job as well.

TM 11-4

Text Reference: Figure 11-7

FLOWCHARTING

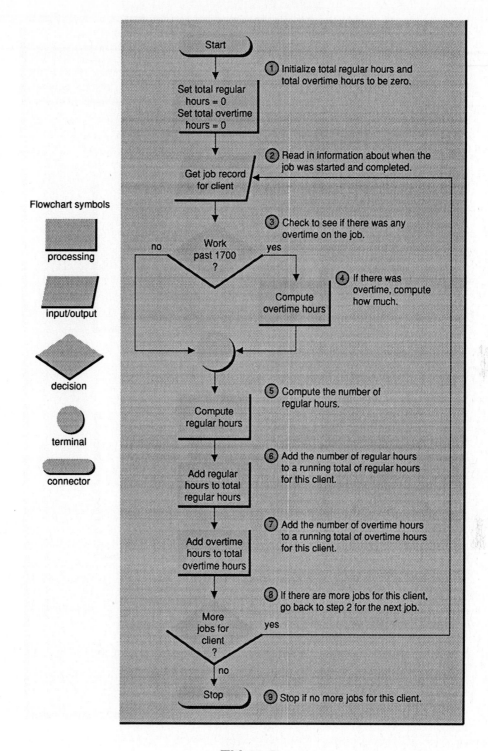

Flowchart symbols

- processing
- input/output
- decision
- terminal
- connector

Start

Set total regular hours = 0
Set total overtime hours = 0

① Initialize total regular hours and total overtime hours to be zero.

Get job record for client

② Read in information about when the job was started and completed.

Work past 1700 ?
no — yes

③ Check to see if there was any overtime on the job.

Compute overtime hours

④ If there was overtime, compute how much.

Compute regular hours

⑤ Compute the number of regular hours.

Add regular hours to total regular hours

⑥ Add the number of regular hours to a running total of regular hours for this client.

Add overtime hours to total overtime hours

⑦ Add the number of overtime hours to a running total of overtime hours for this client.

More jobs for client ?
yes
no

⑧ If there are more jobs for this client, go back to step 2 for the next job.

Stop

⑨ Stop if no more jobs for this client.

TM 11-5

Text Reference: Figure11-8

SEQUENCE LOGIC STRUCTURE

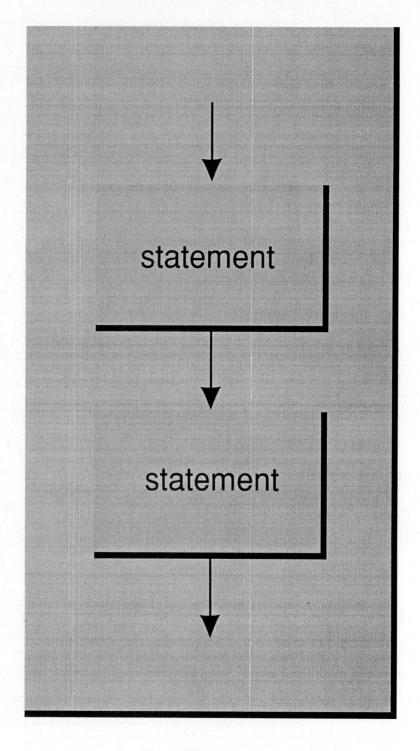

statement

statement

TM 11-6

Text Reference: Figure 11-9

SELECTION LOGIC STRUCTURE

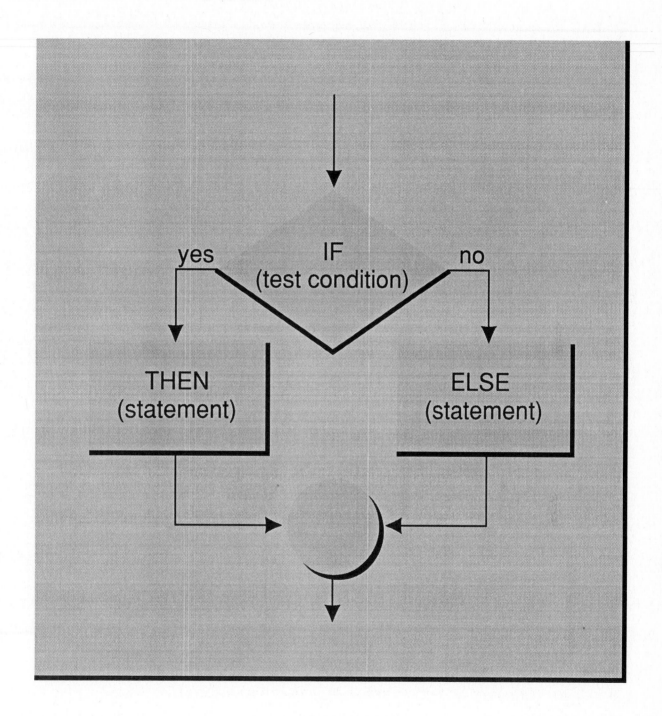

TM 11-7

Text Reference: Figure 11-10

LOOP LOGIC STRUCTURE

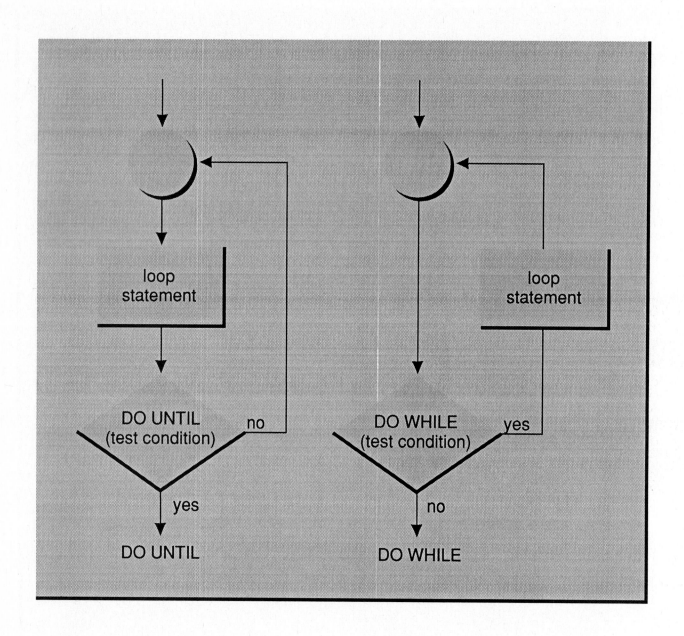

TM 11-8

Text Reference: Figure 11-11

PROGRAMMING LANGUAGE CODE

```
Program compute_time:

var
  input_file : text;
  total_regular,
  total_overtime,
  regular,
  overtime : real;
  hour_in,
  minute_in,
  hour_out,
  minute_out : integer;


begin
assign (input_file,'time.txt');
reset (input_file);

total_regular := 0;
total_overtime  := 0;
while not eof(input_file) do
 begin
 readln (input_file,hour_in,minute_in,hour_out,minute_out);
 if (hour_out >= 17) then
    overtime := (hour_out – 17) + (minute_out/60)
 else
    overtime := 0;
 regular := (hour_out-hour_in) + ((minute_out-minute_in)/60) _overtime;
 total_regular := total_regular + regular;
 total_overtime := total_overtime + overtime;
 end;

writeln('regular = ',total_regular);
writeln('overtime = ',total_overtime);
end.
```

TM 11-9

Text Reference: Figure 11-15

SIX PROGRAMMING STEPS

Programming Steps

Step	Primary activity	
1. Program specification	Determine:	program objectives desired output required input processing requirements
2. Program design	Use:	structured programming technique
3. Program code	Select:	programming language
	Write:	the program
4. Program test	Perform:	desk check manual check translation attempt test with sample data
5. Program documentation	Write procedure for:	users operators programmers
6. Program maintenance	Adjust for:	errors inefficient or ineffective operations nonstandard code changes over time

TM 11-10

Text Reference: Figure 11-19

PERSONAL INFORMATION MANAGERS

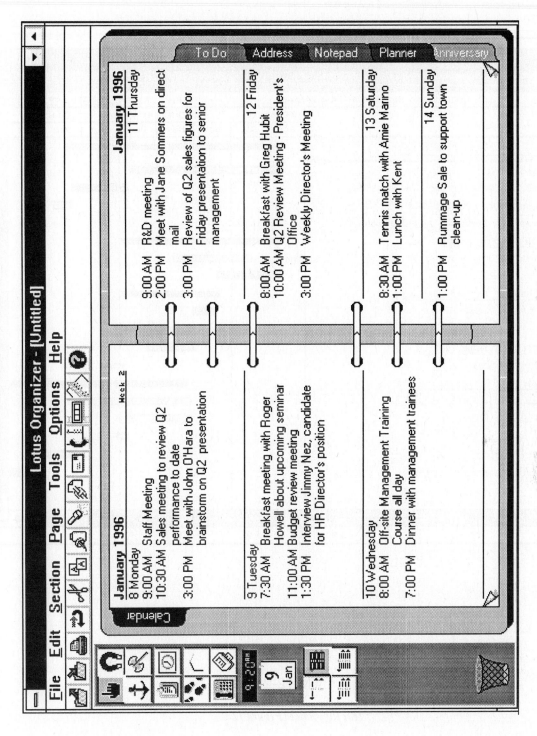

TM 12-1

Text Reference: Figure 12-1

GANTT CHART

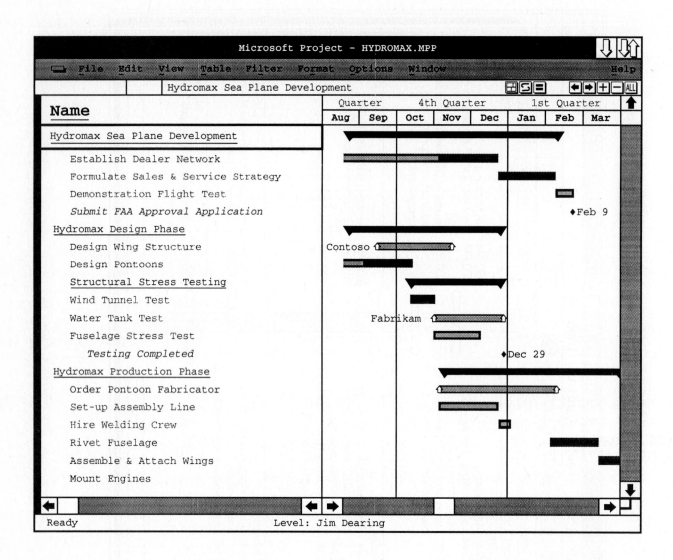

Microsoft Project - HYDROMAX.MPP

File   Edit   View   Table   Filter   Format   Options   Window   Help

Hydromax Sea Plane Development

Name	Quarter	4th Quarter	1st Quarter
	Aug Sep	Oct Nov Dec	Jan Feb Mar

Hydromax Sea Plane Development
  Establish Dealer Network
  Formulate Sales & Service Strategy
  Demonstration Flight Test
  Submit FAA Approval Application   ◆Feb 9
Hydromax Design Phase
  Design Wing Structure   Contoso
  Design Pontoons
  Structural Stress Testing
  Wind Tunnel Test
  Water Tank Test   Fabrikam
  Fuselage Stress Test
    Testing Completed   ◆Dec 29
Hydromax Production Phase
  Order Pontoon Fabricator
  Set-up Assembly Line
  Hire Welding Crew
  Rivet Fuselage
  Assemble & Attach Wings
  Mount Engines

Ready   Level: Jim Dearing

TM 12-2

Text Reference: Figure 12-2

PERT CHART

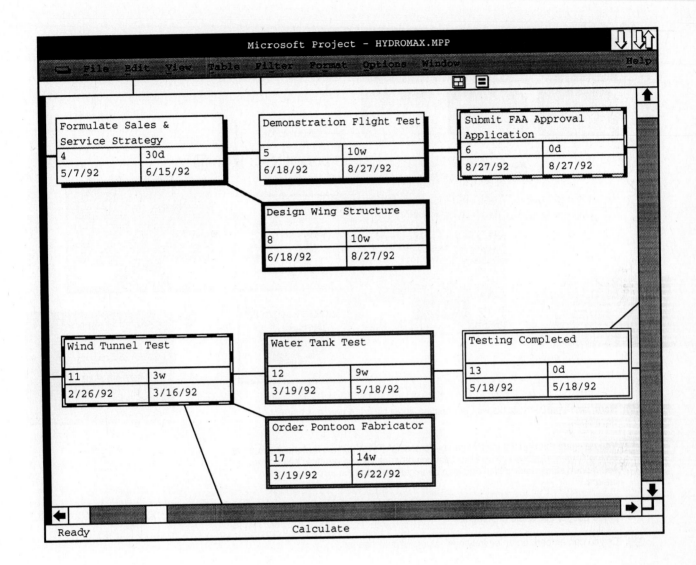

TM 12-3

Text Reference: Figure 12-3

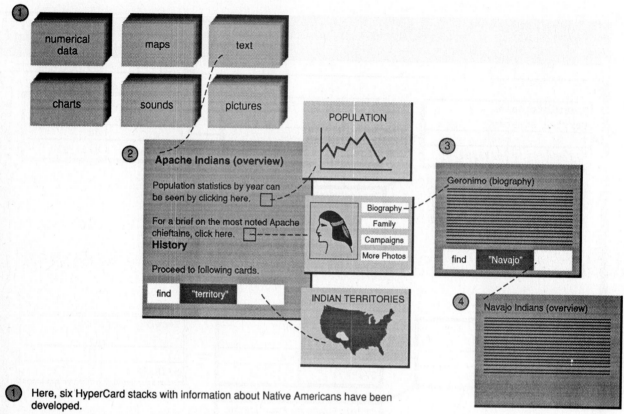

1. Here, six HyperCard stacks with information about Native Americans have been developed.

2. You navigate through the information by "pressing" ("clicking") on buttons that appear on the screen. Buttons call up linked data on other cards and promote self-paced, self-guided study. Information can also be accessed using the HyperCard "Find" feature.

3. Linking data is not a one-way street. From any card, you can access other cards to probe deeper into a line of thought.

4. Or you can embark on an entirely new course of investigation.

TM 12-4

Text Reference: Figure 12-6

MULTIMEDIA

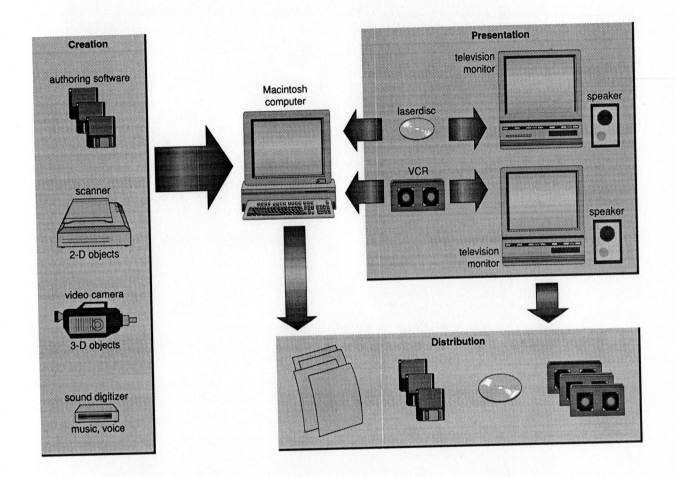

TM 12-5

Text Reference: Figure12-7

PERCEPTION SYSTEMS

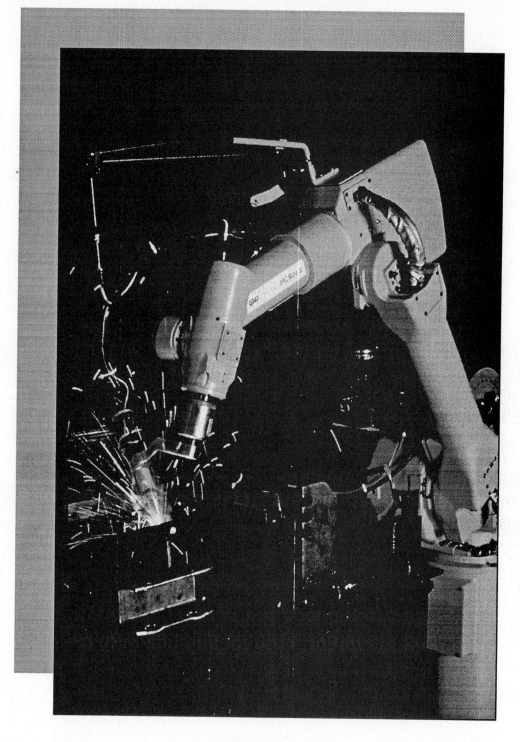

TM 12-6

Text Reference: Figure 12-12

EXPERT SYSTEMS

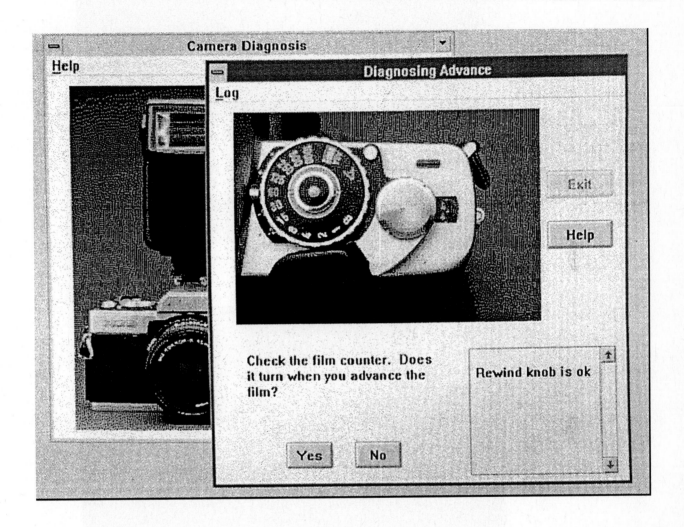

TM 12-7

Text Reference: Figure 12-13

VIRTUAL REALITY

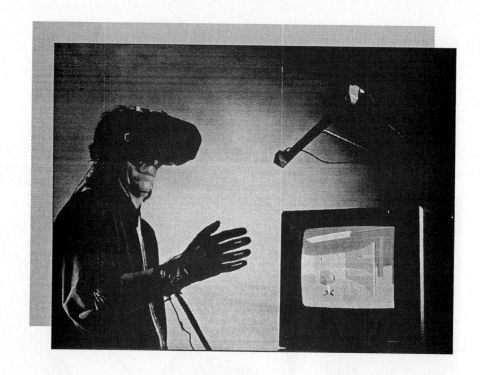

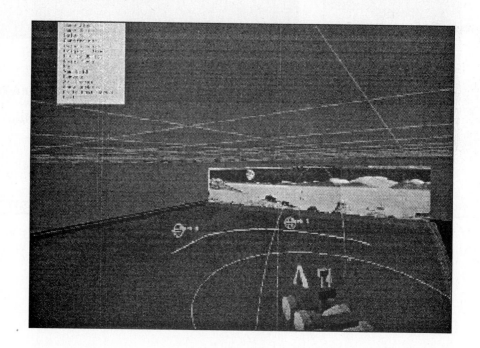

TM 12-8

Text Reference: Figure 12-14

THE ERGONOMIC WORKSTATION

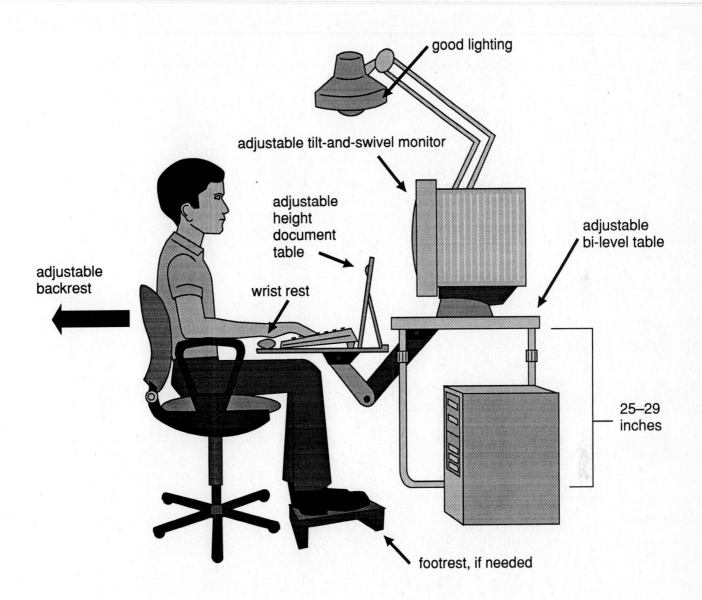

good lighting

adjustable tilt-and-swivel monitor

adjustable height document table

adjustable bi-level table

adjustable backrest

wrist rest

25–29 inches

footrest, if needed

TM 13-1

Text Reference: Figure 13-1

PRIVACY LAWS

Privacy Laws

Law	Protection
Fair Credit Reporting Act	Gives right to review and correct personal credit records; restricts sharing of personal credit histories
Freedom of Information Act	Gives right to see personal files collected by federal agencies
Privacy Act	Prohibits use of federal information for purposes other than original intent
Right to Financial Privacy Act	Limits federal authority to examine personal bank records
Computer Fraud and Abuse Act	Allows prosecution of unauthorized access to computers and databases
Electronic Communications Privacy Act	Protects privacy on public electronic-mail systems
Video Privacy Protection Act	Prevents sale of video-rental records
Computer Matching and Privacy Protection Act	Limits government's authority to match individual's data

TM 13-2

Text Reference: Figure 13-4

CODE OF FAIR INFORMATION PRACTICE

1. *No secret databases:* There must be no record-keeping systems containing personal data whose very existence is kept secret.

2. *Right of individual access:* Individuals must be able to find out what information about them is in a record and how it is used.

3. *Right of consent:* Information about individuals obtained for one purpose cannot be used for other purposes without their consent.

4. *Right to correct:* Individuals must be able to correct or amend records of identifiable information about them.

5. *Assurance of reliability and proper use:* Organizations creating, maintaining, using, or disseminating records of identifiable personal data must make sure the data is reliable for its intended use. They must take precautions to prevent such data from being misused.

TM 13-3

Text Reference: Figure 13-5

HOW A COMPUTER VIRUS SPREADS

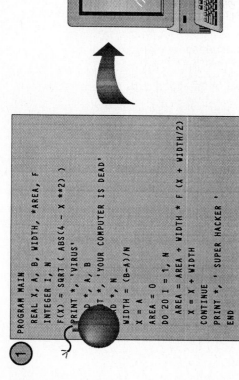

```
PROGRAM MAIN
  REAL X, A, B, WIDTH, *AREA, F
  INTEGER I, N
  F(X) = SQRT ( ABS(4 - X **2) )
  PRINT *, 'VIRUS'
  ...D *, A, B
  ...T *, 'YOUR COMPUTER IS DEAD'
  ...D *, N
  WIDTH = (B-A)/N
  X = A
  AREA = 0
  DO 20 I = 1, N
    AREA = AREA + WIDTH * F (X + WIDTH/2)
    X = X + WIDTH
  CONTINUE
  PRINT *, ' SUPER HACKER '
  END
```

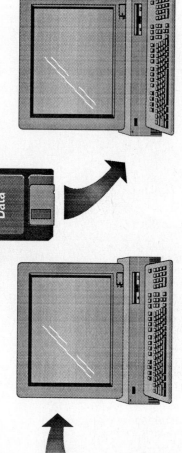

Data

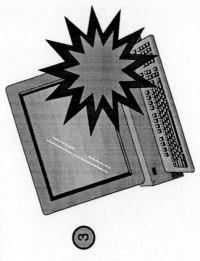

1. A virus begins when a "cracker" or programmer writes a program that attaches itself to an operating system, another program, or piece of data.

2. The virus travels via floppy disk or downloading from networks or bulletin boards anywhere that the operating system, program, or data travels.

3. The virus is set off. A nondestructive virus may simply print a message ("Surprise!"). A destructive virus may erase data, destroy programs, and even (through repeated reading and writing to one location) wear out a hard disk. The virus may be set off either by a time limit or by a sequence of operations by the user.

TM 13-4

Text Reference: Figure 13-7

HOW TO MINIMIZE VIRUS DAMAGE

1. Make backup copies of your data on a frequent basis.
2. Protect data on your floppy disks by using write-protect tabs.
3. Turn off your microcomputer when you're not using it.
4. Don't use master disks. Make a working copy and store the master.
5. Avoid downloading computer games from electronic bulletin boards.
6. Limit your use of "shareware" programs.
7. Do not loan out your utility or other software programs.

TM 13-5

Text Reference: Figure 13-8

BEING a WINNER in the INFORMATION REVOLUTION

- New technology requires people who are capable of using and working with it.

- Ability and a positive attitude can help develop confidence to learn and to manage the new technology.

- Know how to integrate the technology with the people who use it.

- Learn the most current technology and use it to your advantage to become a winner in the information revolution.

TM 14.01

HOW YOU CAN BE a WINNER

- Progressive organizations are using the technology of the information age.

- If an individual desires to increase the chances for success in today's business world, the following ideas may provide sound advice:

  Stay current with your field

  Stay current with technology

  Develop professional contacts

  Develop specialty skills as well as general skills

  Be alert for organizational change

  Look for innovative opportunities

TM 14.02

1) The term "End User" describes people who use microcomputers or have access to large computers.

2) Computer competency means the same for all people.

3) Powerful expert systems make end users experts.

4) An individual taking a computerized test is an end user.

5) Computers are categorized into four types - microcomputer, minicomputer, midrange and mainframe.

6) Laptop or transportables are types of minicomputers.

7) People should be a key consideration in designing a microcomputer system.

8) Hardware usually contains the step-by-step instructions necessary for the computer to meet end user's needs

9) Data and information are the same.

10) Software is another name for program instructions.

11) Information is processed data meeting an end user's needs.

12) Procedures are manuals with instructions containing rules or guidelines to follow when using software, hardware, and data.

13) The operating system is the most important part of applications software.

14) Systems software is considered "background" software.

15) Today, organizations hire programmers to customize all their programs.

16) Communications programs and electronic spreadsheets are applications software programs.

17) Systems software is a special type of applications software.

18) Applications software and systems software are basically the same.

19) Systems software interacts between the applications software and the computer.

20) Four of today's most popular microcomputer operating systems include DOS, OS/2, Macintosh, and VMS.

21) Computer use for business needs are usually information related or for a decision making purpose.

22) Being computer competent means as individual must learn how to run a microcomputer.

23) Microcomputers are also known as personal computers.

24) Developing a computer competency should improve personal and professional productivity.

25) Hardware usually contains the step-by-step instructions necessary for the computer to meet end user's needs.

26) Hardware consists of monitor, keyboard and software.

27) Microsoft Windows extends the capability of DOS in IBM and compatible systems.

28) The central processor is where data is stored temporarily while awaiting processing.

29) Primary storage must hold both the program and the data while executing the program for processing.

30) Secondary storage may be built into the system unit cabinet of a microcomputer.

31) DOS is the standard operating system for Apple Corporation's Macintosh.

32) Secondary storage is considered temporary storage for data and programs.

33) A data diskette is usually blank and must be prepared so that a computer system can store data on it.

34) Memory is also known as primary storage.

35) Many computer system units are configured with two floppy disk drives referred to as drive A and drive C.

36) Drive C is the designator for the hard disk in a microcomputer.

37) A modem is used to send electronic signals over telephone lines.

38) Connectivity is the concept of connecting a microcomputer to appliances found in most homes.

39) Computer competence is in a constant state of change in terms of what an individual must know.

40) Successful end users should know how to integrate new technology to improve the quality and accessibility of information.

41) A modem is a device used for formatting large quantities of floppy disks very rapidly.

42) The hard disk is typically removable from the system unit cabinet.

43) It is possible to have hard-disk and floppy-disk drives external to the system unit cabinet.

44) Flexible disks and hard disks hold data or programs in the form of magnetized spots.

45) Communications hardware sends data and programs from one computer or secondary storage device to another.

46) A field is an item of data made up by one or more logically related characters.

47) A record is a collection of related files.

48) A database can give people access to data located in different files to produce information.

49) Artificial intelligence attempts to develop computer systems that:

a) mimic human thought processes.
b) includes robotics development.
c) includes knowledge-based systems.
d) includes expert systems.
e) All of the above are part of artificial intelligence.

50) Virtual reality

   a) has the user wear headgear and a glove(s).
   b) allows the user to alter the physical world.
   c) allows one to experience alternative realities to their
      physical world.
   d) All the above are true of virtual reality.
   e) Only answers a and c above are true of virtual reality.

51) Packaged software is

   a) custom-made.
   b) written by in-house programmers.
   c) applications software.
   d) systems software.

52) Files containing highly structured and organized data are:

   a) documents.
   b) worksheets.
   c) databases.
   d) graphics.
   e) communications.

53) Which of the following is considered part of an information
    system?

   a) people
   b) procedures
   c) hardware
   d) data
   e) All the above are part of an information system.

54) Systems software is

   a) background software.
   b) a "basic tool".
   c) integrated software.
   d) All the above are true of systems software.

55) Someone that has practical working knowledge of computers that
    allows one to obtain the necessary
    information to solve problems is said to be

   a) a hacker.
   b) a computer programmer.
   c) computer competent.
   d) none of the above

56) Which of the following is not a classification of computer systems?

a) microcomputer
b) supercomputer
c) maxicomputer
d) minicomputer
e) mainframe

57) High-capacity computers used primarily for research purposes are:

a) microcomputers.
b) minicomputers.
c) mainframes.
d) supercomputers.
e) personal computers.

58) Programs can also be called

a) software.
b) hardware.
c) procedures.
d) information.

59) Which of the following is most closely associated with a microcomputer?

a) programmer
b) data-entry clerk
c) computer operator
d) end-user

60) The end user, in business, working with a microcomputer system will likely

a) use a "prewritten program".
b) be seeking solutions to an information-related problem.
c) need the services of a programmer.
d) All the above.
e) Both answers a and b above.

61) Which of the following is not considered hardware?

a) keyboard
b) monitor
c) programs
d) printer

62) Which of the following packaged software would most likely be used to write documents?

    a) electronic spreadsheets
    b) word processing
    c) graphics programs
    d) none of the above

63) Electronic spreadsheets are generally used for

    a) creating written documents.
    b) analyzing and summarizing data.
    c) transmitting and receiving data.
    d) all of the above

64) Which of the following is not one of the five categories of microcomputer hardware?

    a) input devices
    b) output devices
    c) communications devices
    d) all of the above

65) All of the following are considered temporary storage except

    a) secondary storage.
    b) primary storage.
    c) main memory.
    d) internal storage.

66) A floppy disk is considered to be

    a) software
    b) hardware
    c) primary storage
    d) none of the above

67) Which of the following statements about secondary storage is false?

    a) it may be built into the system cabinet
    b) it is designed to store programs and data permanently
    c) it is part of the central processor
    d) it may consist of either flexible diskettes, hard disks or both

68) The most commonly used floppy disk sizes for microcomputers are

   a) 3 1/2 cm and 5 1/4 cm.
   b) 3 1/2 inch and 5 1/4 inch.
   c) 5 1/4 inch and 8 inch.
   d) 3 1/2 cm and 8 cm.

69) When electrical power is disrupted or cut off, data and programs
   are lost in:

   a) secondary storage.
   b) basic tools.
   c) memory.
   d) operating system.
   e) hard disk.

70) A hard disk is usually designated as drive

   a) A
   b) B
   c) C
   d) none of the above

71) Which of the following are possible features of a printer?

   a) capable of producing softcopy output
   b) capable of producing hardcopy output
   c) capable of producing print in color
   d) both b and c above
   e) All of the above are available features

72) Which of the following devices is used to change the digital
   signal of the computer into an analog signal that can travel over
   telephone lines?

   a) transformer
   b) video display terminal
   c) modem
   d) CRT

73) Which of the following terms does not represent a microcomputer
   output device?

   a) video display screen
   b) monitor
   c) cathode ray tube
   d) keyboard

74) The central processing unit (CPU) is located in the:

a) hard disk.
b) system unit.
c) memory.
d) monitor.
e) keyboard.

75) Which of the following is true of systems software?

a) programs helping the computer manage its resources
b) includes the operating system
c) makes it easier for the end-user to use the hardware
d) all the above are true of systems software

76) A program that can be purchased by an end-user for entertainment, solving business problems or countless other applications is a(n)

a) prewritten program.
b) customized program.
c) systems software program.
d) operating system program.

77) Which is true of a microcomputer system?

a) requires special needs for environment and wiring
b) used by organizations for voluminous amounts of data
c) allows the end user to produce sophisticated output
d) All the above are true of a microcomputer system.

78) Which of the following is true of a program diskette?

a) It holds instructions for the computer.
b) It holds raw data.
c) It holds processed information ready for output.
d) None of the above are true for a program diskette.

79) Which of the following is true of a local area network?

a) connects computers within a building
b) connects computers in a regional network
c) connects computers in a national network
d) requires the use of telephone lines to work

80) Computers are electronic devices that accept instructions, process input, and produce:

   a) information.
   b) prewritten programs.
   c) data.
   d) end users.
   e) system software.

81) Being computer competent will require individuals to have an understanding of

   a) powerful software.
   b) powerful hardware.
   c) connectivity.
   d) All of the above are needed.

82) Multimedia connects text files with

   a)   graphics.
   b)   video.
   c)   sound.
   d)   All of the above can be connected together with multimedia.

1)	T		53)	e
2)	F		54)	a
3)	F		55)	c
4)	T		56)	c
5)	F		57)	d
6)	F		58)	a
7)	T		59)	d
8)	F		60)	e
9)	F		61)	c
10)	T		62)	b
11)	T		63)	b
12)	T		64)	d
13)	F		65)	a
14)	T		66)	a
15)	F		67)	c
16)	T		68)	b
17)	F		69)	c
18)	F		70)	c
19)	T		71)	d
20)	F		72)	c
21)	T		73)	d
22)	F		74)	b
23)	T		75)	d
24)	T		76)	a
25)	F		77)	c
26)	F		78)	a
27)	T		79)	a
28)	F		80)	a
29)	T		81)	d
30)	T		82)	d
31)	T			
32)	F			
33)	T			
34)	F			
35)	F			
36)	T			
37)	T			
38)	F			
39)	T			
40)	T			
41)	F			
42)	F			
43)	T			
44)	T			
45)	T			
46)	T			
47)	F			
48)	T			
49)	e			
50)	e			
51)	c			
52)	c			

1) Applications software performs useful work such as word processing or database management.

2) The exporting feature is common to many applications programs and allows word processing files to be retrieved into spreadsheet files.

3) Packaged software can be on disks of 3 1/2 inch or 5 1/4 inch format.

4) The cursor indicates where you may enter data next.

5) Packaged software is also called off-the-wall software.

6) A word processing program is considered to be a general-purpose software application.

7) The scriptor is a blinking symbol on the screen that shows where you may enter data next.

8) The electronic spreadsheet is based on the traditional accounting worksheet.

9) Scrolling allows the user to roll text up or down on the screen.

10) Word wrap is a feature of word processing that causes the cursor to automatically move to the next line during typing when the end of a line is reached.

11) Word wrap is a feature common to database managers.

12) When using a word processor, you must press a carriage return key to begin typing on a new line.

13) An integrated package is a communications application program with data bank, message, exchange, and financial service capabilities.

14) The portion of text you wish to move using a word processor is called a block.

15) The block of text you wish to move using a word processor is usually identified by the use of underlining.

16) The CTRL key is an example of a special-purpose key on a microcomputer keyboard.

17) Database management programs are used to keep track of details such as inventory records or client lists.

18) A databank resembles a huge electronic encyclopedia.

19) Programs are available that will automatically check the spelling throughout a document.

20) A cell holds a single unit of data in a spreadsheet.

21) Analytical graphics look more sophisticated than presentation graphics because they use color, titles, three-dimensional look, and other features that graphic artists might employ.

22) A number contained in a spreadsheet cell is called a label.

23) Labels in a spreadsheet are always centered in the cell.

24) Microsoft Works and Lotus Works are low-end integrated packages.

25) Automatic recalculation can occur within a spreadsheet each time an entry is made in the worksheet.

26) WordPerfect 5.1 has a "pull-down" menu system.

27) Quattro Pro is a widely used word processor.

28) A menu is often found in software packages. It lists commands available for manipulating data.

29) A pull-down menu displays a list of commands in a menu that usually "drops-down" from a menu bar at the top of the screen.

30) With communications programs, you can look up airline reservations and stock quotations.

31) Many databases can handle calculations such as finding the average of the data in a specific field.

32) It is possible today to do banking from home using a personal computer.

33) Some electronic spreadsheet programs link cells in one file to cells in another file to automatically update the file and perform recalculations, if necessary.

34) Word processing software is designed to handle any kind of text material in the form of letters, memos, term papers, reports, contracts, etc.

35) LOTUS 1-2-3 is a popular word processing software package.

36) Communications software lets you send and receive data from another computer.

37) A package that allows you to do word processing, database management, spreadsheets and graphics is known as an integrated package.

38) Desktop publishing allows text and graphics to be combined in documents.

39) Some word processors have the ability to automatically outline ideas and phrases as they are entered into a document.

40) Some electronic spreadsheets have the capability of creating three dimensional graphs from numeric values entered into the worksheet.

41) A dynamic file link allows a word processing program and a spreadsheet to use the same file.

42) "Format" in an electronic spreadsheet means to change the appearance of the content value(s) of a cell or cells.

43) A basic feature of all database programs is the capability to locate records in the file quickly.

44) The process of sorting a database means to locate a specific record the user desires.

45) An add-on console with special cartridges can be plugged into a microcomputer keyboard and used to interpret complex commands in spreadsheet programs.

46) Many database programs contain built-in math formulas.

47) Business graphics help convey information and to show relationships in numeric data, they include

a) analytical graphics.
b) presentation graphics.
c) both a and b above
d) none of the above

48) The feature common to most application packages that allows you to store a sequence of keystrokes
   as a single command:

   a) export
   b) menu bar
   c) macro
   d) import
   e) replace

49) A tool used frequently by marketing people to communicate a message or to persuade clients:

   a) word processors.
   b) spreadsheets.
   c) analytical graphics.
   d) database managers.
   e) presentation graphics.

50) Features like justification, mail-merge, and boldface are more commonly found in a(n)

   a) electronic spreadsheet.
   b) database management program.
   c) word processing program.
   d) desktop management program.

51) The important principle of "connectivity" is most likely established by

   a) a word processing program
   b) a communications program.
   c) a database manager.
   d) a graphics program.

52) Which of the following is not a publisher of packaged software?

   a) Lotus Corporation
   b) Ashton-Tate
   c) Microsoft
   d) All the above are publishers of packaged software.

53) Which of the following would probably not be produced using a word processor?

   a) an income statement
   b) a letter
   c) a memo
   d) a term paper

54) Which of the following is the blinking symbol on the screen that
shows where you may enter text or data next?

a) scroll bar
b) cursor
c) data light
d) light pen

55) The feature of word processing systems which automatically moves
the cursor to a new line during typing is called

a) automatic line advance.
b) a carriage return.
c) word wrap.
d) left justification.

56) Which of the following is the term used to describe the portion
of text you wish to move using a word processing system?

a) chunk
b) paragraph
c) cut and paste selection
d) block

57) All of the following are popular word processing programs except

a) dBASE.
b) WordPerfect.
c) Word.
d) MacWrite.

58) The intersection of a row and column in a spreadsheet is known as
a

a) worksheet area.
b) cell.
c) window.
d) none of the above

59) Which of the following are important features of most integrated
package software programs?

a) cursor and scrolling
b) menus
c) format
d) function keys
e) all the above are important features

60) All of the following are popular spreadsheet programs except

a) Lotus 1-2-3.
b) Quattro Pro.
c) SuperCalc.
d) dBASE.
e) All the above are electronic spreadsheets.

61) All of the following are popular database management programs except

a) dBASE.
b) FoxPro.
c) Paradox.
d) All the above are database programs.

62) All of the following are popular business graphics programs except

a) DisplayWrite.
b) Harvard Graphics.
c) Freelance Plus.
d) Draw Applause.

63) Which of the following packages would you be most likely to use to produce a business graph?

a) Microsoft Word
b) Freelance Plus
c) DisplayWrite
d) dBASE III Plus

64) Which of the following packages would you be most likely to use to communicate over telephone lines?

a) Smartcom
b) Lotus 1-2-3
c) Quattro Pro
d) MultiMate

65) Which of the following is not generally included in an integrated package?

a) a database manager
b) a communications program
c) the operating system
d) a spreadsheet program

1)	T	53)	a
2)	T	54)	b
3)	T	55)	c
4)	T	56)	d
5)	F	57)	a
6)	T	58)	b
7)	F	59)	e
8)	T	60)	d
9)	T	61)	d
10)	T	62)	a
11)	F	63)	b
12)	F	64)	a
13)	F	65)	c
14)	T		
15)	F		
16)	T		
17)	T		
18)	T		
19)	T		
20)	T		
21)	F		
22)	F		
23)	F		
24)	F		
25)	T		
26)	T		
27)	F		
28)	T		
29)	T		
30)	T		
31)	T		
32)	T		
33)	T		
34)	T		
35)	F		
36)	T		
37)	T		
38)	T		
39)	T		
40)	T		
41)	F		
42)	T		
43)	T		
44)	F		
45)	T		
46)	T		
47)	c		
48)	c		
49)	e		
50)	c		
51)	b		
52)	d		

1) One computer can only run one kind of system software.

2) MS-DOS is only available on 5 1/4 inch diskettes.

3) System software is generally written by the end user.

4) Booting the system means that the computer has been turned on and the operating system has been loaded into memory.

5) MS-DOS is the standard operating system for IBM-compatible computers.

6) OS/2 allows users to run only one program at a time in the microcomputer.

7) MS-DOS and Macintosh operating systems are compatible.

8) OS/2 was developed for a new generation of more powerful microcomputers.

9) One limitation of MS-DOS is the amount of RAM it can access and use.

10) Virtual memory increases the amount of memory available to run applications programs.

11) The bootstrap loader is a program stored permanently in the computer's electronic circuitry.

12) One form of a diagnostic routine would be to test the computer's RAM memory.

13) Of all the microcomputer operating systems, DOS is able to run on the least expensive hardware.

14) The basic input output system is stored on a disk until it is needed by the computer.

15) A computer's operating system is usually a permanent part of a computer's electronic circuitry.

16) Mainframe and minicomputer systems tend to focus on multiple users of a single computer system.

17) The operating system is a collection of programs that helps the computer manage its own resources.

18) Macintosh computers are designed to use the '486 microprocessor.

19) Every computer has to have an operating system.

20) Formatting a disk is a basic function of the computer's basic input output system.

21) MVS and OS/VS are two popular operating systems for IBM mainframe computers.

22) A 3.2 version of an operating system means that it has had 2 major revisions and 3 minor revisions since it was introduced on the market.

23) Window NT is an operating system.

24) Two advantages of MS-DOS are the enormous number of applications programs available and its multitasking capabilities.

25) One of Unix's primary strengths is the large number of applications written for it.

26) Advantages of UNIX include multitasking, multiuser, and networking capabilities.

27) The disadvantages of OS/2 is that it is expensive and has few applications presently available to use its features.

28) The System file and the Finder are the two primary files in the Macintosh operating system.

29) The Apple Macintosh has had many of the same features that OS/2 offers.

30) The disadvantages of the Apple Macintosh are its image as a business machine, difficulties with compatibility with the DOS environment, and the expense.

31) UNIX was originally developed by IBM as an operating system for its first microcomputer system.

32) The lack of a standard version for UNIX is likely its most significant disadvantage.

33) An advantage of the UNIX operating system is the universal standard version of UNIX the microcomputer industry employs.

34) Disadvantages of UNIX includes limited applications software and no graphical user interface.

35) The multiuser microcomputer operating system:

   a) Unix
   b) OS/2
   c) DOS with Windows
   d) Desqview
   e) Macintosh

36) All of the following are considered to be part of system software except

   a) utility programs.
   b) language translators.
   c) operating systems.
   d) application packages.

37) The newest operating system for microcomputers is

   a) MS-DOS.
   b) OS-DOS.
   c) OS/2.
   d) UNIX.

38) Which of the following would be a good reason for learning more about systems software?

   a) to help determine the best computer system for your needs
   b) to understand the limitations of systems software
   c) to get the most benefit from the computer system
   d) all the above

39) Systems software consists of four kinds of programs, which of the following is not one of them?

   a) bootstrap loader
   b) diagnostic routines
   c) applications software
   d) basic input output system

40) Which of the following is true of a bootstrap loader?

   a) stored permanently in the computer's electronic circuitry
   b) starts up when the computer is turned on
   c) loads the operating system from a disk into memory
   d) All the above are true of a bootstrap loader.

41) Which of the following are true of diagnostic routines?

   a) programs stored in the computer's electronic circuitry
   b) start up when the computer is turned on
   c) test the primary storage of the computer
   d) makes sure the computer is running properly
   e) all the above are true of diagnostic routines

42) A part of system software that enables the computer to interpret
    keyboard characters and transmit them to a monitor or disk is

   a) the bootstrap loader.
   b) application software.
   c) the basic input output system.
   d) diagnostic routines.

43) A part of system software that enables the computer to manage its
    own resources and take much of this burden from the user is

   a) the boot strap loader.
   b) application software.
   c) the operating system.
   d) the basic input output system.

44) Which of the following is not part of the operating system's
    utility programs?

   a) formatting disks
   b) duplicating disks
   c) testing RAM
   d) erasing files from a disk

45) Which of the following is not a mainframe operating system?

   a) MVS
   b) OS/2
   c) OS/VS
   d) VAX/MVS

46) Which of the following would not likely work in an IBM PS/2 with
    a 386 processor?

   a) PC-DOS
   b) OS/2
   c) UNIX
   d) Macintosh

47) Which of the following is not an advantage of PC-DOS?

    a) popularity
    b) numerous available application programs
    c) runs on inexpensive hardware
    d) multitasking capability

48) Which of the following is not an advantage of OS/2?

    a) numerous application programs available
    b) multitasking capability
    c) compatibility with DOS
    d) graphical user interface
    e) all the above are advantages of OS/2

49) Which of the following are advantages of the Apple Macintosh
    systems software?

    a) quality graphics
    b) ease of use
    c) compatibility with DOS
    d) both a and b above
    e) all the above

50) Which of the following are advantages of the UNIX systems
    software?

    a) multitasking capability
    b) multiuser capability
    c) works well in a network
    d) not limited by primary memory
    e) all the above

51) DOS used with Windows

    a) can run several programs at once.
    b) can share data between programs.
    c) has a graphical user interface.
    d) All the above are true.
    e) None of the above are true.

52) Integrated software

    a) can access more primary storage.
    b) allows the user to work on more than one application at the
       same time.
    c) allows the user to work on more than one application, one at a
       time.
    d) Both A and B above.

53) Windowing software with DOS
a) creates an operating environment.
b) still is limited by 640KB of RAM.
c) limits the capability of DOS.
d) All of the above are true.

54) Which of the following is not true of a graphical user interface (GUI)?

a) can work with a keyboard
b) can work with a mouse
c) uses icons
d) None of the above are true of GUI.

55) Multitasking means

a) more than one operating system can run in the system.
b) more than one application program can run in the system, at the same time.
c) the computer has more than one processor.
d) DOS has to be present in RAM.

56) The collection of programs that helps the computer manage its resources:

a) bootstrap loader
b) applications
c) operating system
d) diagnostic routines
e) backup

57) The most widely used microcomputer operating system:

a) DOS
b) DOS with Windows
c) MVS
d) Macintosh
e) Unix

58) The ability to have a number of applications running at the same time:

a) GUI
b) integrated
c) windowing software
d) multitasking
e) networking

59) An operating system developed jointly by IBM and Microsoft
Corporation:

a) Unix
b) OS/2
c) Windows NT
d) Desqview
e) Macintosh

1)	F	53)	a
2)	F	54)	d
3)	F	55)	b
4)	T	56)	c
5)	T	57)	a
6)	F	58)	d
7)	F	59)	b
8)	T		
9)	T		
10)	T		
11)	T		
12)	T		
13)	T		
14)	F		
15)	F		
16)	T		
17)	T		
18)	F		
19)	T		
20)	F		
21)	T		
22)	F		
23)	T		
24)	F		
25)	F		
26)	T		
27)	T		
28)	T		
29)	T		
30)	T		
31)	F		
32)	T		
33)	F		
34)	T		
35)	a		
36)	d		
37)	c		
38)	d		
39)	c		
40)	d		
41)	e		
42)	c		
43)	c		
44)	c		
45)	b		
46)	d		
47)	d		
48)	a		
49)	d		
50)	e		
51)	e		
52)	c		

1) EBCDIC is the most widely used binary code for microcomputers.

2) Main memory is contained on ROM chips.

3) The system board is also called the add-on board.

4) Registers are high-speed areas for temporarily holding data and instructions.

5) Portable computers are gaining in popularity because of their versatility which allows the end user to work on a computer almost anywhere.

6) Workstations are classified as minicomputers.

7) The part of a computer that executes program instructions is known as the computer programming unit (CPU).

8) Microcomputers are presently available that cost as little as $200, or less.

9) A pocket personal computer is very small and can easily be held in one hand.

10) Microcomputers process data in speeds measured in picoseconds.

11) Mainframe computers are also known as midrange computers.

12) Mainframe computers can process millions of instructions per second.

13) An extra bit automatically added to a byte to test for transmission errors is called a parity bit.

14) Another name for a system board is a motherboard.

15) The control unit is the section of the CPU that tells the rest of the computer system how to carry out a program's instructions.

16) ROM memory chips are volatile and lose their contents if the power to the computer is turned off or disrupted.

17) The CPU has two main sections, the ALU and main memory.

18) All peripheral devices are inside the system unit cabinet.

19) Supercomputers process instructions at speeds measured in milliseconds.

20) A nanosecond is one thousandth of a second.

21) The control unit directs the movement of electronic signals between main memory and the ALU.

22) ROM holds data or application instructions for processing.

23) The computer represents data using the decimal number system.

24) A bit, or binary digit, represents one character.

25) One kilobyte is equal to 1,024 bytes.

26) One megabyte represents 1,024,000 bits.

27) A gigabyte is a term often used to measure main memory of midrange and mainframes computers.

28) EBCDIC is the standard coding format for mainframe computers.

29) The arithmetic-logic unit performs fundamental math operations and logical operations.

30) Main memory is part of the system unit.

31) A smaller bus connecting the CPU with other devices makes the operation of the system faster and more powerful.

32) A serial port is used to connect devices that transmit several bits simultaneously.

33) Microcomputers require the use of a system clock.

34) The internal speed of the computer is measured in megahertz.

35) The user can read from ROM chips but cannot write to them.

36) Additional devices may be attached to a microcomputer through the use of processor chips.

37) Network adapter cards are used to connect the system unit to a communication network.

38) Minicomputers work well in distributed data processing or decentralized computer systems.

39) Supercomputers are used for such tasks as weather forecasting and weapons research.

40) Some computers do not have a CPU.

41) Serial ports are widely used for a variety of purposes including connecting a mouse, keyboard, modem, and other devices to the system unit.

42) Registers are a type of storage location used by the ALU.

43) To locate characters of data or instructions in main memory, the computer stores them at locations known as addresses.

44) A megabyte is larger than a terabyte.

45) Most microcomputers have open architecture that allows users to expand their systems by plugging boards into available expansion slots inside the system unit.

46) All of the following are temporary storage except

   a) primary memory.
   b) secondary storage.
   c) main memory.
   d) internal storage.

47) Which of the following is not found in main memory?

   a) data awaiting processing
   b) programs
   c) processed data awaiting output
   d) All of the above may be found in main memory.

48) In a microcomputer, the CPU is contained on a single chip called:

   a) RAM
   b) ROM
   c) bus
   d) microprocessor
   e) memory

49) The bus IBM developed to support the '386 chip:

   a) MCA
   b) ISA
   c) OS/2
   d) EISA
   e) CD ROM

CHAPTER 4
THE CENTRAL PROCESSING UNIT
Corresponds to Computing Essentials Annual Edition, 1994-1995

50) All of the following are names for microcomputers except

a) personal computers.
b) laptop computers.
c) transportable computers.
d) movables.
e) All of the above are considered to be a microcomputer.

51) The processing speed of supercomputers is in the range of

a) thousands of instructions per second.
b) hundreds of thousands of instructions per second.
c) millions of instructions per second.
d) over one billion instructions per second.

52) The abbreviation CPU stands for

a) cabinet power unit.
b) central processing unit.
c) central power unit.
d) computer programming unit.

53) If a microcomputer system is listed as having 2MB of main memory, this is approximately

a) 2,000 bits.
b) 2,000 bytes.
c) 2 million bytes.
d) 2 billion bytes.

54) The computer system used for large special-purpose applications like predicting weather worldwide:

a) mainframe
b) supercomputer
c) microcomputer
d) workstation
e) minicomputer

55) The pathway connecting parts of the CPU to each other is called a

a) motherboard.
b) bus.
c) serial port.
D) parallel port.

56) A port is a

a) cable that links the CPU to other devices.
b) device which controls how fast all the operations within a computer take place.
c) carrier package for memory cables.
d) connecting socket on the outside of the system unit to plug in other devices.

57) The type of portable microcomputer that fits comfortably into most briefcases:

a) workstation
b) personal computer
c) midrange computer
d) notebook
e) remote

58) The control unit directs the movement of the electronic signals between

a) the CPU and input devices.
b) the CPU and output devices.
c) main memory and the ALU.
d) all of the above

59) Which of the following companies would be least likely to own a mainframe computer?

a) a bank
b) a small florist shop
c) an insurance company
d) a large mail-order firm

60) Random access memory

a) is permanently programmed at the factory.
b) is permanent storage.
c) is used to store data and programs temporarily.
d) is also called firmware.
e) all the above

61) Which of the following is true regarding read-only memory (ROM) chips?

a) they are programmed at the factory
b) data or instructions can be read from them
c) the user cannot write on them
d) a and b above
e) all the above

62) Which of the following symbols is not used in a logical operation?

a) =
b) >
c) <
d) +
e) all the above

63) One billion twenty four million (1,024,000,000) bytes of storage
are represented by the symbol

a) KB.
b) MB.
c) GB.
d) QB.
e) TB.

64) Lines that transmit bits one at a time would be connected to a

a) serial port.
b) parallel port.
c) bus
d) motherboard.

65) The speed of operations within the computer is controlled by the

a) bus.
b) motherboard.
c) parallel port.
d) system clock.

66) An open architecture computer system will

a) have a faster bus.
b) limit the efficiency of the system.
c) have ports to expand the system.
d) All of the above are true of open architecture.
e) None of the above are true of open architecture.

67) The silicon chip which contains the CPU of a personal computer is
called a

a) microcomputer.
b) microprocessor.
c) RAM chip.
d) PROM chip.

68) Expansion boards are used to

   a) add main memory to a computer.
   b) add a color monitor to the system.
   c) add a hard drive to the system.
   d) all the above

69) Expansion boards are also known as

   a) plug-in boards.
   b) controller cards.
   c) interface boards.
   d) all of the above

70) The IBM PC and PS/2 models use microprocessor chips manufactured by

   a) Intel.
   b) Motorola.
   c) MOS Technology.
   d) all of the above

71) Which of the following is not a peripheral device?

   a) keyboard
   b) main memory
   c) hard disk
   d) monitor

72) Which number system do computers use to represent data?

   a) decimal
   b) binary
   c) tertiary
   d) none of the above

73) A character is represented in a computer by

   a) 8 bits.
   b) 8 bytes.
   c) a "0" or a "1".
   d) none of the above

74) The capacity of main storage in a microcomputer is usually represented in

   a) bits
   b) bytes
   c) characters
   d) none of the above

75) Which set of numbers listed below correctly represents the binary
number system?

a) 0, 1
b) 0, 1, 2
c) 1, 2
d) 0, 1, 2, 3, 4, 5, 6, 7, 8, 9

1) F		53) c	
2) F		54) b	
3) F		55) b	
4) T		56) d	
5) T		57) d	
6) F		58) d	
7) F		59) b	
8) T		60) c	
9) T		61) e	
10) F		62) d	
11) F		63) c	
12) T		64) a	
13) T		65) d	
14) T		66) c	
15) T		67) b	
16) F		68) d	
17) F		69) d	
18) F		70) a	
19) F		71) b	
20) F		72) b	
21) T		73) a	
22) F		74) b	
23) F		75) a	
24) F			
25) T			
26) F			
27) T			
28) T			
29) T			
30) T			
31) F			
32) F			
33) T			
34) T			
35) T			
36) F			
37) T			
38) T			
39) T			
40) F			
41) T			
42) T			
43) T			
44) F			
45) T			
46) b			
47) d			
48) d			
49) a			
50) d			
51) d			
52) b			

1) Voice input is much easier than voice output to successfully implement in a computer system.

2) Computers process electronic signals of 0s and 1s.

3) A plotter is a device that can be used to trace or copy a drawing or photograph.

4) Ergonomics studies the human factors related to computers.

5) There are commercially available hand-held computers with a one-inch screens.

6) Input devices convert human communication to computer readable formats.

7) A digitizer is used to convert a drawing or photograph to digital data.

8) Direct keyboard entry of data is not generally necessary when using an image scanner for input.

9) Microcomputers are increasingly being used in place of dedicated terminals as a link to larger computer systems.

10) Input devices translate symbols that people understand into symbols that computers can process.

11) A monochrome monitor cannot display graphic images.

12) Banks use a method called magnetic-ink character recognition (MICR) to automatically read and sort checks.

13) A smart terminal can do some editing of data prior to sending it to the CPU of the host computer.

14) A POS terminal can directly input data via a keyboard.

15) A monitor's resolution is measured by the density of pixels on the screen.

16) A mouse, touch screen, digitizer and light pen are all types of input pointing devices.

17) All data for computer systems are input via keyboard entry.

18) A source document is the original version of a piece of text that is stored on secondary storage in the computer system.

19) A directional arrow key is categorized as a function key.

20) The numbers 1 and 0 are interchangeable with the letters L and O when entering data through the keyboard.

21) Laser printers are highly reliable but the quality of their output limits their use to rough drafts and in-house communications.

22) Function keys are used primarily to input numbers.

23) Voice-output devices make sounds that resemble human speech.

24) Plotters are special-purpose drawing devices.

25) Many printers can print a line either right to left or left to right. This feature is called bi-directional printing.

26) Fax machines are popular office machines because they can transfer documents at electronic speeds.

27) A chain printer is one of the best suited printers for a microcomputer.

28) Voice-output can be used as a reinforcement tool for learning.

29) A smart terminal has memory, a processing unit and storage similar to a microcomputer.

30) The higher a screen's resolution, the sharper the letters and images appear.

31) The dot-matrix printer is a reliable, inexpensive printer that forms letters by a series of small pins on a print head.

32) Flat-panel displays are used primarily for color graphics applications.

33) Another name for the mouse that has a ball that is controlled with the thumb is trackball or rollerball.

34) Most portable microcomputers use cathode ray tube technology in their monitors.

35) Information output on paper is called softcopy.

36) MICR is a direct-entry method used in banks.

37) The gas-plasma display produces the best resolution quality of the flat screen displays.

38) Dot-matrix printers are only capable of printing letters and numbers, not graphics.

39) A pixel is the smallest unit on a screen that can be turned on and off or made in different shades.

40) Dot-matrix printers are the most popular printers used with microcomputers.

41) A daisy-wheel printer produces letter-quality output.

42) Desktop publishing allows users to create professional looking documents using daisy-wheel printers.

43) A dumb terminal cannot process data.

44) Daisy-wheel printers are considered slow speed printers.

45) Most laser printers can produce eight pages of text in about one minute or less.

46) Bidirectional printers are faster than those having a simple carriage return.

47) A smart terminal allows users to do some editing of data prior to sending it to the computer.

48) Microcomputers are increasingly being used as intelligent terminals.

49) Direct entry requires data to be keyed by someone sitting at a keyboard.

50) A flatbed plotter may produce multi-colored output.

51) Voice output is easier to create than voice input.

52) A terminal is a form of input and output device that consists of a keyboard, a monitor, and a communications link.

53) Which of the following would be least likely to be produced using a plotter?

    a) text document
    b) architectural drawing
    c) bar chart
    d) map

54) Esc, Ctrl, Del, and Ins are _____ keys.

   a) function
   b) numeric
   c) directional arrow
   d) cursor control
   e) special-purpose

55) The document the user reads data from in a data entry application
    is called the

   a) source document.
   b) original.
   c) data entry form.
   d) computer input.

56) Which of the following is not a plotter type?

   a) flatbed
   b) drum
   c) disk
   d) All the above are types of plotters.

57) A device that converts images on a page to electronic signals
    that can be stored in a computer:

   a) monitor
   b) scanner
   c) plotter
   d) MICR
   e) POS

58) Which of the following is not a type of terminal?

   a) dumb terminal
   b) smart terminal
   c) very smart terminal
   d) intelligent terminal

59) Which of the following is not considered a direct entry device?

   a) image scanner
   b) mouse
   c) digitizer
   d) keyboard

60) Which of the following is not a graphics monitor?

   a) XGA
   b) EGA
   c) LCD
   d) VGA

61) Which of the following devices directs the location of the cursor
    on the screen by rolling it about on the table top?

   a) digitizer
   b) mouse
   c) light pen
   d) image scanner

62) Which of the following is not a printer feature that is possible
    on a microcomputer system?

   a) bidirectional
   b) tractor feed
   c) type style
   d) shared use
   e) All the above are printer features.

63) Which of the following devices can be used to scan a photograph
    and convert it to digital data?

   a) mouse and bit-mapping device
   b) digitizer and light pen
   c) light pen and image scanner
   d) digitizer and image scanner
   e) All of the above can be used to scan a photograph.

64) The type of portable color panel that can display more colors,
    faster, and brighter:

   a) active-matrix
   b) passive-matrix
   c) monochrome
   d) CGA
   e) VGA

65) Which of the following devices is not generally found in a
    point-of-sale terminal?

   a) mouse
   b) keyboard
   c) screen
   d) printer

66) A bit-mapping device is also known as a(n)

a) mouse.
b) voice-input device.
c) digitizer.
d) image scanner.

67) Which of the following is a direct-entry device used with a
point-of-sale terminal?

a) bit-mapping device
b) digitizer
c) bar code reader
d) voice-input device

68) Which of the following is not a typical microcomputer display
type?

a) bit-mapping display
b) alphanumeric monitor
c) graphics monitor
d) flat-panel display

69) Which of the following terminal types can be used to input and
receive data, but not process it independently?

a) dumb terminal
b) smart terminal
c) intelligent terminal
d) all of the above

70) Which of the following best describes a smart terminal?

a) It can be used to input and receive data, but not process it
independently.
b) It has some memory, data editing capability, verification of
data can be performed on it.
c) It has a processing unit, primary and secondary storage, and
it can process data independently.
d) none of the above

71) Which of the following printer types is not commonly used with
microcomputers?

a) laser printers
b) ink-jet printers
c) daisy-wheel printers
d) chain printers

72) Which of the following printer types is the most popular for use
with a microcomputer?

a) ink jet
b) dot-matrix
c) laser
d) daisy-wheel

73) Which of the following is not generally considered a
letter-quality printer?

a) daisy-wheel
b) dot-matrix
c) laser
d) ink-jet

74) Which of the following printers is most generally the slowest
type of printer?

a) daisy-wheel
b) ink-jet
c) dot-matrix
d) laser

75) Which of the following printer types is most generally the
fastest type of printer?

a) daisy-wheel
b) ink-jet
c) dot-matrix
d) laser

76) Which of the following printer types has encouraged the
development of a new microcomputer industry called desktop
publishing?

a) daisy-wheel
b) ink-jet
c) dot-matrix
d) laser

77) Which of the following printer types would be best suited to
reproduce a color graph visible on the monitor?

a) daisy-wheel
b) ink-jet
c) dot-matrix
d) laser

78) Which of the following are not found on a typical microcomputer keyboard?

a) typewriter keys.
b) function keys.
c) numeric keys.
d) all are on a microcomputer keyboard

79) The printer that produces very high quality images using heat elements on heat-sensitive paper:

a) dot-matrix
b) laser
c) ink-jet
d) plotter
e) thermal

80) Which of the following is not another name for a microcomputer output device?

a) monitor
b) video display terminal (VDT)
c) cathode-ray output device (COD)
d) screen

81) Which of the following is not a flat-panel technology?

a) liquid-crystal display
b) video graphics array
c) electroluminescent
d) gas-plasma display
e) all the above are flat-panel technologies

82) Which of the following is not an ergonomic factor?

a) the positioning of the display with relation to the users eye level
b) reduction of glare on the screen
c) the study of well designed computer furniture with relation to the users application
d) the reduction of electromagnetic fields in computer monitors
e) all the above are ergonomic factors

83) What is the usual display size of an alphanumeric monitor?

a) 12 lines with 40 characters per line
b) 40 lines with 24 characters per line
c) 24 lines with 80 characters per line
d) 20 lines with 60 characters per line

84) Screen resolution is measured in terms of

a) rows and columns of characters.
b) dots.
c) pixels.
d) all of the above

85) Which of the following display types is most often used with portable computers?

a) flat-panel displays
b) flat tension mask displays
c) alphanumeric monitors
d) graphics monitors

86) The plotter that creates images using heat-sensitive paper and electrically heated pins:

a) pen
b) ink-jet
c) direct imaging
d) scanner
e) electrostatic

1) F		53) a	
2) T		54) e	
3) F		55) a	
4) T		56) c	
5) T		57) b	
6) T		58) c	
7) T		59) d	
8) T		60) c	
9) T		61) b	
10) T		62) e	
11) F		63) d	
12) T		64) a	
13) T		65) a	
14) T		66) d	
15) T		67) c	
16) T		68) a	
17) F		69) a	
18) F		70) b	
19) F		71) d	
20) F		72) b	
21) F		73) b	
22) F		74) a	
23) T		75) d	
24) T		76) d	
25) T		77) b	
26) T		78) d	
27) F		79) e	
28) T		80) c	
29) F		81) b	
30) T		82) e	
31) T		83) c	
32) F		84) c	
33) T		85) a	
34) F		86) c	
35) F			
36) T			
37) T			
38) F			
39) T			
40) T			
41) T			
42) F			
43) T			
44) T			
45) T			
46) T			
47) T			
48) T			
49) F			
50) T			
51) T			
52) T			

1) Magnetic tape is a direct access storage.

2) RAM is the internal temporary storage of the computer.

3) A floppy disk has high capacity and fast sequential access.

4) Secondary storage holds information within the CPU.

5) The primary advantages of optical disks over the other kinds of external storage are direct access and high capacity.

6) Floppy disks are also known as flexible disks and as floppies.

7) The two forms of tape storage are magnetic tape streamers and magnetic tape reels.

8) A track is the same as a sector.

9) External storage is volatile.

10) Secondary storage may be either within, or external to the system cabinet.

11) Data transfer time measures how long it takes to move data from the hard-disk track to memory.

12) Data is recorded on a disk in rings called tracks.

13) Internal hard disks have two advantages over floppy disks: capacity and speed.

14) The search operation occurs when the disk drive rotates the disk to the proper position.

15) Either a seek or a search operation is necessary to locate data on a disk.

16) Secondary storage is considered to be a nonvolatile form of storing data.

17) Laser beams are used to record data on optical disks.

18) A 3 1/2 inch floppy diskette is encased in a rigid plastic jacket.

19) To write to a disk means to obtain data from a diskette or hard disk.

20) Cross formatting occurs when a disk is formatted to a different capacity than the manufacturer's recommended capacity.

21) Cross formatting can cause problems when double-density disks are formatted at high density.

22) Most microcomputers require at least two floppy disk drives to be operational.

23) Most software programs are initially entered into the computer using a floppy disk drive.

24) Saving a new file onto a disk or hard disk will overwrite an existing file having the same name.

25) The program disk is generally inserted in drive B of a two-drive system.

26) Drive A is the left-hand or upper drive in a system unit cabinet of a microcomputer having two disk drives.

27) Data is stored in concentric circles called sectors on floppy disks.

28) A sector is a pie-wedge shaped section of a diskette used to organize data on a disk.

29) Soft-sectored disks must be formatted by the user.

30) If tracks and sectors are already in place when you purchase diskettes, they are soft-sectored floppy diskettes.

31) Formatting or initializing is required for both hard- and soft-sectored diskettes.

32) A 5 and 1/4-inch double-sided, double density diskettes may hold 360 K bytes of data.

33) The write-protect notch on a 3 1/2 inch diskette is covered with a sliding shutter to prevent accidental erasure of valuable data.

34) A 5 1/4 inch diskette has a sliding shutter to cover the write protect notch.

35) A 5 1/4 inch diskette is more durable than a 3 1/2 inch diskette.

36) A 5 1/4 inch diskette generally has more storage capacity than a 3 1/2 inch diskette.

37) Disk caching improves hard-disk performance.

38) Retrieving data and programs is much faster with tape than it is with disks.

39) If a microcomputer is already equipped with two diskette drives and additional hard disk storage is desired, it must always be in a device external to the system cabinet.

40) Write-once optical disk drives can be written on only by the manufacturer.

41) Data is recorded on optical disks using lasers.

42) Data is recorded on hard-disk cartridges using lasers.

43) Disk storage is a direct access storage.

44) Some or all of the data on a hard disk may be lost when a head crash occurs.

45) A tape streamer is used to backup diskettes onto itself.

46) Tape storage is sequential access storage.

47) The storage capacity of tape backup units is

   a) 360 KB.
   b) 1 MB.
   c) from 10 to 60 MB.
   d) from 500 to 1,000 MB.

48) Which of the following is not a type of secondary storage?

   a) diskette
   b) hard disk
   c) CD-RAM
   d) optical disk
   e) magnetic tape

49) Which of the following is exclusively a sequential access storage media?

   a) floppy disk
   b) hard disk
   c) magnetic tape
   d) CD-ROM
   e) WORM

50) Finding the correct part of the disk from which to read data is called

   a) a read/write operation.
   b) seek and then search operation.
   c) search then seek operation
   d) head positioning.

51) Which of the following is not considered external storage for microcomputers?

   a) memory
   b) diskette
   c) hard disk
   d) magnetic tape

52) _____ improves disk performance by reducing the amount of space required to store data and programs.

   a) Data compression
   b) RAIDS
   c) CD-ROM
   d) WORM

53) Seek time is

   a) the speed which the access arm gets into position over a track.
   b) the time it takes for the read-write head to activate.
   c) the time it takes the disk to rotate into position.
   d) the time it takes for data to transfer.

54) Which of the following means obtaining data from disk?

   a) reading
   b) writing
   c) searching
   d) seeking

55) RAIDS

   a) improves performance by expanding external storage.
   b) uses groups of inexpensive disks.
   c) out performs a single disk.
   d) All of the above is true of RAIDS

56) Data are recorded on diskette in

a) spiral grooves.
b) concentric circles on a smooth surface.
c) concentric circles on a grooved surface.
d) either concentric circles or spirals on a smooth surface.

57) How are data organized on a diskette?

a) in tracks
b) in sectors
c) in both tracks and sectors
d) in pie wedges

58) What is the purpose of formatting a diskette?

a) tell the computer if it is soft- or hard-sectored
b) set up tracks and sectors on a soft-sectored diskette
c) set up tracks and sectors on a hard-sectored diskette
d) none of the above

59) If a box of diskettes is labeled 2S/2D, it means

a) the disks are soft-sectored, with two in a box.
b) 3 1/2 inch, two sided disks.
c) double sided, double density disks.
d) not enough information is given

60) A typical double-sided, double density 5 1/4 inch diskette can hold

a) 80 KB.
b) 160 KB.
c) over 360 KB.
d) over 1 MB.

61) Which of the following has the largest storage capacity?

a) a 5 1/4 inch, high-capacity diskette
b) a 5 1/4 inch, double-density diskette
c) a 3 1/2 inch diskette
d) a hard disk

62) A head crash occurs

a) when the disk is unable to rotate.
b) frequently with floppy disks.
c) with magnetic tape.
d) when the read-write head contacts the disk surface or particles on the disk.

63) Which of the following is likely to cause damage to a 5 1/4 inch
diskette?

a) writing on the label with a ballpoint pen
b) touching the disk through an opening in the jacket
c) leaving it in the car trunk in the summer
d) leaving it on top of the monitor
e) all the above

64) On a floppy-disk drive, data signals are transferred to the
computer through:

a) read-write heads.
b) access arms.
c) drive gate.
d) drive A.
e) sectors

65) A hardcard is

a) an external disk.
b) a 3 1/2 inch diskette.
c) a circuit board with a disk that plugs into an expansion slot
   in the computer.
d) none of the above

66) Which of the following are examples of mass storage?

a) floppies and hard disks
b) hard disks and hardcards
c) hard-disk cartridges and optical disks
d) optical disks and hardcards

67) Which of the following devices uses a laser beam to burn data
into the surface of an aluminum disk?

a) optical disk
b) hard-disk cartridge
c) hardcards
d) 3 1/2 inch flexible disks

68) Which of the following devices would have the largest storage
capacity?

a) hard disk
b) memory
c) hardcard
d) optical disk

69) Which of the following storage devices allows the user to write their own data, but not erase it?

a) WORM devices
b) hard disks
c) hardcards
d) CD-ROM

70) The hard-disk type that has several platters aligned one above the other:

a) internal hard disk
b) hard-disk pack
c) floppy-disk array
d) hard-disk cartridge
e) disk cache

71) The method of improving hard-disk performance by anticipating data needs is:

a) disk compression
b) disk caching
c) disk decompression
d) RAIDS
e) virtual processing

1) T		53) a	
2) T		54) a	
3) F		55) d	
4) F		56) b	
5) T		57) c	
6) T		58) b	
7) T		59) c	
8) F		60) c	
9) F		61) d	
10) T		62) d	
11) T		63) e	
12) T		64) a	
13) T		65) c	
14) T		66) c	
15) F		67) a	
16) T		68) d	
17) T		69) a	
18) T		70) b	
19) F		71) b	
20) T			
21) T			
22) F			
23) T			
24) T			
25) F			
26) T			
27) F			
28) T			
29) T			
30) F			
31) F			
32) T			
33) T			
34) F			
35) F			
36) F			
37) T			
38) F			
39) F			
40) F			
41) T			
42) F			
43) T			
44) T			
45) F			
46) T			
47) c			
48) c			
49) c			
50) b			
51) a			
52) a			

1) Half-duplex is the fastest and most efficient form of communication.

2) A local area network connects two or more computers within a limited area, such as within the same building.

3) All long-distance communication requires the use of modems.

4) A front-end processor is used to process a database in a large mainframe network.

5) Wide area networks are countrywide and worldwide networks that connect users over long distances.

6) Full-duplex communication requires special equipment.

7) Downloading is the process of transferring information from a microcomputer to a mainframe.

8) CompuServ and Prodigy are two well-known protocols.

9) Because microwaves travel in straight lines through the air and cannot bend with the curvature of the Earth, they can transmit data only over short distances (by themselves).

10) Electronic mail may be used internally within a company, or between companies.

11) Fiber-optic cables transmit more slowly than copper cable.

12) A cable is required to directly connect all computers for data communications.

13) Transferring data from your microcomputer to a minicomputer or mainframe is called uploading.

14) In a client/server, each node on the network has equal responsibility for coordinating the network's activities.

15) Data in a simplex transmission travels in only one direction.

16) A standalone computer is not connected to a network.

17) A direct-connect modem requires a telephone receiver.

18) Telephone lines are typically made of coaxial cable.

19) Coaxial cable is often used for transoceanic communications.

20) An external modem is connected by a cable to a serial port.

21) All communications in a ring network pass through a central host unit.

22) A bus network has no host computer.

23) A ring network is the least frequently used of the network types.

24) Microwave transmission consists of low-frequency radio waves travelling through the air.

25) The telephone usually requires an analog signal, while the computer requires a digital signal.

26) Local area networks frequently use a bus form of organization.

27) Local area networks frequently use a bus form of organization.

28) Polling is used to control communications in a star network.

29) A star network does not have a central host.

30) Local area networks allow many users to share microcomputer peripherals.

31) Local area networks generally connect two or more mainframe computers.

32) In half-duplex communication, data flows in both directions at the same time.

33) A peer-to-peer system typically has several users who equally share the responsibility of coordinating the activities on a network.

34) Serial transmission uses an asynchronous communication port.

35) In full-duplex communication, data is transmitted back and forth at the same time on the line.

36) A protocol defines the set of rules each device must follow to allow data communications.

37) Voice messaging systems are computer systems linked to telephones that convert the human voice into digital bits.

38) Access to an electronic mailbox usually requires a password.

39) A microcomputer can be used to shop for appliances and many other products.

40) In synchronous transmission, data is sent and received one byte at a time.

41) Asynchronous transmission requires a synchronized clock in both the sending and receiving device.

42) Synchronous transmission is faster than asynchronous data communications.

43) Three types of networks include LAN, MAN and WAN.

44) The hierarchical network is also known as a hybrid network.

45) Most telephone traffic is in the form of parallel data transmission.

46) Each bit in a character flows through a separate line simultaneously in parallel data transmission.

47) Transmission between the CPU and a printer is generally serial.

48) Frequently, computer communications over telephone lines require a modem.

49) Connectivity puts the power of a mainframe on an end-user's desk.

50) Which of the following devices are not required to gain access to an electronic bulletin board?

   a) microcomputer
   b) printer
   c) telephone connection
   d) modem

51) Transferring data from a larger computer to your microcomputer is called:

   a) a LAN.
   b) time-sharing.
   c) downloading.
   d) networking.
   e) uploading.

52) Which of the following is provided by many commercial services?

a) home banking
b) stock trading
c) teleshopping
d) All of the above are offered by commercial services.

53) A special sequence of numbers or letters that limits access to electronic mail boxes is a:

a) combination.
b) code.
c) fax.
d) password.
e) modem.

54) Which of the following channels is not typically need for data communications?

a) telephone lines
b) coaxial cable
c) fiber-optic cable
d) all are used in data communications

55) Which type of channel uses tubes of glass to transmit messages?

a) coaxial cable
b) twisted pair telephone cable
c) fiber optic cable
d) microwave

56) What communications channel transfers data as pulses of light?

a) telephone lines
b) coaxial cable
c) fiber-optic cable
d) microwave
e) satellite

57) Which of the following communications channels transmits through the air?

a) fiber-optic
b) microwave
c) coaxial
d) none of the above

58) Which of the following is not an advantage of fiber-optic cable over coaxial cable?

a) It is more reliable at transmitting data.
b) It is faster than copper cable.
c) It is immune to electronic interference.
d) All are advantages of fiber-optic over coaxial cable.

59) Which of the following communications channels uses high-frequency radio waves to transmit data through the air?

a) coaxial cable
b) microwave
c) fiber-optic cable
d) telephone wire

60) ISDN

a) is concerned with international-exchange standards for telephones.
b) will make the telephone system completely digital.
c) will replace modems with terminal adapters.
d) allows data, fax, voice, and video to transmit at one time.
e) All the above are true of ISDN.

61) A modem is a device that

a) is attached to the microcomputer to speed up data communications.
b) is required only for voice communication.
c) transmits data between a microwave tower and a satellite.
d) converts data from digital to analog, or analog to digital.

62) Which of the following is not a typical microcomputer data transmission speed?

a) 700 baud
b) 1200 baud
c) 2400 baud
d) 9600 baud

63) Which of the following communications channels do not require modems?

a) microwave and satellites
b) coaxial and fiber-optic cables
c) telephone lines
d) All of the above require modems.

64) A specialized computer used to manage communications in complex computer systems is

a) a front-end processor.
b) a modem equalizer.
c) a modem/line distributor.
d) an internal modem.

65) In a star network, the central computer asks each connecting device whether it has a message to send in a process known as

a) requesting.
b) polling.
c) dispatching.
d) servicing.

66) Which of the following network types uses polling to control communications traffic?

a) star network
b) ring network
c) bus network
d) All of the above use polling.

67) Downsized applications means

a) computers are getting smaller.
b) mainframe applications are now available for the microcomputer.
c) sophisticated software features are removed for ease of use.
d) Answers a and c above are both true of downsizing.

68) The era of the portable office means

a) a portable computer could be linked to a network.
b) sophisticated programs can run on microcomputers.
c) a fax machine could be hooked to a network.
d) people can operate efficiently while traveling.
e) All the above are true of the portable office concept.

69) Supernet

a) is a project to build a national data highway.
b) is a computer system designed to track illegal drugs.
c) is a project to connect all police forces to a central point.
d) allows users to make long distance calls more cheaply.

70) Which of the following allows users to leave messages on the computer for access by another user?

   a) electronic mail
   b) teleshopping
   c) travel reservations
   d) All of the above permit messaging.

71) Which of the following is a system linked to telephones that convert the human voice into digital bits?

   a) electronic mail
   b) voice-messaging
   c) electronic bulletin board
   d) fax

72) Which of the following networks has a central computer?

   a) ring
   b) star
   c) bus
   d) All of the above have a central computer.

73) Bits flow in a continuous stream when using any of the following except

   a) an RS-232C connector.
   b) an asynchronous communications port.
   c) a parallel port.
   d) a serial port.

74) Rules for exchanging data on a network:

   a) protocol
   b) asynchronous transmission
   c) configuration
   d) channel
   e) serial transmission

75) Which of the following modes of data flow would not be suitable for communications with an electronic bulletin board?

   a) full-duplex
   b) half-duplex
   c) simplex
   d) all are suitable

76) Which of the following modes of transmission is most likely to be used for microcomputer communications?

a) simplex
b) half-duplex
c) full-duplex
d) All are equally popular for microcomputer communications.

77) Which of the following is the fastest method of two-way communications?

a) simplex
b) half-duplex
c) full-duplex
d) triplex

78) The rules governing the exchange of information in a data communications environment are called the

a) protocol.
b) communications hierarchy.
c) serial/parallel conventions.
d) none of the above

79) Networks where all the devices are within one building are known as

a) wide area networks.
b) campus gateways.
c) local area networks.
d) building communications networks

80) The purpose of a network gateway is

a) to link two wide area networks.
b) to link a microwave and satellite network together.
c) to allow a microcomputer to access a computer bulletin board.
d) to link two LANs or a LAN and a wide area network.

81) New developments in hardware suggest

a) more computers will be networked.
b) that there will be fewer standalone computers.
c) the era of the portable office will be a reality.
d) downsizing of applications is now possible.
e) All of the above are true of new technological developments.

82) A system frequently used in decentralized organizations in which computing power is located and shared at different sites:

   a) client/server
   b) ring
   c) centralized
   d) mainframe
   e) distributed

1)	F	53)	d
2)	T	54)	d
3)	F	55)	c
4)	F	56)	c
5)	T	57)	b
6)	T	58)	d
7)	F	59)	b
8)	F	60)	e
9)	T	61)	d
10)	T	62)	a
11)	F	63)	b
12)	F	64)	a
13)	T	65)	b
14)	T	66)	a
15)	T	67)	b
16)	T	68)	e
17)	F	69)	a
18)	F	70)	a
19)	T	71)	b
20)	T	72)	b
21)	F	73)	c
22)	T	74)	a
23)	T	75)	c
24)	F	76)	c
25)	T	77)	c
26)	T	78)	a
27)	T	79)	c
28)	T	80)	d
29)	F	81)	e
30)	T	82)	e
31)	F		
32)	F		
33)	T		
34)	T		
35)	T		
36)	T		
37)	T		
38)	F		
39)	T		
40)	F		
41)	F		
42)	T		
43)	T		
44)	T		
45)	F		
46)	T		
47)	F		
48)	T		
49)	T		
50)	b		
51)	c		
52)	d		

1) A corporate database is usually stored on a mainframe computer.

2) An organization's database must be located on a single computer system.

3) CompuServe is a good example of a distributed database.

4) A record is a collection of related files.

5) A record in a file is uniquely identified by a key field.

6) A microcomputer database is the same as an individual database.

7) Purchases made by a department store credit card customer posted to a statement once a month is an example of batch processing.

8) Microcomputers may be used to prepare the input for batch processing on mainframes.

9) Sequential files must be identified using a key field.

10) A database consists of logically related files and records.

11) The most flexible data organization is the relational database.

12) Consistency of data throughout an organization's database is an example of data integrity.

13) Processing rights are typically determined by the database administrator to specify which people have access to what kind of data.

14) A data dictionary describes the structure of the data in a database.

15) In direct file organization, the computer uses the record's key to go directly to the record being sought.

16) Indexed sequential file organization requires the use of magnetic tape.

17) A database is a collection of integrated data.

18) Indexed file organization is good both for locating specific records and for updating all or a large part of an entire file.

19) Data redundancy is one problem of data management that is not solved by using a database.

20) Data integrity is generally not a problem in database systems.

21) Database management software is made up of a flowchart and a query language.

22) A distributed database has data located in more than one location.

23) Company databases are of two types, common operational databases and common user databases.

24) Reserving a specific seat on a departing flight is an example of real-time processing.

25) The key uniquely identifies each record.

26) A column entry in a relational database is called an attribute, and resembles a field.

27) It is difficult to add, delete or modify data when using a relational database.

28) A corporate database is usually controlled by computer professionals.

29) Large organizations employ database administrators to help determine database structures and evaluate database performance are countrywide and worldwide networks that connect users over long distances.

30) In batch processing, data is processed at the same time the transaction occurs.

31) Relational databases are more flexible and easier to use than hierarchical and network databases.

32) Microcomputers cannot perform in real-time processing applications.

33) Direct file organization requires the computer to check every record's key field beginning with the first record in the file until it finds the desired information.

34) Sequential files are stored in ascending or descending order based on a key field.

35) In direct file organization, the computer does not sort records in sequential order.

36) When the direct file organization method is used, data may be stored on disk or tape.

37) Computer viruses are hidden instructions that attach themselves to network programs, operating systems, and databases.

38) The database structure most frequently used for microcomputers is the hierarchical database.

39) Batch processing is done when data is grouped together and processed right away.

40) Data may be structured in two forms, files or database.

41) In a hierarchical database, fields and records are structured in nodes (points connected like tree branches).

42) A temporary holding file that accumulates a patient's hospital expenses during his/her stay is called a master file.

43) Each entry has one parent node in a hierarchical database.

44) A zip code would be a good key field for a customer file.

45) A pointer is a connection between the rows and columns in a relational database.

46) Proprietary database are accessible by individuals who have a microcomputer and modem and pay a fee.

47) Index sequential file organization is a compromise between sequential and direct file organizations.

48) A database administrator determines who has access to an individual database.

49) The transaction file contains recent changes to records that will be used to update a master file.

50) A query language is an easy-to-use language understandable to most users of the database.

51) Security is concerned with protecting information, hardware, and software from unauthorized use, damage from intrusions, sabotage, and natural disasters such as fires or hurricanes.

52) Security is the right to keep personal information such as credit ratings and medical histories from being accessed by unauthorized people.

53) The data dictionary defines the field names, lengths and characteristics (alphabetical, numeric, or alphanumeric) of data in the database.

54) Real-time processing occurs when data is processed at the same time the transaction occurs.

55) In a hierarchical database, a child node cannot be added without first adding a parent node.

56) In a hierarchical database, if a parent node is deleted, so are all the subordinate child nodes.

57) Which of the following contains a description of the structure of the data used in a database management system?

a) data flow diagram
b) data dictionary
c) system flowchart
d) query language

58) Which of the following is not a database management system organization?

a) indexed-sequential
b) relational
c) network
d) hierarchical

59) Which of the following database structures does not have parent/child relationships among nodes?

a) relational
b) hierarchical
c) network
d) All of the above have parent/child relationships.

60) In which database structure may a node be reached through more than one path?

a) indexed-sequential
b) relational
c) hierarchical
d) network

61) The most flexible database organization is

a) relational.
b) hierarchical.
c) direct.
d) network.

62) A column in a relational database is known as a(n)

    a) relation.
    b) attribute.
    c) record.
    d) field.

63) A row in a relational database is known as a(n)

    a) attribute.
    b) record.
    c) relation.
    d) field.

64) A collection of related fields:

    a) bytes
    b) words
    c) characters
    d) record
    e) file

65) All of the following are database types except

    a) sole proprietor.
    b) individual.
    c) company.
    d) distributed.

66) Each of the following is a proprietary database except

    a) Dow Jones News/Retrieval.
    b) CompuServe.
    c) Hypertext.
    d) Mead Data Central.

67) Which of the following is probably not the responsibility of a
database administrator?

    a) setting up an individual database
    b) determining processing rights for shared databases
    c) determining the structure of large databases
    d) evaluating company database performance statistics

68) Which of the following is a temporary holding file that contains recent changes to records?

a) key file
b) transaction file
c) master file
d) change file

69) Which of the following is the unique identifier chosen to identify a record?

a) key field
b) index field
c) record name
d) disk address

70) Which file organization method would be best if the data is to be used for both batch and real-time processing?

a) direct
b) sequential
c) indexed-sequential
d) All are equally well suited for batch and real-time processing.

71) Which of the following types of files would be stored on magnetic tape?

a) sequential
b) direct
c) index-sequential
d) none of the above

72) Which of the following would not be directly associated with the updating process of data?

a) transaction file
b) hierarchical database
c) master file
d) none of the above

73) Which of the following is not an advantage of sequential files?

a) must be ordered in a specified way and searched one at a time
b) useful when all or a large part of the records in a file needs to be accessed
c) can use a less expensive storage medium than disk
d) All the above are advantages of sequential files.

74) Which of the following is the best example of a batch processing system?

a) an automated teller machine
b) monthly invoicing to customers
c) an airline reservation system
d) None of the above would use batch processing.

75) Which of the following is the best example of a real-time processing system?

a) printing monthly statements for credit card customers
b) processing payroll and producing paychecks
c) telephone company directory assistance
d) All the above are real-time processing applications.

76) Which of the following is not a type of file organization?

a) direct
b) indexed sequential
c) sequential
d) non-sequential

77) Which of the following file organizations must be stored on magnetic disk?

a) non-sequential
b) indexed sequential
c) sequential
d) direct
e) both b and d

78) Which of the following organization methods use a record key to locate the record being sought?

a) sequential
b) direct
c) indexed sequential
d) All of the above use a record key.

79) The type of database that is sometimes called an information utility or a data bank:

a) individual
b) common operational
c) common user
d) distributed
e) proprietary

80) The database organization in which fields and records are structures in nodes with each child node having only one parent.

a) hierarchical
b) network
c) proprietary
d) relational
e) individual

81) Hidden instructions that "migrate" through networks and operating systems:

a) file servers
b) viruses
c) nodes
d) relation
e) pointer

1) T		53) T	
2) F		54) T	
3) F		55) T	
4) F		56) T	
5) T		57) b	
6) T		58) a	
7) T		59) a	
8) T		60) d	
9) T		61) a	
10) T		62) d	
11) T		63) b	
12) T		64) d	
13) T		65) a	
14) T		66) c	
15) T		67) a	
16) F		68) b	
17) T		69) a	
18) T		70) c	
19) F		71) a	
20) T		72) b	
21) F		73) a	
22) T		74) b	
23) T		75) c	
24) T		76) d	
25) T		77) e	
26) T		78) d	
27) F		79) e	
28) T		80) a	
29) T		81) b	
30) F			
31) T			
32) F			
33) F			
34) T			
35) T			
36) F			
37) T			
38) F			
39) F			
40) T			
41) T			
42) F			
43) T			
44) F			
45) F			
46) T			
47) T			
48) F			
49) T			
50) T			
51) T			
52) F			

1) Moving applications from microcomputers to minicomputers and mainframes is called downsizing.

2) Executive information systems are specially designed, simplified systems for top-level executives.

3) Middle management utilize periodic reports more often than upper- and lower-level management.

4) The opposite of a periodic report is a demand report that is produced on request of management.

5) A DSS helps decision makers analyze unanticipated situations.

6) A transaction processing system is the same as a data processing system.

7) Information needs are different for each level of management.

8) The four parts of a decision support system are the programmer, system software, data and decision models.

9) A decision support system is interactive between the user and the computer system.

10) Management information systems record daily transactions.

11) The term supermicro suggests a class of computers with larger memory (measured in megabytes), increased processing speed, and the handling of more powerful programs with greater amounts of data.

12) An organization is structured by two aspects: functional areas (departments or divisions) and management levels.

13) The flow of information in an organization is different at each level of management.

14) Standardized reports are produced be data processing and decision support systems.

15) Services of a computer professional are usually required for a decision support system.

16) Decision support systems summarize the detailed data of the transaction processing system in standard reports.

17) Transaction processing systems record day-to-day activities such as customer orders and inventory levels.

18) CEO stands for chief executive officer.

19) Top-level managers are concerned with long-range planning.

20) An information system is a collection of hardware, software, people, procedures, and data.

21) The production department takes in raw materials and puts people to work to turn out finished goods (or services).

22) The research department relates new discoveries and does product development.

23) In smaller organizations such titles as vice president of marketing and director of human resources are often combined.

24) A sales order processing system is an example of a data processing system.

25) A data processing system requires a database management system.

26) Tactical planning is usually the responsibility of lower management.

27) Summarized information is most often used by lower- and middle-level management.

28) Data processing systems record routine and daily transactions.

29) An executive support system is the same as an executive information system.

30) Forecasting future events is a responsibility of top-level management.

31) Microcomputers may be connected to a mainframe database using a local area network.

32) Marketing is an example of a function within an organization.

33) Lower management would be responsible for supervising bank tellers.

34) An MIS will generally draw data from several departments.

35) Periodic reports are typically produced only on request.

36) Electronic spreadsheets are often used for predictive reports.

37) Middle management implements the long-term goals of an organization.

38) Lower-level managers are most likely to need information from outside the organization.

39) Detailed transaction information is most needed by lower-level managers.

40) Data processing systems usually combine both internal and external information in summarized form.

41) Data processing systems record the day-to-day transactions of an organization.

42) Management information systems produce structured, summarized reports.

43) Each functional area of a company generally has a data processing system.

44) Strategic planning is usually the responsibility of middle management.

45) Microcomputers can be used to help make decisions.

46) Older microcomputers are limited by their processing capacity and speeds.

47) One limitation of microcomputers is that they do not have the capability to access data stored in databases on mainframe computers.

48) Accounting transactions in large organizations are generally handled on microcomputers.

49) A management information system requires a database management system.

50) Management information systems are used to help management deal with unanticipated questions.

51) Interactive terminals and software are generally required for decision support systems.

52) A decision support system generally provides both internal and external information useful to management.

53) Depending on the services or products they provide, most organizations have departments that perform the five basic functions of accounting, production, marketing, personnel and research.

54) All of the following are examples of periodic reports except

   a) a monthly report showing sales by district.
   b) a yearly income statement for the organization.
   c) a report showing products having lower-than-average profit margins.
   d) All of the above are periodic reports.

55) Which of the following report types call attention to unusual events?

   a) scheduled reports
   b) predictive reports
   c) exception reports
   d) demand reports

56) Which of the following is the opposite of a scheduled report?

   a) periodic report
   b) exception report
   c) predictive report
   d) demand report

57) All of the following would be activities of a lower-level manager except

   a) operational matters.
   b) supervising assembly line workers.
   c) tactical planning.
   d) monitoring day-to-day events.

58) The computer-based information system that provides a flexible tool for analysis:

   a) database management system
   b) transaction processing system
   c) management information system
   d) executive information system
   e) decision support system

59) This department finds and hires people and handles such matters as sick leave and retirement benefits:

   a) accounting
   b) production
   c) marketing
   d) human resources
   e) research

60) The key technology advance supporting downsizing that describes the importance of microcomputers replacing terminals:

   a) faster processing
   b) easier access to large databases
   c) more secondary storage
   d) more memory
   e) executive information systems

61) Which management level would be most likely to oversee inventory control activities?

   a) lower-level
   b) middle
   c) top
   d) executive

62) The level of managers whose information is primarily vertical:

   a) supervisors
   b) top management
   c) middle management
   d) executive
   e) vice presidents

63) The level of manager who deals with control and planning:

   a) executive
   b) top management
   c) middle management
   d) supervisors
   e) vice presidents

64) Which of the following levels of management supervises the employees or workers?

   a) lower-level management
   b) middle management
   c) top-level management
   d) executive management

65) Middle-level management is responsible for

   a) operational control.
   b) tactical planning.
   c) strategic planning.
   d) All of the above are responsibilities of middle-level
      management.

66) Which management level is responsible for implementing the
   long-term goals of the organization?

   a) lower management
   b) middle management
   c) top management
   d) All levels of management are responsible for implementation of
      long-term goals.

67) Which level of management is most concerned with long-range
   planning?

   a) lower-level
   b) middle-level
   c) top-level
   d) first-line

68) Summarized information is most useful to

   a) top-level management.
   b) middle-level management.
   c) both a and b
   d) none of the above

69) Detailed, day-to-day transaction information is most useful to

   a) lower-level management.
   b) middle-level management.
   c) top-level management.
   d) all the above

70) Which of the following records the day-to-day transactions of an
   operation?

   a) management information system
   b) data processing system
   c) decision support system
   d) management support system

71) Which of the following systems produces standardized reports of summarized, structured information?

a) data processing system
b) decision support system
c) management information system
d) All of the above produce standardized reports.

72) Which of the following produces flexible, on-demand reports based on information drawn from both inside and outside the organization?

a) management information system
b) data processing system
c) demand processing system
d) decision support system

73) Which of the following systems can be called a transaction processing system?

a) data processing system
b) decision support system
c) management information system
d) management support system

74) All of the following are part of a typical accounting system except

a) inventory control.
b) sales order processing.
c) payroll.
d) All of the above are typical of accounting systems.

75) Which of the following show what money has been received from or is owed by customers?

a) accounts payable
b) accounts receivable
c) sales order processing
d) general ledger

76) Top management is most likely to be involved in which of the following activities?

a) strategic planning
b) tactical planning
c) operational control
d) monitoring day-to-day events

77) Information from outside the organization is most likely a requirement of

a) lower-level management.
b) middle-level management.
c) top-level management.
d) All levels require outside information equally.

78) Income statements and balance sheets are produced by which accounting system?

a) payroll
b) sales order processing
c) accounts payable
d) general ledger

79) Which of the following is not a category of report produced by a management information system?

a) scheduled
b) repetitive
c) predictive
d) exception

80) Which of the following is most likely to require interactive terminals and software?

a) data processing system
b) decision support system
c) management information system
d) both a and c above

81) Which type of information system would be most likely to use statistical packages, simulations and other models?

a) data processing system
b) decision support system
c) management information system
d) All the above use these models

82) Which of the following is most likely to use data from external sources?

a) data processing system
b) database management system
c) management information system
d) decision support system

83) Which of the following is not a function within an organization?

    a) middle management
    b) marketing
    c) accounting
    d) personnel

1)	F		53)	T
2)	T		54)	c
3)	T		55)	c
4)	T		56)	d
5)	T		57)	c
6)	T		58)	e
7)	T		59)	d
8)	F		60)	b
9)	T		61)	a
10)	F		62)	a
11)	T		63)	c
12)	T		64)	a
13)	T		65)	b
14)	F		66)	b
15)	F		67)	c
16)	F		68)	c
17)	T		69)	a
18)	T		70)	b
19)	T		71)	a
20)	T		72)	d
21)	T		73)	a
22)	T		74)	d
23)	T		75)	b
24)	T		76)	a
25)	F		77)	c
26)	F		78)	d
27)	F		79)	b
28)	T		80)	b
29)	T		81)	b
30)	T		82)	d
31)	T		83)	a
32)	T			
33)	T			
34)	T			
35)	F			
36)	T			
37)	T			
38)	F			
39)	T			
40)	F			
41)	T			
42)	T			
43)	T			
44)	F			
45)	T			
46)	T			
47)	F			
48)	F			
49)	T			
50)	F			
51)	T			
52)	T			

1) RAD can shorten the development time in the systems life cycle.

2) CASE development software may be part of rapid applications development.

3) The phased approach of systems conversion is usually the most expensive but least risky methods of implementing a new system.

4) Training people and making them aware of the advantages of the new system is very critical to the success of the new system.

5) People may be considered part of an information system.

6) The last phase of the systems life cycle is systems maintenance.

7) A prototype is a model of a system.

8) In pilot conversion, one part of the organization initially tries out the new system.

9) Defining the problem is a task in Phase 2, design.

10) Once the new system is operational, a system audit is performed to compare the original design specifications with the actual system.

11) Software is either purchased or developed in the implementation phase.

12) Data flow diagrams trace data from its origination through processing, storage, and output.

13) In large organizations, the person who uses the systems life cycle the most is called a database administrator.

14) Systems implementation includes the acquisition of new hardware.

15) Required inputs, processes, and outputs are shown with HIPO charts during systems analysis.

16) A system may be technically but not economically feasible.

17) Designing alternative systems and selecting the best one are done during the systems development phase of the life cycle.

18) Requirements of the new information system are specified in the systems design phase.

19) Testing the new system is usually done during the development phase of the systems life cycle.

20) Systems analysis is concerned with gathering data, analyzing the data, and completed with summarizing documentation.

21) Automation and functional feasibility are two tasks handled during the design phase of the systems life cycle.

22) A systems design report describes alternative designs and makes recommendations for higher management.

23) Defining the problem, suggesting alternative systems, and preparing a short report are all parts of preliminary investigation.

24) Systems analysis and design is a way to reduce the chance of creating an ineffective information system.

25) The six phase problem-solving procedure for systems analysis and design is the systems analysis and design.

26) Systems analysis is the first step in the system life cycle.

27) Conversion and systems development mean the same thing.

28) Parallel conversion is when old and new systems are operated side be side until the new one is deemed reliable.

29) The direct approach to conversion is the riskiest.

30) Information needs of an organization are identified during the preliminary investigation.

31) Most information systems projects are requested by a systems analyst.

32) Top-down analysis methodology is a tool used during the preliminary investigation.

33) A decision table can show the decision rules that apply in the completion of a task for an organization.

34) Problem definition is done by a systems analyst when a large project is being requested.

35) The preliminary investigation phase of a proposed project should involve end users.

36) A company's organization chart may be useful during the data gathering phase of systems analysis.

37) System flowcharts and program flowcharts generally depict the same thing.

38) Determining if the benefits of a new system will justify the costs is a task handled during the design phase of the systems life cycle.

39) The relationship between input and output documents can be shown with a grid chart.

40) The modules of a computer program can be shown with a decision table.

41) Purchasing off-the-shelf packaged software circumvents the need for systems analysis.

42) System testing may take from days to months depending on the complexity of the system.

43) Prototyping is generally considered less risky than the traditional method of system analysis and design.

44) New hardware and software are acquired, developed, and tested during the systems development phase of the systems life cycle.

45) A new or alternative information system is designed during the systems analysis phase of the systems life cycle.

46) The present information system is studied in depth during the systems design phase of the systems life cycle.

47) Systems maintenance is an ongoing phase that involves the evaluation and updating of the system periodically.

48) The systems analyst is concerned with a brief definition of the problem, suggesting an alternative solution and preparing a short report during the preliminary investigation.

49) Data is gathered from observations and interviews during the analysis phase of the systems life cycle.

50) Custom design software specifically created to meet the needs of the organization is generally the most economical approach of software selection.

51) External factors, such as a change in government regulations, may cause an organization to change its information system.

52) Which of the following is the first phase of the systems life cycle?

    a) systems analysis
    b) preliminary investigation
    c) systems maintenance
    d) systems development

53) Which of the following shows the phases of the systems life cycle in the correct order?

    a) preliminary investigation, systems maintenance, systems
       analysis, systems implementation, systems development,
    systems design
    b) systems maintenance, preliminary investigation, systems
       analysis, systems implementation, systems design,
    systems development
    c) preliminary investigation, systems analysis, systems design,
       systems development, systems implementation,
    systems maintenance
    d) systems design, systems analysis, systems development, systems
       maintenance, systems implementation,
    preliminary investigation

54) During which phase of the systems life cycle is the new software installed for productive use?

    a) systems analysis
    b) preliminary investigation
    c) systems implementation
    d) systems development

55) Which of the following is the last phase of the systems life cycle?

    a) systems analysis
    b) systems maintenance
    c) systems implementation
    d) systems development

56) Who is most likely to request a new information system?

    a) programmer
    b) end user manager
    c) systems analyst
    d) data processing manager

57) During which phase is the problem definition done?

a) systems analysis
b) preliminary investigation
c) systems implementation
d) systems development

58) Which of the following is not a part of the systems analysis phase?

a) creating data flow diagrams and system flowcharts
b) gathering detailed data about how the current system works
c) using an organization chart to understand the functions and levels of management
d) creating program flowcharts

59) Which of the following shows the relationship between input and output documents?

a) grid charts
b) system flowcharts
c) data flow diagrams
d) All of the above relates inputs and outputs.

60) An overview chart showing the inputs, processes, and outputs of a particular module of a system is typical of which of the following systems analysis tools?

a) grid charts
b) system flowcharts
c) data flow diagrams
d) HIPO charts

61) Which of the following is not part of the definition of system feasibility to be determined during the design phase?

a) operation feasibility
b) technical feasibility
c) economic feasibility
d) All the above are reviewed during the design phase.

62) Which of the following is not accomplished during systems development?

a) developing software
b) hardware acquisition
c) selecting the best hardware system
d) software testing and debugging

63) Conversion is another word for

   a) system development.
   b) hardware installation.
   c) software installation.
   d) system implementation.

64) The riskiest method of implementation is probably

   a) the direct approach.
   b) the pilot approach.
   c) parallel conversion.
   d) the phased approach.

65) The parallel approach to systems implementation is characterized by

   a) old and new systems operating side by side until the new one is deemed reliable.
   b) abandoning the old system and starting up the new one simultaneously.
   c) the greatest risk of any method.
   d) gradual implementation.

66) In which approach is the new system implemented in one part of the organization prior to general implementation?

   a) the direct approach
   b) the pilot approach
   c) parallel conversion
   d) the phased approach

67) Prototyping

   a) may involve greater risk than systems analysis and design.
   b) involves building a model users can try before the actual system is installed.
   c) is generally faster than systems analysis and design.
   d) All the above are true of prototyping.

68) System testing is generally done during which phase of the systems life cycle?

   a) systems design
   b) systems implementation
   c) systems development
   d) systems maintenance

69) A management report describing progress to date is generally prepared during which phase of the systems life cycle?

a) systems design
b) preliminary investigation
c) systems analysis
d) A management report is prepared in all of the above.

70) Which of the following are tools used to assist the systems analysts and end users in the analysis phase?

a) checklists
b) top-down analysis methodology
c) grid charts
d) All the above tools are used to assist the systems analysts.
e) none of the above

71) Which of the following shows rules that apply to a business related task within an organization when certain conditions occur?

a) checklists
b) decision table
c) system flowchart
d) grid chart

72) Which of the following terms describe tools that enable several systems analysts and programmers to automate and to coordinate their efforts on a project?

a) automated design tools
b) CASE tools
c) computer-aided software engineering tools
d) All the above are synonymous terms.

73) Applications software for the new information system can be

a) purchased off-the-shelf as packaged software and modified.
b) custom designed.
c) both answers a and b
d) none of the above

74) In the systems audit

   a) A systems analyst compares the new system to the design specifications.
   b) A systems analyst may decide to scrap the system and start all over from the beginning.
   c) The analyst determines if the new procedures are actually furthering productivity.
   d) The analyst may elect to redesign the system.
   e) All the above except answer b.

75) All of the following are considered part of an information system except

   a) people.
   b) software.
   c) hardware.
   d) All the above are part of an information system.

76) Which of the following is generally not a reason organizations need to change their information systems?

   a) growth
   b) acquisition by another company
   c) competitive pressures
   d) All of the above may cause an organization to change information systems.

77) The final step in Phase 4, development, is:

   a) designing alternative systems
   b) selecting the best system
   c) developing software
   d) acquiring hardware
   e) testing the new system

78) The evaluation of economic, technical, and operational feasibility is made during this phase:

   a) preliminary investigation
   b) systems design
   c) systems development
   d) systems implementation
   e) systems maintenance

79) Phase 2, analysis, involves gathering data, analyzing the data, and:

a) designing the new system.
b) creating programs.
c) auditing the existing information system.
d) documenting the systems analysis stage.
e) training.

80) This phase in the systems life cycle focuses on evaluating and determining the need for a new information system:

a) preliminary investigation
b) systems design
c) systems development
d) systems implementation
e) systems maintenance

81) A collection of hardware, software, people, procedures, and data:

a) analysis and design
b) system
c) network
d) microcomputer
e) design

1) T			53) c	
2) T			54) c	
3) T			55) b	
4) T			56) b	
5) T			57) b	
6) T			58) d	
7) T			59) a	
8) T			60) d	
9) F			61) d	
10) T			62) c	
11) F			63) d	
12) T			64) a	
13) F			65) a	
14) F			66) b	
15) T			67) d	
16) T			68) c	
17) F			69) d	
18) F			70) d	
19) T			71) b	
20) T			72) d	
21) F			73) c	
22) T			74) e	
23) T			75) d	
24) T			76) d	
25) T			77) e	
26) F			78) b	
27) F			79) d	
28) T			80) a	
29) T			81) b	
30) T				
31) F				
32) F				
33) T				
34) T				
35) T				
36) T				
37) F				
38) T				
39) T				
40) F				
41) F				
42) T				
43) F				
44) T				
45) F				
46) F				
47) T				
48) T				
49) T				
50) F				
51) T				
52) b				

1) A program is a list of instructions for the computer to follow to accomplish the task of processing data into information.

2) All documentation is performed in the last step in the programming.

3) COBOL is the most frequently used language in business programming.

4) CASE stands for computer association of scientific engineers.

5) Seventy-five percent of software costs can be attributed to program maintenance.

6) Debugging is another name for testing the program.

7) Assembly is in the first generation of programming languages.

8) The logic structure IF-THEN-ELSE is used when a decision must be made.

9) In program specifications, you should specify outputs before inputs.

10) A translator converts a programming language into machine language.

11) A programmer's work can be made easier and more reliable using CASE tools.

12) CASE is a programming tool that can make a programmer's work easier, faster and more reliable.

13) Object-oriented programming languages (OOPS) manipulate "objects" (graphic symbols, modules or blocks of programming code, or data). This allows programmers to isolate, combine, and reuse programming code very efficiently.

14) Programming will only become more important in the future.

15) The first step in the programming process is coding.

16) Inputs should generally be specified before outputs.

17) Program definition should be done prior to program design.

18) A make-or-buy decision regarding software is made during the development phase of the system life cycle.

19) The program design phase follows the make-or-buy decision if it is decided that the software must be custom-made.

20) Program design is not necessary if an off-the-shelf package is chosen.

21) A program module should have only one entry point and one exit point, according to the rules of structured design.

22) Program modules should have between 50 and 100 program statements.

23) Pseudocode provides a graphic representation of the steps needed to solve a programming problem.

24) A rectangle in a program flowchart represents a process.

25) Input and output are represented by a parallelogram in a program flowchart.

26) A decision is represented in a program flowchart by an ellipse.

27) A circle in a program flowchart represents a connector.

28) The three basic logic structures of programming are the sequence, selection and iteration (loop) structures.

29) The selection structure is also known as an IF-THEN-ELSE structure.

30) The selection structure is also known as an iteration.

31) Typing the program into the computer is called coding.

32) In the sequence structure, one program statement follows another.

33) The loop structure may be repeated multiple times.

34) DO UNTIL and DO WHILE are variations of the sequence structure.

35) The most popular language for microcomputers has been COBOL.

36) DO PROCESS HOURS WORKED UNTIL THERE IS NO MORE DATA TO PROCESS, is an example of an iteration structure.

37) Debugging involves finding and correcting both syntax and logic errors.

38) Logic errors are encountered when the programmer has used an incorrect formula or left out a programming procedure.

39) Syntax errors can be detected by a language translator; logic errors cannot.

40) Desk checking usually involves looking for logic errors only.

41) A program should be tested, with both correct and incorrect data, to check for correct processing results.

42) Program documentation is generally not needed by end users.

43) Word processors and spreadsheets are examples of custom-made programs.

44) Machine language is the lowest level language.

45) Lower level languages are closer to machine language; higher level languages are closer to English.

46) Assembly language is written as a series of Os and 1s.

47) Machine languages vary from one make of computer to another.

48) Assembly languages are intended to solve general business or scientific problems.

49) Programs written in a procedural language are translated from object code to source code.

50) No object code is saved when an interpreter is used.

51) Most versions of BASIC use an interpreter.

52) COBOL and FORTRAN must be translated by an interpreter prior to execution.

53) A programmer wanting to do interactive programming would most likely select an interpreter rather than a compiler.

54) Programming is usually done during the systems analysis phase of the systems life cycle.

55) COBOL is used for programming mainframes only.

56) An engineer requiring the ability to process complex formulas would be most likely to select COBOL for programming his/her application.

57) Problem-oriented languages generally do not require users to learn a complex programming languages.

58) Lotus 1-2-3 is an example of a fourth generation language.

59) A well written program is one that is structured, correctly performs the task for which it was designed, and is maintainable.

60) A natural language is consider to be a fifth generation language.

61) Fourth generation languages are problem-oriented languages.

62) The last step in programming:

   a) design
   b) analysis
   c) test
   d) maintenance
   e) coding

63) The last thing to do before leaving the program design step:

   a) determine outputs
   b) document
   c) test
   d) select programming language
   e) code

64) The structured programming technique that graphically presents the detailed steps needed to solve the problem:

   a) top-down design
   b) pseudocode
   c) flowcharts
   d) logic structures
   e) object-oriented programming

65) Which of the following is not specified during program definition

   a) the desired output.
   b) the prototype procedures.
   c) the program's objectives.
   d) all the above are specified

66) Which of the following shapes is used to represent input and output in a program flowchart?

   a) diamond
   b) ellipse
   c) circle
   d) parallelogram

67) A rectangle in a program flowchart depicts

   a) input or output.
   b) a process.
   c) a connection point.
   d) a decision.

68) Which of the following shapes represents a decision in a program flowchart?

   a) diamond
   b) ellipse
   c) circle
   d) parallelogram

69) In which of the following programming structures are program statements executed one after the other without looping or branching?

   a) sequence
   b) selection
   c) iteration
   d) all of the above

70) The selection structure is characterized by

   a) one program statement executing after the other without variation.
   b) IF-THEN-ELSE logic.
   c) DO UNTIL logic.
   d) DO WHILE logic.

71) DO UNTIL and DO WHILE logic is found in which programming structure?

   a) sequence
   b) selection
   c) loop
   d) all of the above

72) The loop structure

   a) causes a process to be repeated as long as a certain condition is true.
   b) has two variations: DO UNTIL and DO WHILE.
   c) is also called the iteration structure.
   d) all of the above

73) Testing and elimination of programming errors is known as

   a) program coding.
   b) debugging.
   c) error detection and correction.
   d) none of the above

74) All of the following are examples of syntax errors except

   a) misspelled words.
   b) misplaced punctuation.
   c) using an incorrect formula.
   d) All the above are syntax errors

75) When three or four programmers, including the author, review a
program for errors it is known as

   a) desk checking.
   b) manual testing with sample data.
   c) structured walkthrough.
   d) debugging.

76) Translator that converts procedural languages one statement at a
time into machine code before it is to be executed:

   a) BASIC
   b) interpreter
   c) Pascal
   d) query language
   e) compiler

77) A translation program will identify

   a) logic errors.
   b) syntax errors.
   c) both a and b above
   d) neither a or b above

78) Which of the following is not considered program documentation?

   a) program flowcharts
   b) procedures describing how to use the program
   c) pseudocode
   d) All of the above are program documentation.

79) Which of the following groups is least likely to use program
documentation?

   a) users
   b) computer operators
   c) programmers
   d) All of the above use program documentation.

80) All of the following represent computer language generations except

a) machine languages.
b) natural languages.
c) control languages.
d) procedural languages.

81) Which of the following is considered the first generation computer language?

a) machine languages
b) natural languages
c) assembly languages
d) procedural languages

82) Which of the following is the third generation of computer languages?

a) problem-oriented languages
b) assembly languages
c) machine languages
d) procedural languages

83) Which of the following represents the correct order for programming languages, from lowest level to highest?

a) machine language, assembly language, problem-oriented language, procedural language
b) procedural language, assembly language, natural language, problem-oriented language
c) machine language, assembly language, procedural language, problem-oriented language
d) natural language, problem-oriented language, assembly language, machine language

84) Data represented in 1s and 0s is written in

a) machine languages
b) natural languages
c) assembly languages
d) procedural languages

85) Which of the following is probably not portable?

a) a machine language program
b) a COBOL program
c) a program written in a problem-oriented language
d) all the above are portable

86) Which of the following is not a procedural language?

   a) COBOL
   b) BASIC
   c) Pascal
   d) Lotus 1-2-3

87) Translation of a procedural language is done

   a) by an interpreter.
   b) by a compiler.
   c) either a or b above
   d) neither a or b above

88) An example of a procedural language using an interpreter is

   a) Lotus 1-2-3.
   b) Framework.
   c) BASIC.
   d) COBOL.

89) A programmer's COBOL program, known as source code, is converted
    to object code by

   a) a machine language program.
   b) a compiler.
   c) an assembly language program.
   d) an interpreter.

90) Source code is to object code as COBOL instructions are to

   a) machine language instructions.
   b) an interpreter.
   c) a compiler.
   d) an assembly language program.

91) What is the main advantage of compiler languages over interpreter
    languages?

   a) they are better suited to interactive programming
   b) the object code runs faster
   c) they are easier to learn
   d) all of the above

92) Which of the following is the first step of the programming process?

   a) deciding whether to make or buy software
   b) defining the problem
   c) coding the program
   d) documenting the program

93) Which of the following represents the correct sequence of programming steps?

   a) defining the problem, designing the program, coding the program, testing the program
   b) deciding whether to make or buy software, documenting the program, designing the program, coding the program
   c) designing the program, testing the program, coding the program, defining the problem
   d) documenting the program, coding the program, defining the problem, testing the program

94) Which language is useful for writing operating systems and database programs?

   a) COBOL
   b) BASIC
   c) C
   d) FORTRAN

95) Which programming language is the most widely used scientific and mathematical language?

   a) Ada
   b) FORTRAN
   c) COBOL
   d) BASIC

96) Which programming language was developed under the sponsorship of the Department of Defense primarily for weapons systems applications?

   a) BASIC
   b) RPG
   c) Ada
   d) FORTRAN

97) Which language is intended primarily as a tool to create business
reports quickly and easily?
a) COBOL
b) Ada
c) BASIC
d) RPG

98) All of the following are problem-oriented languages except

a) COBOL.
b) Lotus 1-2-3.
c) dBASE IV.
d) Framework.

99) Nonprogrammers would be most likely to search a database using a
language such as

a) a compiler.
b) an interpreter.
c) a query language.
d) an application generator.

100) Which of the following represents the fifth generation of
programming languages?

a) machine language
b) natural language
c) problem-oriented language
d) procedural language

101) Which of the following languages are still being developed to
give people a more human connection with computers?

a) a compiler
b) an interpreter
c) RPG
d) natural languages

102) Which of the following is not considered an off-the-shelf program?

a) a word processor
b) a spreadsheet program
c) a database manager
d) BASIC

1)	T	53)	T
2)	F	54)	F
3)	T	55)	F
4)	F	56)	F
5)	F	57)	T
6)	T	58)	T
7)	F	59)	T
8)	T	60)	T
9)	T	61)	T
10)	T	62)	d
11)	T	63)	b
12)	T	64)	c
13)	T	65)	b
14)	T	66)	d
15)	F	67)	b
16)	F	68)	a
17)	T	69)	a
18)	T	70)	b
19)	T	71)	c
20)	T	72)	d
21)	T	73)	b
22)	F	74)	c
23)	T	75)	c
24)	T	76)	b
25)	T	77)	b
26)	F	78)	d
27)	T	79)	d
28)	T	80)	c
29)	T	81)	a
30)	F	82)	d
31)	F	83)	c
32)	T	84)	a
33)	T	85)	a
34)	T	86)	d
35)	F	87)	c
36)	T	88)	c
37)	T	89)	b
38)	T	90)	a
39)	T	91)	b
40)	F	92)	b
41)	T	93)	a
42)	F	94)	c
43)	F	95)	b
44)	T	96)	c
45)	T	97)	d
46)	F	98)	a
47)	T	99)	c
48)	T	100)	b
49)	F	101)	c
50)	T	102)	d
51)	T		
52)	F		

1) PIMs typically include electronic calendars, to-do lists, address books, and notepads.

2) A knowledge-based system might show a employee how to use new equipment or the tasks involved in a new job.

3) A financial executive might use an expert system to help in business planning.

4) An expert system might provide advice to managers who are working in fields unfamiliar to them.

5) A page description language is used to interpret the page to a printer in a standard way.

6) Computer aided design is replacing most industrial designers and engineers.

7) Lotus Organizer is an example of a personal information manager.

8) Expert system shells are special programs that allow a person to custom-build an expert system.

9) PIM software helps an individual to get organized and to stay organized.

10) A project is a one-operation composed of several tasks to be completed within a stated time period.

11) In desktop publishing, a style sheet helps you to create the basic appearance of single or multiple pages.

12) Multimedia sales are expected to remain constant for the next few years.

13) Expert systems are programs that give advice to individuals who would otherwise rely on human experts.

14) A user concurrently working on more than one application is multitasking.

15) An internal newsletter could be produced using desktop publishing software.

16) A mouse is a useful input device for both desktop publishing and computer aided design.

17) Desktop publishing software helps you to plan, schedule, and control the people, resources, and costs of a project.

18) Dot matrix printers would be required desktop publishing software.

19) A full general ledger accounting system could be managed with project management software.

20) Desktop publishing produces near professional quality output.

21) A style sheet is the same as a page description language.

22) Aldus PageMaker is a type of desktop publishing software.

23) Hypertext allows the linking of text, graphics, and digital information.

24) Desktop publishing software makes it possible to mix text and graphics.

25) A page description language is used with desktop publishing to describe the shape and position of letters and graphics to the printer.

26) Desktop managers can be held in primary memory at the same time you are running another application on the microcomputer.

27) Expert systems are not sophisticated enough to handle complex situations found in the fields of law and engineering.

28) CAD and CAM programs together are too massive to work in a microcomputer environment.

29) Memory-resident programs stay in the computer's primary memory until the computer is turned off.

30) Some desktop publishers have the ability to automatically realign text around a graphic image inserted on a page.

31) Plotters are frequently employed as output devices for computer aided design.

32) The goal of artificial intelligence is to replace human intelligence.

33) Most data processing systems up to now have concentrated on computerizing tasks performed by managers.

34) Expert systems are based primarily on surface knowledge of a particular field or subject matter.

35) Current microcomputers are not large or fast enough to run expert systems.

36) One application of knowledge-based systems is to store an organization's operating procedure and make them available to employees in lower-level positions in the organization.

37) CADD is a variation of CAD by adding the component of detailing (Computer-Aided Design and Detailing).

38) Shells are special kinds of software that allow a person to custom-build a particular kind of expert system.

39) The ability to connect any two files together is an application for hypertext.

40) Managing people and resources would be an application of project management software.

41) Personal information managers are memory resident programs.

42) The ability to link video, music, voice and animation is an application for hypertext.

43) Project management software assist in the planning, scheduling and costs of a project.

44) Unlike most assembly-line machines, robots can be reprogrammed to do more than one task.

45) In hypertext, a stack in the basic filing unit.

46) Multitasking software is also known as operating environments, which is software that allows the user to work on a number of applications programs simultaneously.

47) Ventura Publisher in a powerful project management software program.

48) Which of the following would not be an application for a project management software program?

a) planning
b) publishing
c) scheduling
d) controlling resources.

49) Which of the following projects could be handled by a project management software?

a) construction project
b) aerospace project
c) political campaign
d) All the above would be well served by project management software.

50) Which of the following is less likely than the others to be produced using desktop publishing?

a) an internal newsletter
b) a glossy trade magazine
c) a single-page marketing brochure
d) a menu for a restaurant

51) Which of the following output devices is required for desktop publishing?

a) dot matrix printer
b) ink-jet printer
c) laser printer
d) color plotter

52) Which of the following products is not a desktop publishing package?

a) AutoCad
b) Ventura Publisher
c) PageMaker
d) Postscript

53) Which of the following printers may be used for CAD output?

a) dot-matrix
b) laser
c) ink-jet
d) all of the above

54) Which of the following is not an input device used for CAD systems?

a) mouse
b) plotter
c) keyboard
d) digitizer

55) Programs that control factory equipment and robots are known as

   a) CAD.
   b) CADD.
   c) CAM.
   d) none of the above

56) All of the following are examples of artificial intelligence except

   a) robotics.
   b) knowledge-based systems.
   c) expert systems.
   d) computer-aided design.

57) Expert systems would be useful in all of the following fields except

   a) law.
   b) medicine.
   c) accounting.
   d) Expert systems would be useful in all of the above.

58) Which of the following is true of hypertext software?

   a) links files together
   b) links items of text and pictures together
   c) can link video, music, voice, and animation together
   d) all the above
   e) none of the above

59) Which of the following is not an example of project management software?

   a) Windows
   b) Harvard project manager
   c) Project Scheduler 4
   d) all of the above

60) Which of the following is not true of page description languages?

   a) It describes the shape and position of letters and graphics to the printer.
   b) It works with desktop publishing software.
   c) The various languages available are interchangeable.
   d) none of the above is true of page description languages

61) Which of the following is true of expert systems?

   a) They are based on surface knowledge.
   b) They are based on deep knowledge of a particular field.
   c) They incorporate textbook knowledge and "tricks of the trade".
   d) all of the above

62) Which of the following is not true of a shell?

   a) It can automate several redundant tasks for the user.
   b) It allows a person to custom-build a particular kind of expert system.
   c) Some shell programs can work with Lotus or dBASE programs.
   d) none of the above are true of a shell program

63) Which of the following are not true of knowledge-based systems?

   a) They are programs based on surface knowledge.
   b) They are programs based on textbook knowledge.
   c) They are programs based on facts and widely accepted rules.
   d) They tell how certain decisions should be made or tasks accomplished.
   e) all of the above are true of knowledge-based systems

64) Which of the following has a different meaning than the others?

   a) windowing software
   b) expert systems
   c) multitasking software
   d) operating environments

65) Which of the following is a tool included in personal information management software?

   a) desktop publishing
   b) Rolodex file
   c) Gantt chart
   d) All the above are part of a PIM software.

66) A style sheet

   a) can assist in determining the appearance of a page.
   b) can assist in the shading of a drawing.
   c) is part of a page description language.
   d) All the above are true of a style sheet.

67) Multimedia

   a) is the same as hypermedia.
   b) can link text, graphics, animation, video, music and voice.
   c) is the same as hyper text.
   d) All the above are true of multimedia.
   e) Both answers a and b are true of multimedia.

68) Virtual reality

   a) is the same as perception systems.
   b) is a form of AI which produces a simulated experience.
   c) requires the use of robots.
   d) All the above are true of virtual reality.

69) Virtual reality

   a) can be used as a form of entertainment.
   b) replaces lost senses of smell or sight.
   c) is a type of expert system.
   d) None of the above are true of virtual reality.

70) Artificial life

   a) is a new life form created with computer technology.
   b) can be used to simulate living systems.
   c) may assist in the defense against computer viruses.
   d) All of the above are true of artificial life.
   e) Answers b and c above are true.

71) An area of artificial intelligence that simulates certain
    experiences using special headgear, gloves, and software that
    translates data into images:

   a) virtual reality
   b) expert system
   c) CADD
   d) CAD/CAM
   e) shell

72) Clothing, furniture, industrial products, and just about anything
    else can be designed using _____ software:

   a) CAM
   b) CAD
   c) AI
   d) PIM
   e) knowledge-based system

CHAPTER 12
APPLICATIONS SOFTWARE: POWER TOOLS
Corresponds to Computing Essentials Annual Edition, 1994-1995

73) The application that can link all sorts of media into one form of presentation:

a) organizer
b) word processor
c) multimedia
d) spreadsheet
e) hypertext

74) The applications software that allows you to mix text and graphics to create documents of nearly professional quality:

a) AI
b) PIM
c) CAD/CAM
d) desktop publishing
e) hypertext

75) A one-time operation composed of several tasks that must be completed during a stated period:

a) plan
b) organizer
c) manager
d) schedule
e) project

1)	T	53)	d
2)	T	54)	b
3)	T	55)	c
4)	T	56)	d
5)	T	57)	d
6)	F	58)	d
7)	T	59)	a
8)	T	60)	c
9)	T	61)	d
10)	T	62)	a
11)	T	63)	e
12)	F	64)	b
13)	T	65)	b
14)	T	66)	a
15)	T	67)	e
16)	T	68)	b
17)	F	69)	a
18)	F	70)	e
19)	F	71)	a
20)	T	72)	b
21)	F	73)	c
22)	T	74)	d
23)	T	75)	e
24)	T		
25)	T		
26)	T		
27)	F		
28)	F		
29)	T		
30)	T		
31)	T		
32)	F		
33)	T		
34)	F		
35)	F		
36)	T		
37)	F		
38)	T		
39)	T		
40)	T		
41)	T		
42)	T		
43)	T		
44)	T		
45)	F		
46)	T		
47)	F		
48)	b		
49)	d		
50)	b		
51)	c		
52)	a		

1) Noninterlaced is a type of monitor that does not flicker.

2) Carpal tunnel syndrome is a type of repetitive motion injury.

3) The National Institute of Occupational Safety and Health found no statistical link between VDTs and miscarriages.

4) Our legal system is the essential element used to control computers today.

5) Computer ethics are guidelines for the morally acceptable use of computers in our society.

6) EMF stands for electromagnetic field.

7) More than 10 million American use VDT every day.

8) About one half of Americans used a computer at work in 1989.

9) Ergonomics is the study of computer crime.

10) An injury that can be sustained when using a computer is called repetitive strain injury.

11) The new word technostress is used to describe harmful stress associated with computer use.

12) A Trojan horse is a virus that keeps replicating itself until the computer system's operations are slowed or stopped.

13) Over 20 percent of business search through employees' electronic messages and computer files.

14) People are part of a complete computer system.

15) It can be physically unhealthy to use a computer.

16) Most people who use computers are midlevel managers.

17) Software piracy is the unauthorized copying of programs for personal gain.

18) People who gain unauthorized access to a computer system for fun and challenge are called hackers.

19) The electromagnetic field emitted from a computer monitor is totally safe for all user.

20) In an open office environment where workstations are situated close together, one can have greater exposure to EMF emissions from a co-worker's workstation than their own.

21) The strongest EMF emissions come from the front screen of the monitor.

22) Noise and stress related to computers are both a form of mental health concerns in technology.

23) Electronically monitored employees tend to be more efficient and less stressed than employees monitored in a traditional manner.

24) To be successfully implemented, studies have shown that expert systems must appear to think like humans.

25) We have few worries as individuals about the personal information contained in large databases.

26) Electronic networks have been recently challenged for infringing on our right to Freedom of Speech.

27) Credit agencies may share information with anyone they reasonably believe has a legitimate business need.

28) The Freedom of Information Act of 1970 entitles you to look at any and all information the government has collected.

29) The Privacy Act of 1974 restricts the manner in which federal agencies may share information about American citizens.

30) The Right to Financial Privacy Act of 1979 sets strict procedures about the way federal agencies can examine bank records.

31) The Computer Fraud and Abuse Act of 1986 allows for prosecution of anyone who accesses a computer system and is not authorized to do so.

32) Spreading personal information without personal consent rarely occurs in our society.

33) Inaccurate information contained in databases are automatically corrected by the computer.

34) Which of the following would prohibit a retailer from disclosing
information about a customers video tape rental preferences?

a) Privacy Act of 1974
b) Right to Financial Privacy Act of 1979
c) Video Privacy Protection Act of 1988
d) all of the above

35) Which of the following is not part of the Code of Fair
Information Practice?

a) No secret databases
b) Right of consent
c) Right to correct
d) Assurance of reliability and proper use
e) All the above are part of this code.

36) Computer criminals are likely to be

a) employees.
b) suppliers and clients.
c) hackers or crackers.
d) part of organized crime
e) All of the above.

37) Computer theft usually is in the form of stealing

a) hardware.
b) software.
c) data.
d) computer time.
e) All of the above

38) Which of the following is not dangerous to a computer system?

a) worm
b) virus
c) Trojan horse
d) bacteria
e) All are dangerous to a computer system.

39) Some viruses

a) erase all files from a disk.
b) cannot be detected.
c) are good for computer systems.
d) Both A and B above.
e) All of the above.

40) Unauthorized copying of software

    a) is fine if you don't get caught.
    b) is allowed if you are the original purchaser of the software.
    c) is called software piracy.
    d) All of the above

41) Which of the following is considered to be a technological failure?

    a) civil strife
    b) watching television
    c) a voltage surge
    d) develop specific skills

42) Security of a computer system includes

    a) restricting access.
    b) making back-up copies of data.
    c) anticipating disasters.
    d) All of the above
    e) None of the above

43) Security for microcomputers includes all the following except,

    a) avoiding extreme temperatures
    b) guarding the computer with locks
    c) guarding programs and data
    d) All of the above.
    d) None of the above.

44) The ethical issue that deals with the responsibility to control the availability of data:

    a) privacy
    b) accuracy
    c) property
    d) ownership
    e) access

45) The largest category of computer criminals:

    a) students
    b) hackers
    c) outside users
    d) employees
    e) data

46) Restricting access, anticipating disasters, and making backup
copies of data are all aspects of:

   a) security
   b) virus protection
   c) computer ethics
   d) privacy
   e) computer design

47) A repetitive strain injury that causes damage to nerves and
tendons in hands:

   a) RSI
   b) carpal tunnel syndrome
   c) EMF
   d) hacker
   e) virus

48) The study of human factors related to computers:

   a) data analysis
   b) human system performance
   c) ergonomics
   d) expert analysis
   e) personal design

1) T
2) T
3) T
4) F
5) T
6) T
7) T
8) F
9) F
10) T
11) T
12) F
13) T
14) T
15) T
16) F
17) T
18) T
19) F
20) T
21) F
22) T
23) F
24) T
25) F
26) T
27) T
28) F
29) T
30) T
31) T
32) F
33) F
34) c
35) e
36) e
37) e
38) e
39) d
40) c
41) b
42) d
43) d
44) e
45) d
46) a
47) b
48) c

CHAPTER 14
YOUR FUTURE: USING INFORMATION TECHNOLOGY
Corresponds to Computing Essentials Annual Edition, 1994-1995

1) Most businesses are making formal plans to track and to implement technology into their competitive strategies.

2) Being computer-competent means taking positive control.

3) Grapevine is another name for the informal lines of communication within an organization.

4) Technology has made it possible to combine savings, checking, credit card and investment account information into one monthly financial statement for an individual.

5) Technology has changed the way businesses compete.

6) Informal office communications is very important means for obtaining information to stay current with new developments and changes in the organization.

7) In all fields, successful professionals have to be experts in their own fields as well as in computer technology.

8) The person who thinks that microcomputers are overrated can be classified as a cynic.

9) Infoworld, PC World, and MacWorld are magazines that specifically cover microcomputers and information.

10) The office grapevine can be a good source to alert you to organizational changes.

11) Technology helps create products that operate faster and are priced cheaper.

12) Three common reactions to the prospect of encountering new technology are: cynicism, naivete, and frustration.

13) Businesses never allow customers access to their information systems.

14) Reading trade journals about the use of technology is a good way to stay current.

15) ATM cards, home banking, and programs to analyze cursive writing are examples of how some banks are looking to use technology in their competitive strategies.

16) Developing professional contacts is critical to the continued success of an individual in business today.

17) It is not possible, using scanners, to read data directly into the computer without retyping it.

18) Voice-recognition systems are not yet available for industrial applications.

19) Current voice-recognition equipment is often limited to a vocabulary of less than 100 words.

20) Low-cost laser printers do not compare in quality to the output from professional typesetting machines.

21) Workstations are useful in applications where employees need to download files from a mainframe onto their own hard disk.

22) Microcomputers are replacing terminals in many organizations.

23) Communications standards for microcomputers are not well established.

24) Optical disks will allow users to download larger databases from mainframes than is now possible.

25) Teleconferencing is an important component of telecommuting.

26) ATM's have become vital to the banking industry.

27) Technology creates products that operate faster, are usually priced cheaper, are often of better quality, or are wholly new.

28) Information technology can build entire new businesses and industries.

29) Successful professionals of the future will need to stay current in their own field and with the world as it relates to them.

30) Reading the daily newspaper is the best way for professionals to stay current in their respective professions.

31) Microcomputers have generally been introduced to most organizations without affecting operations.

32) Today's microcomputers have more powerful microprocessors than earlier models.

33) A good approach to present your innovative ideas is to
present them:

   a) in terms of improving decision making
   b) to coworkers
   c) in terms of improving information
   d) to the union chief
   e) in terms of saving money

34) By staying in touch with others in your field, you are:

   a) developing professional contacts
   b) staying current
   c) developing specialties
   d) maintaining computer competence
   e) being alert to organizational changes

35) The type of person who underestimates the difficulty of
changing computer systems or of generating information is

   a) a cynic
   b) frustrated
   c) naive
   d) a loser
   e) a winner

36) By giving their customers access to their package
tracking information system, Federal Express is developing new:

   a) global computer facilities
   b) customer and supplier relationships
   c) airline reservation procedures
   d) serious security problems
   e) governmental delivery systems

37) The real issue with new technology is:

   a) how to make it better
   b) which printer is better
   c) how to control it
   d) how to integrate with people
   e) managing its impact on government

38) Which of the following problems was associated with the early
introduction of microcomputers in organizations?

   a) software was difficult to use
   b) microcomputers were incompatible with company mainframes
   c) corporate data became fragmented in individual personal files
   d) all of the above

39) Which of the following is not a current trend in the
microcomputer industry?

    a) more powerful processors
    b) single-tasking operating systems
    c) multi-tasking operating systems
    d) better graphics capabilities

40) Developing professional contacts

    a) can be accomplished by joining professional associations.
    b) can be accomplished by maintaining contacts with other
       professionals.
    c) help you be successful in your career.
    d) all of the above

41) Technology related articles can be frequently found in

    a) Business Week.
    b) Fortune.
    c) Inc.
    d) Wall Street Journal.
    e) all of the above

42) The practice of using computers equipped with communications
capabilities to work at home is called

    a) teleconferencing.
    b) facsimile transmission.
    c) telecommuting.
    d) electronic mail.

43) Technology changes the nature of competition by

    a) creating new products faster, cheaper and with improved
       quality than in the past.
    b) creating entirely new industries.
    c) building improved customer supplier relationships.
    d) all of the above

44) Which of the following are common emotional reactions that people
have toward computer technology?

    a) cynical
    b) naive
    c) frustrated
    d) all of the above

45) Which of the following is not a suggested method of the text for
staying current and being a successful professional of the future?

a) reading trade journals
b) watching television
c) developing professional contacts
d) develop specific skills

ANSWER KEY FOR TEST14- CHAPTER 14

1) T
2) T
3) T
4) T
5) T
6) T
7) F
8) T
9) T
10) T
11) T
12) T
13) F
14) T
15) T
16) T
17) T
18) F
19) T
20) T
21) F
22) T
23) T
24) T
25) F
26) T
27) T
28) T
29) T
30) F
31) F
32) T
33) e
34) a
35) c
36) b
37) d
38) d
39) b
40) d
41) e
42) c
43) d
44) d
45) b